A North Oxfordshire Village

OVER NORTON

S. Rhona Arthur

published by S. Rhona Arthur

©S. Rhona Arthur 2000
cover illustration from the painting *Lizzie Saunders* (neé Webb) 1891 by William Gregory Dawkins. By courtesy of George Harris, her grandson.
Photo: Joe Arthur

isbn 0-9539118-0-2

A North Oxfordshire Village

Over Norton

S. Rhona Arthur

This book is sold subject to the condition that it shall not be re-sold, lent, hired out or otherwise circulated in any binding or cover other than that in which it is published and without a similar condition being imposed upon the subsequent purchaser without the express consent of the publishers.

Printed and bound by
Lazarus Press
Unit 7 Caddsdown Business Park
Bideford
Devon
EX39 3DX

For Joe, my husband, with gratitude for his unstinting support

Acknowledgements

My thanks to my sons Ronald and Richard, to my daughter-in-law Christine, and granddaughter Helen, who all helped in many different ways.

I am extremely grateful to Bill Asbridge, my friend, who read the typescript and made many constructive suggestions.

To everyone mentioned in this book I say thank you for the many pleasurable hours I have spent in collecting the information. It has indeed been pure joy. A special thank you must go to Dorothy Rudge who has guided me on walks in the area, has shared her knowledge with me and has shown great patience in answering my numerous questions.

My sincere thanks to Jane and Stephen Hanks who gave freely of their time to prepare the two maps : *Over Norton Parish and Over Norton Village.*

Thank you to everyone who provided photographs. The unused ones will be preserved for future village reference.

Chipping Norton Museum has kindly granted permission for the Packer photographs to be used and extracts from publications.

Copies of the William Gregory Dawkins paintings were made by kind permission of Fred Moulder, Mrs Lewis, George Harris and Roy Worvill.

Most of the photographic work was carried out by Joe Arthur.

My grateful thanks to Over Norton Parish Council for a grant towards the production of this book planned to mark the year 2000.

Oxfordshire Archives (County Record Office) for permission to quote the Workhouse Agreement (Chapter 7); Probate records (Chapter 5); Over Norton Board School Log Book (Chapter 10). Reference numbers to these within the text. Reference to Martha Gardner (PAR/64/5/63/2 – Chapter 2).

Wendy Turner who prepared the discs for publication.

Janet Thornton, Head Teacher St. Mary's C.E. Primary School, Chipping Norton, for allowing me to quote from the National School Log Books (Chapter 10).

Sarah Duffield, National Society Archivist Church of England Record Centre. (Four letters 1896 quoted in Chapter 10).

The Shakespeare Birthplace Trust Records Office, Stratford-upon-Avon (Chapter 14 and 4).

John D. Mitchell for a copy of 'The Inclosures & Allotments 1769, Chipping Norton Over Norton Little Rollright Salford'.

Oxfordshire County Council for permission to use the 'Definitive Statement of Public Rights of Way for the Parish of Over Norton' and David Coleman for help regarding same (Chapter 2).

Revd. Stephen Weston, St. Mary's Church, Chipping Norton, for permission to quote from the following documents: Window Tax; Orders of Removal/Settlement Certificates; Items from the Churchwardens' Accounts deposited in Chipping Norton Library.

Record Office, House of Lords for permission to include the Protestation Return 1641 and for help on this subject from Robert Harrison, Archive Officer. (Chapter 5)

Jack Sutcliffe for extracts from his transcription of William Wright's will 64/5/L1/1 (Chapter 7).

Revd. Ralph Mann for his large contribution to Chapter 5 (Probate documents of the Huckvale and Busby families).

Extract (Chapter 3) by permission of the British Geological Survey ©NERC All rights reserved IPR/6-23 .

Quotations from the *Victoria History of Oxfordshire* volumes ii and xi are included by permission of the general editor.

The Domesday extract (Chapter 4) is reproduced by kind permission from the Phillimore edition of DOMESDAY BOOK (General Editor – John Morris) volume 14 Oxfordshire pub. 1978 by Phillimore & Co. Ltd. Shopwyke Manor Barn, Chichester, West Sussex PO20 6BG.

Extracts from the *Wigginton Constables' Book*, 1691-1836 (ed. F.D. Price) pub. 1971 are by kind permission of Phillimore & Co. Ltd. as above.

Brian Little, Chairman, Banbury History Society (*Wigginton Constables' Book*) extract.

Bodleian Library University of Oxford quotation from *Memoirs of Dr William Smith* by John Phillips 1844. (44.1490) Extract by permission of County Archives from *Oxford Church Courts Depositions* 1542- 1550 paragraph 14 pub. 1991 Oxfordshire County Council (Leisure & Arts). Written by Jack Howard-Drake.

For general advice I thank Elizabeth Sleight, The Bookshop, Chipping Norton, and David Eddershaw.

Rosalind Garrod (née Adams) for permission to use extracts from her tapes and handwritten book on Over Norton.

Extracts from Mrs K.V. Cambray's book (typescript) *Memories 1933-1964 Over Norton W.I.* and *A History of Over Norton in the War Years* have been used with the blessing of her son, Don Cambray. Mrs Cambray's book is held by Over Norton History Group having been passed to it by the O.N.W.I.

Dennis Hudson for his boyhood drawings of war-time 1935-45 events in Over Norton.

E.G. Cuthbertson from Wagga Wagga, Australia for correspondence and photographs reference Hippolyte Langlois (Chapter 1 and 14 Firs Farm).

George Fawdry of Village Farm, Salford. (ref. Choicehill Farm)

Alan Gibbs for his poem XVII from *Oxfordshire Memories* pub. 1983 (Chapter 14).

Revd. Michael Roden, Rector of Steeple Aston Church, for permission to print a drawing of the Steeple Aston Cope and Barbara Johnston, Sacristan (1997) for information on this cope (Chapter 4).

Carl Boardman and staff at the Oxfordshire County Record Office.
Chris Edbury at the Oxfordshire Museum's Store, Standlake.
Dr. Graham and staff at the Centre of Oxfordshire Studies, Oxford.
Martin Allitt and staff at the Centre for Banburyshire Studies.
The staff of Chipping Norton Library.

Chipping Norton Museum's voluntary staff including John Howells, Curator; Ted Jones, Chairman; and Peter Tyrell, Archivist.

The late Dennis Lewis helped with information about the Over Norton public houses.

C. John Dawkins gave freely of his time (Chapter 6) and provided many original documents and anecdotes.

Rebecca Pearman for providing a copy of *A Diary of a Foxhunting Lady*. (Chapter 9).

Jane & Eric Runacres for general information from their library.

To Peter and Jan Combellack of Kellow Books, Chipping Norton, my thanks for book searches

George Lambrick for allowing me to use information from his lecture on The Rollright Stones (Chapter 9).

Mr & Mrs Jim Wiggins for allowing study of Priory Farm.

Paraphrased section and quotes from: *The Oxfordshire Election of 1754. A study in the Interplay of City, Council, County and University Politics* by R.J. Robson (1949) by permission of Oxford University Press (Chapter 6).

Robert Moulder for help with research.

The Rudge family (Tom, Mavis, Dorothy) for the loan of reference books, documents and maps.

Evelyn Warner for general information.

John Wilson for advice and encouragement over a long period.

Anthony Hobbs for farming information.

Bert Hallett for enthusiastic support.

Contents

Acknowledgements   *page*   4

Chapter 1   'There's No History Here'
Over Norton: Village Green—Geographical Situation—Communications—Roads from 1770 and 1730 Act (Turnpike)—Railway 1887
page   13¹

Chapter 2   Up the Town—Down the Village—Along the Fuzz—Over the Folly—Public Rights of Way
page   25

Chapter 3   Geology—Common Land—Stones—Coal Survey—William Smith—Mr & Mrs Jack Joines—Water
page   34

Chapter 4   Archaeological Finds—Domesday—Cold Norton Priory—The Steeple Aston Cope—Chapel House from 1770—Window Tax—The Naming of Over Norton
page   45

Chapter 5   Taxes (1634/5, 1649 and 1650) collected by the Constable of Over Norton—Hearth Tax and returns for 1665—Burying the Dead in Woollen Cloth—Sheep farming restrictions—Huckvale and Busby families: their wills and inventories—Dissenters applications—Over Norton's Protestation Return 1641
page   60

Chapter 6   The Dawkins Family :
James Dawkins bought Upper Norton House 1726 and was labelled a Jacobite—Dawkins connection with Penrhyn Castle—Census Returns Over Norton House—The Memorial Fountain—William Gregory Dawkins (1825-1914)—Oxfordshire Yeomanry 1887 at Over Norton Park—Chipping Norton Church Faculty 1877—Subscriptions 1838/39 for repairs to church—Receipts of Four Days Bazaar at Chapel House 1839
page   81

Contents

Chapter 7	The Laws of Settlement—Over Norton's Workhouse Agreement—Workhouse conditions—Speenhamland System 1795-1834—Wages and Cost of Food 1795—William Wright's Charity—Dawkins' Charity—O.N.P.C.'s fight to have a say in distribution of charities—Captain Daly's donation 1901	
	page	106
Chapter 8	Agricultural Development in Over Norton 1770s to 1900—1770 Plan with Photographs—Field Names—Robert Fowler—Arthur Young—Rowells—Swing Riots 1830—Heythrop—Home Farm—County Fire Mark—Joseph Arch—The Ascott Women—O.N.P. Councillors 1894—Henry Dawkins' Farming Notes mid-1800s—Extracts from Cropredy Farm Ledgers 1818 to 1912 (Mr W. Anker)—Agricultural Wages Scale 1899— Farm Workers and Farmers from Census Returns 1841 to 1891	
	page	123
Chapter 9	The Daly Family and Conversations with: Mr Fred Sole, Mrs Cook, Mr Harry Barnes, Mrs Nolan, Mrs Thomson, Miss Knight, Mrs Pashley and Mr & Mrs Douglas Sheffield—Also included: Extracts from Mrs K.V. Cambray's book, *Memories of Over Norton Women's Institute 1933-1964* — Mrs W. Jasmund's (née Sheffield) Letter from America .	
	page	152
Chapter 10	Schools in Over Norton and Chipping Norton—Dame School and Public Elementary School (Mrs Joines' taped memories)—Fees National School Chipping Norton 1880-1891—Board School, Over Norton and Church letters of opposition 1896—Log Book July 1900 to April 1933—Chipping Norton Schools' Log Books: fairs, holidays, treats and entertainment 1880 to 1913—Over Norton Monitress (Mrs Padbury's Memories)—	continued/....

Contents

.../continued Chapter 10	St. Cecilia's School (Dorothy Rudge)—Banbury County School (Roy Worvill)—Chipping Norton County School —Today, January 2000		
		page	175
Chapter 11	Lest Ye Forget Those Of This Parish Who Fell During The Great War 1914-1918 and During World War Two 1939-1945		
		page	209
Chapter 12	Village Memories of the Second World War—The Women's Institute from 1933—W.I. formed 1933— War-time—A.R.P.—Evacuees—L.D.V.—Home Guard— Food Rationing—War Work for Women—War memories from the Children (Tom and Dorothy Rudge, Don Cambray and Pat Randall, née Cambray)—American Forces—Gas Masks—W.I. Drama Productions— Electricity arrived		
		page	213
Chapter 13	Occupations 1841 to 1891—Gloving Industry— Bliss's Mill, Chipping Norton—Other occupations 1841 to 1891 from Census Returns		
		page	229
Chapter 14	Farming in Over Norton from 1900—Conditions 1900 to 1939—Dawkins Estate Sales 1897,1918, 1925 and 1926—War-time Agriculture—Post War Reconstruction —Fifteen Farms: Witts, Firs,Sandfields, Walk, Home, Cleeves, Choicehill, Halt,Hull Farm and Priory Mill, Chapel House,Merryweather, Wynmere, Shepherd's Dean, Elmsfield—Dawkins involvement from 1950		
		page	240

Contents

Chapter 15 Wilmot Poole Walford—Nos. 1-4 The Green—Laburnum Cottage—Sunnyside—Broadclose and Shanlee—Joe Benfield—Post-war housing—Joe Roughton (Men's Club and Cricket Team)—Motor Bike Scrambles—Public Houses—Coronation 1953—St James' Chapel Group—Sunday School—The Cemetery—Cub Pack—Silver Jubilee 1977—New Village Hall—County Art Week—Youth Club—Play Areas—Caring for the Village—The Allotments—German Band and Goats—Millennium Bells
page 273

Appendices *page* 286

Index *page* 299

First photographic section (black and white)   between pages 32-33
Second photographic section (black and white) between pages 80-81
Third photographic section (black and white)   between pages 128-129
Fourth photographic section (black and white) between pages 176-177
Fifth photographic section (black and white)   between pages 224-225
Sixth photographic section (colour)   between pages 272-273

Map: Over Norton Village *pages* 120-121

Fold out Map: Over Norton Parish *Inside back cover*

A North Oxfordshire Village

OVER NORTON

CHAPTER 1

There's No History Here

Over Norton: Village Green—Geographical Situation—Communications—
Roads from 1770 and 1730 Act (Turnpike)—Railway 1887

'There's no history here', replied a senior inhabitant of Over Norton when questioned by a new-comer to the village who had a voracious appetite for the minutiae of daily life in days gone by. They were standing within yards of the site of the Over Norton Workhouse which was operating in 1780 and of the Village Green where a mighty elm had stood (felled Easter Monday 1914). A wheelwright had used a whip here to chase children away from his property on the green. This was where Maypole dancing had taken place, and just off the green stands a fountain which was erected to the memory of a gentleman and his wife who both died in 1864, the former having served under the Duke of Wellington. None of this was known by the questioner at that time and certainly not all by the senior inhabitant. And then there was Hippolyte who lived in the centre of the village and whose family says that he took out a patent for a mechanical giant.

Over Norton village, adult population 369 (1998) is situated in North West Oxfordshire just three-quarters of a mile north of Chipping Norton and is in the Chadlington Hundred.

Opportunities for travel in 1999 are in complete contrast to earlier days when residents of this village walked and cycled extremely long distances. William and Eliza Moulder of Blue Row who were aged 56 and 55 at the 1881 census walked to Oxhill, Warwickshire, a few miles north of Compton Wynyates to visit Eliza's family (approximately 18 miles). Their son Samuel Moulder walked from Torquay to Over Norton when he was eleven years old. As Samuel had been suffering from ill-health Col. W.G. Dawkins found employment for him as a boot boy in an hotel in Torquay. He longed to return, so walked home! (This distance, measured on minor roads in 2000, is 243 miles and 180 miles if A and B roads used.)

Mrs Albert Saunders, (née Lizzie Webb 1874-1964) and her daughter Mrs May Ruby Harris (1907-1998) from Over Norton Post Office and shop, now the 'Old Post Office', used to cycle to Banbury (13 miles) for shopping on their half-day closing. Mrs Saunders liked to buy a piece of Goss china for her collection and enjoyed the company of her daughter on these shopping expeditions. George Harris, grandson of Mrs Albert Saunders, still has some pieces of her china.

Mrs Beck, with a friend, used to cycle seven miles to work, to her first employment, which was for *The Countryman* magazine at Idbury Manor where it was produced by J.W. Robertson Scott.

> 'We needed a warm by the stove when we arrived', she laughed.

It was considered to be a great privilege to work on this magazine.

Almost every household has at least one car now and there are convenient bus routes available from the centre of the village and from Chipping Norton.

The following record was found in the Over Norton Parish Council Minutes dated February, 1960,

> ... the bus shelter, built in 1957 [by Harry Bennett, from public subscription] had now been paid for ... a request had been made for the building to be handed over to the Parish Council ...

This bus shelter still stands in good condition.

The nearest railway stations are at Kingham, five miles away, and at Banbury, thirteen miles where there is also a coach station. Many people join holiday coach tours there. Seats for the National Express coach company can be booked at the Tourist Information Office which is operating in the Guildhall, Chipping Norton. The M40 motorway junction is eleven miles from Over Norton. To travel to Heathrow and Gatwick airports, by public transport, one would need to go via Oxford (twenty-one miles away) where coaches leave hourly.

Taxis are available in Chipping Norton. Today, 1999, it costs £3 for a return journey from Over Norton to Chipping Norton.

Parish Boundary

There have been some changes to the parish boundary over the years. The ecclesiastical boundary between Chipping Norton and Over Norton is shown on the 1770 enclosure map of Chipping Norton and Salford. It is this boundary, with more recent changes, which is marked on the Ordnance Survey Series SP22/32 and SP23/33 Pathfinder.

Ecclesiastically Over Norton comes under the care of St. Mary's Church, Chipping Norton, through St. James' Chapel of Rest which is situated in Over Norton. A service is held every Sunday in the Chapel; baptisms, weddings and funerals take place there as well.

The 1885 Ordnance Survey map gave the acreage of Over Norton parish as 2418.580 acres including a detached portion of 73.686 acres. In 1999 the area is 1009 hectares (2.471 acres = 1 hectare) a slight increase on the 1885 figures. It followed from a review order in 1932 that Chipping Norton and Over Norton exchanged some land, as did Salford and Over Norton. West Oxfordshire District Council is unable to provide details on these exchanges but confirmed that Priory Farm was taken out of the Over Norton Parish, following the West Oxfordshire Parish Review in 1985, when it was added to Heythrop parish. The owners of Priory Farm were pleased about this change as they already had close associations with Heythrop Parish. Walk Farm was placed in Over Norton at this time.

A dramatic feature in Over Norton Park is the deeply-cut valley, especially enjoyed in autumn with the colourful splendour of the many deciduous trees. The parish's highest point is at Chapel House which is 230m above sea level, falling to 180m in the valley and rising to 219m at St. James' Chapel up to a point 227m in the field opposite to the entrance to Over Norton House. The land falls again to 145m at Choicehill Farm.

The small un-named stream, sometimes referred to as The Cleeve stream, running N.E. to S.W. has its source above the lakes in Over Norton Park. It collects many springs on each side of the valley and provides part of the parish boundary until it reaches the bridge at the bottom of Over Norton hill. The stream flows on under the road and continues until it borders Pool Meadow, Chipping Norton and on to the Evenlode, a tributary of the Thames. At the Over Norton bridge the parish boundary continues for a short distance up the Over Norton road towards Chipping Norton and then cuts across at a 45° angle through the properties Silverdale, No. 62 and Dapple House. The nearby lake and house No. 66 are in Over Norton parish. The pollarded ash marked on the Pathfinder map SP22/32 no longer exists.

After leaving the gardens the boundary continues along the Cleeves footpath for a short distance and makes a 90° turn N.W. and again joins the line of the stream. The boundary skirts north of the castle mound, passes close to Elmsfield Farm, this being in Over Norton parish, and travels N.W. to join the Salford bridle-way at the crossing of the disused rail track. The boundary follows the bridle-way towards Salford and turns north, skirting the Salford lakes, and curves round Choicehill Farm following the Great Rollright stream west to east, taking in Halt Farm and Hull Farm. It continues following the course of the River Swere, the third stream in the parish to guide its route, a tributary of the Cherwell which rises at Kiteney Copse, Hull Farm and has Priory Mill at its head. At map reference 34 38 30 60 the boundary leaves the Swere and turns south to meet Banbury Road and follows this road S.W. for a short distance. At the beginning of Over Norton Common the boundary leaves the road and continues across farm land N.E. and then S.W. until it joins with the Heythrop to Chapel House road at approximately 34 50 29 25 map reference and then continues on this road until Chapel House is reached, just excluding Priory Farm. Chapel House Farm, the boarding kennels 'Paws With Inn', the four cottages on the roadside, Chapel House, Chapel House Cottage and The Courtyard all come within Over Norton Parish. The boundary leaves the Heythrop road, goes left for a very short distance along the A3400, turns right across farmland just beyond the entrance to the Wool Way to Charlbury and goes S.W. to a marker oak tree, then north to Hit or Miss Farm in Chipping Norton Parish. Thence it turns right along the road A361 towards Banbury for a very short distance and left through the wood behind Hit or Miss Farm. It crosses Over Norton Park in a straight line to the deep ditch at the top of 'The Slad' footpath and after a right-angled turn, follows the line of the ditch to its end. A further right-angled turn takes the boundary down in a straight line for a short distance and then turning S.W. it runs almost parallel with the line of the Dawkins family coach route and then down to meet the stream and so completes the parish boundary. (See map)

Roads

One of the main approaches to Over Norton is from Chipping Norton on the B4026. This road into the village was constructed following the 'Inclosures and Allotments Act 1769' [for] 'Chipping Norton, Over Norton, Little Rollright and Salford'. The former link road to Chipping Norton had been along what is now the Cleeves footpath beginning just above the bridge on the Over Norton side and finishing at Clay Lane near the castle mound. The name Cleeves is often used for land or pathway which follows a stream. (Margaret Gelling *The Place Names of Oxfordshire* E.P.N.S.)

The B4026 continues through the village as Main Street and meets the A3400 Oxford to Stratford-upon-Avon road. This road name it is believed, was first used by Mrs Beck who still lives in Over Norton and who for many years collected the information for the electoral roll and found it difficult to 'position' the houses as the sequence of numbering of them is impossible to follow e.g. two semi-detached houses at The Green are numbered 40 and 50; it is thought that originally they were one house. It is noticed however that in 1881 the enumerator used the term Main Road (not Main Street) – but in previous years from 1841 this was not the case, nor was it used in 1891. In early turnpike days there was only one way into Over Norton from the A3400. That was the left turn marked by the Scots pine trees when approached from Chapel House and this road carried on to Choicehill Farm, leaving Little Rollright to the left, and then up to the toll-house at the top of the hill and across the old ridgeway. The Rollright Stones are to the right. On John Cary's new Map of Oxfordshire, 1820, this road is labelled as the 'Birmingham,

Shrewsbury and Holyhead Road'. The present A3400 section from the Over Norton 'Pines' turn, past the two Great Rollright access roads and on to Long Compton did not exist at this time and was constructed after an act was passed in 1825. The Chipping Norton/Banbury road was turnpiked in 1770 and dis-turnpiked in 1871. A turnpike toll gate was situated a short distance from Chapel House roundabout, along the Banbury Road approximately where the road from Hook Norton meets it. It is thought that part of the present A3400 which runs between Chapel House and the cottages and farm on the opposite side did not exist before the enclosure act of 1770 but that the Hook Norton road continued behind Chapel House, the old coaching inn, and linked with the wool way to Charlbury.

There was until fairly recently an 18th century milestone just N.E. of Banbury Lodge. A local inhabitant has told me that it disappeared after snow clearance. The actual date is unknown but is thought to have been between the years 1987 to 1996.

From 1555 the inhabitants of a parish were by common law bound to repair all highways lying within it. An unpaid Surveyor of Highways, who had to organise free labour from within the parish, was appointed by local people. Parishioners were forced to do a few days unpaid labour yearly – at one time four days later increased to six – or find a substitute or pay a fine. It became increasingly difficult for them to cope with the maintenance of the roads particularly once the wheeled traffic had increased. (This statute labour was not completely abolished until 1835 when a highway rate was levied. The responsibility for highways passed to the newly formed County Councils in 1888.)

Many Turnpike Trusts were set up in the 18th century to try to improve the state of the major roads. The trustees introduced an injection of cash for this purpose collected from private subscriptions. Subscribers hoped to make a profit on their outlay. The following extracts from a 1727/30 Act regarding a turnpike road through Over Norton show that the trustees would be entitled to the fees from a newly erected 'Gate' and 'Toll-house'.

An act for repairing the Road from Chappel on the Heath, in the County of Oxon, to the Quarry above Bourton on the Hill, in the County of Gloucester was headed:

At the Parliament begun and holden at Westminster, the Twenty third Day of January, Anno Dom. 1727 in the First Year of the Reign of our Sovereign Lord George II by the Grace of God, of Great Britain, France, and Ireland,King, Defender of the Faith etc.

And from thence continued by several Prorogations to the Twenty first Day of January, 1730 being the fourth Session of this present Parliament.

Whereas the Road from Chappel on the Heath ... to the Quarry above Bourton on the Hill ... being the Great Road leading from the Cities of London and Oxford to the city of Worcester, and extending Eight Miles, or thereabouts, by reason of the Deepness of the Soil thereof and the many heavy carriages passing through the same, are become so ruinous and bad, that in the Winter Season many Parts thereof are impassable for Waggons and Carriages, and also for horses laden, and other parts are dangerous to Travellers ...

One hundred and fifty-two trustees were appointed to oversee the act from the following 'social' categories: Baronets, Esquires, Clerks, Gentlemen and Yeomen. Ten names are listed in the last two categories. Some well known ones appear including Blandford, Sheldon, Chamberlyne, William Diston [?Chipping Norton], John Hacker [?Churchill and Over Norton connections], Robert Parsons [?Radford], Banbury [?Woodstock] and James Dawkins (see chapter 6, Over Norton Park).

Any five or more of them [may put] this Act in Execution.

[They may] cause to be erected a Gate ... Turnpike, and also a Toll-house... and, to receive and take the Tolls and duties ... before any Coach, Berlin, Chariot, Chaise, Calash, Chair, Waggon, Wain, Cart, or other Carriage, Horse, Mule, Ass, or any other sort of Cattle whatsoever shall be permitted to pass through the same; videlicet,

For every Coach, Berlin, Chariot, Chaise, Calash, or Chair Drawn by Six or more horses, the Sum of One Shilling and Six Pence.

As above drawn by Four Horses – One Shilling

If drawn by One or Two Horses – Sixpence

For every Horse, Mule, or Ass, laden or unladen, and not drawing, – One Penny

> For every Drove of Oxen, Cows, or Neat Cattle, the sum of Ten Pence per Score
>
> For every Drove of Calves, Hogs, Sheep, or Lambs – Two Pence per Score

There was a fine of ten shillings for anyone allowing the avoidance of paying toll, e.g. passing through someone's land to avoid the gate.

No tolls were to be collected from vehicles on election days for Knights to parliament.

> [It] be lawful for the said Surveyors ... to dig, gather, take, and carry away, any Gravel, Furze, Heath, Sand, Stones, or any other Materials out of any Waste or Common of any Parish ... for repairing the highways ... without paying anything ... they may remove and prevent all Annoiances ...

The latter included the removal of bushes and trees and clearing of watercourses.

> Travellers through Chipping Norton and Moreton Henmarsh [Moreton in Marsh] having ... to travel there all night, and, having occassion to travel further, shall proceed on his, her, or their journey the next Day, before Twelve of the Clock at noon ... shall be exempt from paying the Toll a second time ... [This included animals.]

The landlord or householder had to sign a ticket as proof of the overnight stay. The above ruling, also applied to Evesham ...

> or any place lying between Chipping Norton and Evesham aforesaid, to fetch coal... (see Workhouse Chapter 7)

There would be no toll charge for

> carrying Materials, for repairing of the said Roads or for manuring of Gardens, or Land, or any Materials for Building.

Certain crops of hay, ploughs and harrows being taken through were exempt from charge.

Free passage to Church on Sundays was given.

> The Post-house carrying the Mail or Pacquet; ... the horses of any Soldiers passing, that are upon their March, or for Carts, Carriages, or Waggons attending them or for Horses, Carts, or Waggons travelling with vagrants sent by passes ...

... were all excused from paying tolls.

On Sat June 22 1782. *Jacksons Oxford Journal* [It was announced that there was to be a]

> ...General Meeting of the Trustees of ... Turnpikes Frid. 26th July, 1782 at the White Hart Chipping Norton at eleven o'clock in the forenoon. ... with the consent of Trustees ... intend to reduce the Tolls upon Carriages payable at ... the Chipping Norton Gate and Chapel-Heath-Gate.
>
> Also the Tolls will be separately Lett by Auction to the Best Bidders.

The outcome of this meeting was published on Saturday August 3rd 1782 *J.O.J.*

> Notice is hereby given, that the Tolls at ... the Chipping Norton Gate, and Chapel Heath Gate, are, by Order of a General Meeting of the Trustees, to be reduced by One Penny per Wheel on all Carriages, from the Twelfth Day of August Instant. Tables of the Tolls to be affixed at the above Gates.

The following appeared in *J.O.J.* on 1 July 1783:

> Chipping Norton, Chapel Heath, and Salt-Way gates to be let to best bidder.

In April 1787 a Working Surveyor was appointed...

> for the whole of the said Road ... about 12 miles ...

A General meeting was held at the White Hart, Chipping Norton, 1st August 1787, at which the details of the money collected at the Toll Gates were given as follows:

> ... 'which Tolls produced last year'
>
> | | | |
> |---|---|---|
> | Burford Gates | 167 | 1 |
> | Chipping Norton Gate | 74 | 1 |
> | Chapel Heath Gate | 46 | 1 |
> | Saltway Gate | 81 | 1 |
>
> Samuel Churchill Clerk to the Trustees

and details of profits were published: 7 July 1790 *J.O.J.*

> Tolls let by auction
> The profits for last year were
> £45 on Chipping Norton Gate
> £30 on Chapel House Gate

The following two reports appeared in *Jackson's Oxford Journal*. The first one shows something of the dangers which were met whilst travelling.

Saturday 27th Jan 1781:

> On Saturday last the Reverend Mr Earle was stopped, about seven o'clock in the Evening, within sight of Chapel-House, in this County, by two Highwaymen, dressed in Carter's Frocks; who robbed him of two Guineas, some Silver, and his watch: – After many Oaths and Threats that they would search for more, they at length gave the Boy a Shilling, and rode off towards Enstone.

and on 25 March 1783 [*J.O.J.*]:

> Lost on Worcester Rd between Chapel House and the first turnpike house Chipping Norton a screw Barrelled pocket-pistol. Made by Hart, Oxford. Reward from maker, half a guinea.

Arthur Young recorded a great improvement in the roads by 1813 compared with his journeys on them in 1773.

> ... Oxfordshire Roads forty years ago [1773] were in a condition formidable to the bones of all who travelled on wheels. The two great turnpikes which crossed the county by Witney and Chipping Norton, ... were repaired in some places with stones as large as they could be brought from the quarry; and when broken, left so rough as to be calculated for dislocation rather than exercise. The parish roads are greatly improved ... The turnpikes are very good, and where gravel is to be had, excellent.

Railways

The coming of the railways caused the decay of the Turnpike Road system. Certainly the village of Enstone which had been very important in the coaching days rapidly became less so as trade was directed to the new railways via Charlbury. When Chipping Norton was linked to the Oxford, Worcester and Wolverhampton railway via Kingham in August 1855, and then to Banbury in 1887, many opportunities were opened up for the town and the surrounding villages.

From the Chipping Norton National School Log Book:

23rd May 1884

> Several children left this week owing to their parents being discharged from working on the new line. They have all left the town and gone too far away to return for the examination.

There are two derelict, brick built cottages, off Choicehill Road, Over Norton – locally called 'Messengers' – the entrance to them being in front of Rose Cottage. Older locals believe they were built from bricks left over from the Hook Norton viaduct. I am told by an eminent local historian that this 'story' could be repeated in many villages which lie alongside a railway line. This area of the village used to be called Paynes' yard. One of the cottages was a shop (See final chapter).

Over Norton inhabitants could make use of the new railway service by starting their journeys at Chipping Norton, or from December 1906 at the Rollright Halt. Both points were within acceptable walking distance being just over a mile from the centre of the village.

In 1910, to celebrate the return of Robert Brassey as a member of parliament, all of the inhabitants of Over Norton were invited by the Dalys (Mrs Daly [née Brassey] see Chapter 9) to a free day's outing by train from Chipping Norton to Oxford to be followed by a river-trip on the Thames. This group of people was photographed at Chipping Norton station but one person was missing. Thomas Webb had decided to stay at home as in his opinion Brassey was returned

> because of his wealth and not because of his ability.

George Harris, a relative of Thomas, related this story. Thomas lived at No. 50 The Green and died aged 96 years during the Second World War and George helped to clear out Thomas's belongings.

A poem written at that time referring to the election included these words:

> The battle's o'er, the victory's won.
> By Captain Brassey (Albert's son).

Elephants were transported by rail to Chipping Norton station for the Chipperfield circus family based at Heythrop. Children at that time would have been very excited to see a procession of elephants walking through the town on their way to their winter quarters. Many other animals were transported by train including horses for a day's hunting with the Heythrop. (See Daly family Chapter 9)

In 1936 'Monthly Return tickets' cost approximately

> one penny per mile third class ... $1^1/2$d per mile first class. ... Break of journey is permitted ...' (Source: The Cotswold Country G.W.R. 1936).

In 1947 a ticket to Banbury cost 3s.1d.

The line from Chipping Norton to Kingham did not carry passengers after December 1962 but goods were transported until 1964. The Chipping Norton to Banbury line stopped carrying passengers in June 1952 but continued to transport a much reduced goods traffic until a later date. At one time there had been sixteen trains daily carrying ironstone. A landslip between Great Rollright and Hook Norton finally closed this part of the line. When the line was built, with great difficulty, through Over Norton and on to Banbury, no one would have considered the possibility that it would only last for 65 years as a passenger service.

The old 685 yard railway tunnel, which begins in Chipping Norton and ends in Over Norton Parish near the Salford Bridle path, makes a perfect hibernaculum for bats because of its controlled air flow and high humidity. It was the Oxfordshire Bat Group who with the cooperation of British Rail closed off the tunnel to protect this important site. It is visited three times a year by licensed members and their surveys show that there is a colony of twenty to thirty bats. There are several species including the greater horse-shoe and four of the rare lesser horse-shoe. The bats hibernate in the tunnel from September to mid-April and then move to a warmer site for breeding.

The Oxfordshire Bat Group and the Wildlife Trust for Berks, Bucks and Oxfordshire continue to care for the site. There is no access to the tunnel for the public. (Information source: Mr L.R. Tipping of Bodicote)

A huge mound of spoil from the tunnel excavations, now tree covered, can still be seen at the side of the Salford Bridle path.

CHAPTER 2

'Up the Town'— 'Down the Village'—'Along the Fuzz'—
'Over the Folly'—Public Rights of Way

As in all villages, the children who lived here in the past had their own names for various parts of the parish. Quite often there is an historical connection and they are well worth serious consideration.

'*Up Raddies*'. Going up Radbone Hill. This has a County Council name sign and was listed as Radbones Hill on the 1851 census but the name does not appear on the 1891 census returns. Road names were not included in the 1841 census. Controversy 'rages' within a group of senior inhabitants as to whether Radbones should have an S or not and several believe that it should be 'Radmans' and not 'Radbones'. Both of these family names are featured in the church records as farmers here.

'*Up the Town*'. This was at the same end of the village as the above and probably meant above the Township as villages and towns were called Townships in the past. On the 1770 Dawkins' estate map there are many buildings nestling lower down in the park. In 1780 the large field opposite the entrance to Over Norton house was called 'Ground Above Town'.

'*Down the Village*'. This area comprised the houses clustering round the Village Green.

'*Along the Fuzz*'. Going along the Salford Bridle path to where the furze grew. It is now (1999) a scrubby area. This path was also described as 'to Safford'. I last heard this pronunciation used by Mr Jack Wearing of Enstone about 1970.

'*Over the Folly*'. There were two semi-detached cottages and a barn called 'The Folly' situated north of the Salford Bridle Path near the railway line. The property was re-named Hill Side Farm by Col. W G Dawkins. In 1926 it was for sale with 52 acres.

'*Round the Warehouse*'. This seems to have referred to the road between Fountain Cottage and No. 40 and No. 50 The Green. What could this mean? One suggestion from local people is that perhaps there was a warehouse used in connection with the gloving trade.

I would like to put forward another possibility. There is original evidence that a workhouse was operating in Over Norton in 1780 (see Chapter 7). This building seems to have been positioned in the centre of the village. Mr Benfield still gives his address as Workhouse Row and in the census 1891 cottages No. 22 and No. 23, occupied by the Betteridge families, were listed as 'Union Row'. (Nuttall's Dictionary 1919 – *Union*: combination of parishes for the support of the poor; a combination workhouse.) On the 1770 map part of this area was a farm and farmyard. I have been told that within living memory there was a path next to the cottage with the war memorial on it which continued below 'Sunnyside' and back to 'The Green'; a garage built across the path now blocks it. I would like to suggest that 'Round the Warehouse' is a corruption of 'Round the Workhouse'. O.N.P.C. 6th February 1959:

> ... it was agreed to ask the County Council to adopt the roadways around the warehouse ...

An example of how names can change was shown very recently, when a new clerk to the Over Norton Parish Council had written 'Rag o' Bone' for 'Radbones Hill'. Fortunately this was corrected.

'*Up the Lane*'. This description is still used today by the senior inhabitants meaning Choicehill Road.

'*Up the Doubles*'. This is the public footpath number 9 situated at the side of Slad Lodge a continuation of the public footpath crossing the field from the village green and passing between Woodhaven House and the Old Village Hall. There was a double band of trees, each having three rows of eight trees in each, growing here in 1770 and may be the origin of the name.

Since its formation meeting held on 18th December 1890 in the School Room (now St. James' Chapel) the Over Norton Parish Council has been looking after various aspects of the village.

(Important historical records have been kept by O.N.P.C. since that time except for three periods: for 1918 and 1919, from February 1935 to April 20th 1937 and from March 1940 to August 1942.

Perhaps these 'missing periods' were recorded elsewhere but they have not come to my notice. The first minutes book was used from 18th December 1894 until 23rd July 1971 when the last entry was signed by the Chairman R.W. Kettlewell. In the second minutes book, six and a half pages were needed to record the annual general meeting in 1988 whereas less than one page was sufficient to cover the A.G.M. in 1894.)

At the first O.N.P.C. meeting in 1894 the following were present:

> Councillors Frederick Allen, William Jarvis, William Moulder and Henry Sandels, also W.C. Hayes, Assistant Overseer. It was proposed by Councillor Sandels, seconded by Councillor Moulder, and carried that Councillor Allen be Chairman of the present meeting. (Colonel William Gregory Dawkins was appointed Chairman of O.N.P.C. in his absence, a position he held for many years.)

1st April 1895 – At this O.N.P.C. meeting the councillors studied a local Government Board Circular:

> ... as to their powers and duties ... with respect to Rights of Way, Roadside Wastes and Commons.

14th July 1896 – They were discussing:

> ... the desirability of the improvement of the path leading to the park ...

15th April 1900:

> Some discussion took place as to the desirability of placing a few loads of stones in the road known as "the Doubles". The Clerk instructed to write to the Rural District Council Surveyor on the matter.

Public Rights of Way (Seven footpaths and two CRB's)
The clerk to the O.N.P.C. recorded in March 1957:

> A survey of eleven bridle roads and footpaths was made and the map and forms completed ... Mr W. Webb assisted the Council in preparing the survey.

This map is unlocated, as yet, and it is a difficult task to make a current list to tally with the above statement. Some public footpaths disappeared in the fifties including the one which ran across

Sandfields Farm to Hull Farm and from Hull Farm to Priory Mill. Mrs Pashley, an Over Norton resident, recalls using the former in about 1947 when she was living at the Caroline Colyear Cottages, Hull Farm.

Public Rights of Way in the Parish of Over Norton 1999

1. FP From Chipping Norton FP9 at the Chipping Norton Parish boundary leading NE, as diverted, along the perimeter of an artificial lake to the foot of Over Norton Hill on the Over Norton to Chipping Norton road (B4026). – Width 12ft

Remarks Diversion Order Confirmed 8.11.89.

The Chipping Norton FP9 plus the Over Norton FP1 is called 'The Cleeves' by local people and follows, with slight changes, the pre-1770 road which connected Over Norton with Chipping Norton as mentioned in Chapter 1.

2. FP From Choicehill Road, at a point SE of the [old] School, leading NNE to the Great Rollright road SW of Over Norton House.

Locally this footpath is referred to as 'across the Penn' and crosses Witts Farm yard before reaching the road to Great Rollright.

The areas named 'The Penn' and 'Penfield' must surely take their names from 'The Pound' where straying animals were impounded by the local officials. The pound, or part of it, was situated in Choicehill Road near the bungalow named 'Cotswold Edge' which is just opposite the present day 'Penn'. (Chambers Dictionary. *Penfold*: a fold for penning cattle or sheep; a pound)

O.N.P.C. 1939 quote:

A cheque was drawn for the following account: Burbidge & Sons New stile £2.7s.11d. [stile on 'The Penn to Witts Farm' footpath].

There is an original document in existence, dated 14th September 1720, which states that sheep, belonging to Martha Gardner of Priory

Farm in the parish, were impounded. (PAR/64/5/L3/2) There were strict rules about the use of the commons for grazing; trespassing animals could be impounded.

3   FP   From Chipping Norton BR10 at the Chipping Norton Parish Parish boundary leading NNW to the 'Mount to Salford BR' (CRB11).

Soon after leaving Chipping Norton Castle Mound and 'The Mount' FP3 passes through The Vicar's Field (awarded 1770) and to the NE is the field named the Vineyards, (note: 'The Winyards' on 1770 Inclosure Act) which was probably connected with the castle.

11   CRB   [Road used as public path] From Salford CRB8 at the bridge on the Salford Parish boundary at Salford Brook leading SE and E along the Chipping Norton boundary, passing the NW end of Chipping Norton FP19, to the Railway Tunnel and continuing NE past FP3 then E to the road at the top of the Hill on the S side of Over Norton Village.

The Salford road CRB11 has many entries about it in the O.N.P.C. minutes including:

1938

Clerk instructed to draw the attention of the District Surveyor to the unsatisfactory condition of the Gate to the Road leading from Over Norton to Salford.

17th April 1946

The question of the obstruction of the free passage of the awarded highway leading from Over Norton to Salford, due to the land being ploughed by the tenant was discussed ... instruction to write ... strongly protesting.

9   FP   From Over Norton Village Green leading E across FP10 to the Chipping Norton Parish boundary where it passes into Chipping Norton at Slad Lodge and

		becomes Chipping Norton FP30, continuing from the E end of Chipping Norton FP30 at the same boundary and leading generally ESE to the junction of the A361 and the A44 at Chapel House Cross Roads.
Remarks		Diversion Order confirmed 9.1.57.
10	FP	From Chipping Norton FP29 at the Chipping Norton Parish boundary leading NNE to FP9 SE of Slad Lodge

Dawkins' Old Coach Road
The most used public footpath of all must be the one which has its entrance through 'The Pillars' [width 3.2 metres] off Over Norton Road. Part of it passes through Chipping Norton Parish FP29 but is on land owned by the Dawkins family of Over Norton Park.

Reliable oral sources have it that this was a Dawkins family coach road to Over Norton House; Mrs Beck of Over Norton has said that her grandmother told her that the women of the village used to weed it. On one occasion, when weeding near the house, one remarked, "I wonder where the old woman is". A quick reply came from a window, "The old woman is here".

The footpath follows the coach road and from it the old ridge and furrow farming pattern can be clearly seen particularly when the sun is in the west. Senior locals call this ground 'Fifteen Lands' but Col. W G Dawkins had recorded it on a map, 1890, as 'The Terrace Field', the size being 32 acres let at 26/8½d per acre. The ridge and furrow markings continue in the fields behind the Chipping Norton Ambulance Station – below the hospital. (Detailed information about field systems is given in *The History of the Countryside*, Oliver Rackham. Pub. J.H. Dent 1986. Paperback Phoenix 1997 Chapter 8.)

At the beginning of this route, if one looks towards Chipping Norton, a large hollow can be seen where clay was dug and bricks were hand-made; some were used to build two cottages, Brick Kiln Cottages, now demolished, which stood a little way off the road bordering the present houses in Park Road.

There are some very ancient trees near this route including a large pollarded ash, which can be seen on the stream side of the path. Before reaching Slad Lodge the road passes over a stone bridge (width 4 metres). It is known that Samuel Moulder built an extension to this cottage using concrete bricks which he had fashioned himself. Sam made the wooden shuttering for casting the blocks. I was told by his son, Fred, that he made his own mortar, collecting the sand by donkey from Hit or Miss Farm. Sam recorded in his ledger on 25th January 1913 ...

> Dig Grave and bury the donkey.

What a hard, sad day he must have had.

There is no mention of a lime kiln in this village but it would have been within easy distance to the lime kiln at Great Rollright just above the railway halt. Mr Beale was operating a lime kiln on the opposite side, during the second World War years. I had the good fortune of meeting Mr Beale when he kindly explained his work to a group of primary school children who were under my care in 1968. Mrs Willis, Mr Beale's daughter, lives in Over Norton (1999).

At the Slad Lodge, FP9 from Over Norton Village Green to Chapel House is met. On turning right from FP29 (CN) the path continues through a wooded area and crosses a deep ditch which is of historical interest. Measured in 1999 it was five metres broad and 0.77 metres at its deepest point and stretches for a distance of approximately one sixth of a mile. It is, probably, a continuation of a ha-ha which was recorded in the garden to the north-east of Over Norton House in 1990. If the two parts did link up in the past it would have made a substantial barrier against animals particularly with the addition of a fence.

In September 1906 Col. W.G. Dawkins acknowledged a letter from Sam Moulder, his estate foreman and wrote,

> I think as you say I had best put a wire fence alongside the Old Ha Ha. What size and length of wire shall I order?

Traces of this wire can still be seen.

In 1957 permission was granted for a slight diversion of the path upon Mr C.J. Dawkins' request. The main reason given was that it would simplify the distribution of water needed for agricultural purposes. The path crosses the field named Boarlands (1770 map) and North Hill (1818 map).

Six Wellingtonias (*Sequoiadendron giganteum*) dominate the landscape here. These trees, named to honour the Duke of Wellington, were discovered in America and brought to this country in 1853 a year after his death. It is probable that the Over Norton ones were planted at about that time in memory of the Duke. Henry Dawkins (m Emma) had close connections with him. (The Dawkins family tradition is to add the wife's name. See Chapters 3 and 6.)

In earlier times the path would have passed through a grand avenue of lime trees, thirty-six trees arranged in a double row, crossing Rond Hill (1770 map) and travellers made their exit by way of 'The Steps' at Chapel House. A few large lime trees have survived. The enclosed corner in that area was sold to the Thames Water Board by Mr C.J. Dawkins in the mid-sixties. It is within this enclosure that a scheduled monument, a Bronze Age round barrow can be found which can be viewed by asking permission at the site (entrance from the A3400). This probably explains the name Rond (Round) Hill although sometimes what seems to be obvious is far from correct.

A route from the village across the fields to Chapel House must have been the scene of many villagers carrying their 'ration' of furze for their fires but in 1770 the route was in a different location from FP9 (1999). It followed the present track from Over Norton House to the bridge and then in a straight line across New Close to Chapel House. The site can at times be clearly seen in New Close. In 1780 when the Churchwarden and the Overseers 'farm let' the Workhouse at Over Norton (see chapter 7) it was a condition that no Person in the Work-House

> shall cut any Gause [Gorse] or Furze from off the Poor's Plot.

At the 1770 Enclosure, 50 acres were set aside for the poor called 'Over Norton Common' – now (1998) 54 acres according to Ian Pearman whose family company rent it – situated on the Banbury

William & Eliza Moulder b. 1825/26 walked 18 miles to Oxhill Warwickshire to visit relatives.

Over Norton residents outing to Oxford 1910. (See story Chapter 1)

Working on the New Road (now A3400)

Working at Over Norton/Great Rollright cross roads.

Felling the elm tree – Village Green Easter Monday 1914.

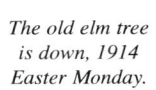

The old elm tree is down, 1914 Easter Monday.

Right: Over Norton Hollow.

Below: The Avenue, Over Norton Park.

Walty Webb, Home Farm.

Work on the engine house for the new water supply. 1927 L to R:
?
Reuben Coleman
Horace Hawton
Sammy Cooper
Unknown
Kenneth Benfield

Barrels of water being delivered due to a water shortage (site of present chapel). The notice reads: For Drinking Purposes Only.

Water cart used due to winter conditions. L to R Jack Tomlin, Mary Barratt (née Moulder, sister to Fred and Cyril), Ivy Moulder (Cyril's wife). Others unknown.

Chapel House Cottage 1925.

Chapel House – the former coaching inn.

A Buck print of 1729 showing the remains of Cold Norton Priory. Pub. by courtesy of The Centre for Banburyshire Studies, Cultural Services, Oxfordshire County Council. (Chapter 4)

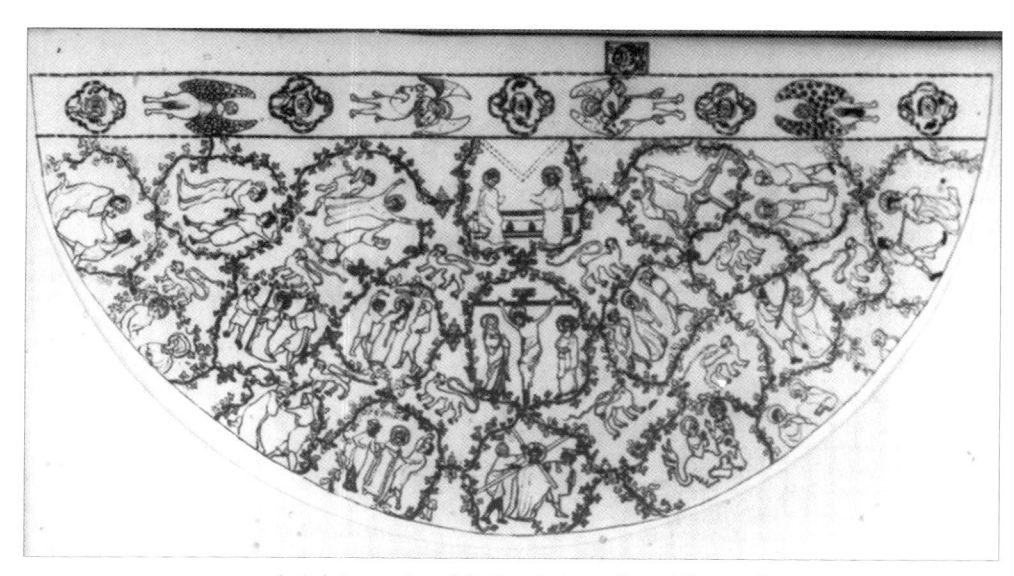

Artist's impression of the Steeple Aston Cope. (Chapter 4)

Poster displayed to the public by William Gregory Dawkins 1898.

EXPLANATION

of Farmer Busby's outrageous and prolonged insolence at Over Norton Election Poll, which, if Mr. Schofield had been a Gentleman he would not have allowed or employed in his behalf, even if I had not paid for his leaving the Ranks, if I had not brought him here and spent £400 on his house where he was my Land Steward.

Mr. Busby was my Tenant for over 10 years. I hesitated at his rent lowering. He himself gave up both Farms.. He claimed full price for hay valuation, falsely asserting that his predecessor had sold the hay elsewhere for full price, while no hay had been grown!

Last year Mr. Busby expected to make unfair gains of several hundreds by his having to settle with me for valuations on the larger Farm. But I sold the Farm, and Busby's annoyance is ludicrously described at his finding he had to deal with an experienced Farmer, who exposed his lying statements and baffled his attempts to cheat.

Mr. Busby, to the great injury of my Farm, had surreptitiously ploughed up 50 acres of grass, but had deservedly lost heavily by it, through drought.

In my own defence I claim to show the above facts the vindictive reasons for Farmer Busby's abuse and his imbecile and contemptible insolence towards me, present and absent, during some hours of the Poll at my Gates.

April 13th, 1898.   WILLIAM DAWKINS, Over Norton House.

Bert Harrison (left) and Harry Barnes served during the 1939-45 war in Southern Italy

Left: Mrs Doris Pashley's father – James Harrison.

Right: Mrs Doris Pashley (née Harrison) with her 1930's style doll's pram.

Road near to the Heythrop Lodge. It would have been quite a trek on foot up to that ground. There is a field named 'Ovens Gorze' at Priory Farm. (No longer in O.N. Parish.) Is it too simplistic to think that it means gorse for fuel'? This field has a dramatic display of yellow gorse, with a complete carpet of bluebells in spring and is a sight which once seen remains in the memory forever. Over Norton History Group has been very privileged to walk in this area several times under the leadership of Jim Wiggins, who is an expert naturalist. (Jim owns Priory Farm.)

4	FP	From the road at Choicehill Farm leading SW to the FP section of Salford 7 at the Salford Parish boundary, NE of the artificial lake.
6	CRB	From the Chipping Norton road (A361) near Banbury Lodge leading E to Heythrop CRB2 at the Heythrop Parish boundary.
12	FP	From Little Tew FP9 at the Little Tew Parish boundary leading W and N to the road at Walk Farm. (The Boundary Commission changes of 1.4.85 transferred all of Heythrop FP1 into Over Norton where it was renumbered as Over Norton FP12.)
Remarks		Added by Parish boundary changes 1.4.85 (Formerly Heythrop FP1)

CHAPTER 3

Geology—Common Land—Stones—Coal Survey—
William Smith—Mr & Mrs Jack Joines—Water

Geology

Over Norton is situated in the north-eastern end of the Cotswolds limestone belt. It comes within the 'stonebrash' area of the county.

The following extract is taken from the British Geological Survey *The Geology of the Country around Chipping Norton* by A. Horton and others 1987.

> The outcrop of the Chipping Norton limestone forms the high ground to the north and east of the town. It is difficult to determine its total thickness because of cambering [*a type of rock-folding that forms rounded hills and valleys*, Chambers Dictionary 1997] but it may be about 7.6m. Pale cream to white, sandy, shelly oolites were seen in several old quarries around Over Norton.
>
> There are several small outcrops along the southern margin of the Swerford trough. The best in Richardson's Beds, is behind a garage at Priory Mill (Richardson 1911).

Despite the co-operation of the owners of Priory Mill I could not find this site in 1998.

There are no obvious signs that the quarrying of stone and the digging of sand are being carried out in this parish now (1999) but the remnants of past work in these trades are many.

The four stone cottages, with brick surrounds to the doors and windows, Nos 1-4 The Green, were built about 1907 by Mr Walford, of stone collected from local farmland by Mr Albert Saunders, his Head Carter.

There was a quarry at the top of Choicehill Road where the present village hall is standing, the site of which has caused much annoyance over the years. John West recalls being told by Walty

Webb that the Choicehill Road was repaired with stone from this quarry. Walty Webb had to spray this road with water during dry spells to keep the dust down. He kept his horse and cart, used for collecting stones and chippings for the council, in the orchard opposite his home, Home Farm. Back in 1910 the O.N.P.C. debated about the ownership of the Choicehill Quarry.

> ... it was found that the land belonged to the parish, and therefore the council would have the right of letting or selling the same... it was agreed to let the land and Mr Sanders was requested to have the gate repaired and find a suitable tenant.

Seventeen days later on 27 July 1910 Mr Sanders reported:

> the land let to Mr Saunders ... yearly rent 10/- [and on] 13 October 1911 O.N.P.C. [paid a] ... cheque for £1.2s.6d. in payment of Mr W.J. Weale's account for repairing the gate at the old quarry.

(Mr Weale, wheelwright, lived at Firs Farm.)

The quarry was used as a rubbish tip by locals and the district council. It was a wonderful source of materials for the village children during the Second World War from which they made 'trackers' and 'tricycles'. John West, as a child, went flying down the Over Norton hill on one of these contraptions and through the bridge railings into the brook. Tom Rudge, Peter Flick, Richard Woolliams and their other pals enjoyed this sport but later they graduated to driving the milk churn trolleys down the hill! (In 1897 three Over Norton men were fined 1s.6d. each for sledging down Over Norton Hill: Brain, Harrison and Worvil.)

In March 1943 it was noted by the O.N.P.C. that they:

> ...discussed the question of the condition of the quarry and a reference was made of a nuisance arising from the practice of tenants of nearby houses emptying night-soil in the quarry ... carried that the Clerk write to the Rural District Council with a view to the nuisance being abated.

14th September 1966 O.N.P.C.
Register of Common Land

It was agreed that the undermentioned lands should forthwith be registered as Common Land with the Oxfordshire County Council

1. Rubbish Tip formerly known as the Stone Pits [1/4 acre].

2. [At the same time the Village Green 1/8 acre was registered too.]

The present village hall was erected on the quarry site. Building began in 1977. It has proved to be a questionable decision as during the last few years huge cracks have appeared across the floor and in the walls.

Quarhill Close gets its name from the quarry.

One quarry was mentioned in a sales notice of Hill View Farm in 1925 as follows:

Roadway – Over Norton to Salford
... is believed to be an old public right of roadway said to have a width of 60 ft, but for a long period of years it has been used as an ordinary roadway or track of its present width and character and the precise position of the boundaries of the old road are believed to be unknown... [and] Part of the Quarry, situate on Enclosure No. 150, is believed to be situated on the old public roadway ... this lot is sold subject to any public rights of quarrying or ownership therein that may exist. [see page 281]

At the Sandfields Farm crossroads there was a substantial stone quarry in the corner of the ground at the beginning of Clinton's Walk (Dawkins family). It is part of Witts farm and in the adjoining fields there were several possible quarry sites. Over Norton parish had a public quarry which was situated on the east side of the Great Rollright hill.

Over Norton Park is surrounded by a well kept dry stone wall. Much of its repair work now falls to Mr Tom Hall. This wall, according to Mr C.J. Dawkins of Over Norton Park was constructed by Napoleonic prisoners of war. Colonel Henry Dawkins served under the Duke of Wellington. The Duke of Wellington was responsible for a huge army of occupation in France after the Battle of Waterloo, 18th June 1815. He was based in Paris until 1818. French prisoners were still here presumably during that period. Two date stones have been located, both of which can only be seen from private property. One stone has 'No. 2 1817' inscribed on it – the inscription taking up a space 30cm x 21cm – and clearly visible on a wax rubbing of the stone. The second stone has 'No. ? 1 Oct 1816' on it and is contained within an oval border 60cm x 53cm. The latter stone has been defaced.

It is rumoured that Burden's, Chipping Norton builders, built the Over Norton Park wall but a descendant, Mrs Eileen Forbes, stated that the late Mr Dennis Lewis, a much respected local historian, told her it was not true. Perhaps they did a major repair at one time or extended the wall.

Mr Tom Hall recalls seeing a date stone on the wall surrounding the school gardens at Chipping Norton when he was working there as a boy. The school gardens were in the apex of Over Norton Road and Banbury Road. This ground was part of the Dawkins (Over Norton Park) estate at one time. No date stone has been located there in 1998 despite British Telecom allowing a search to be made. This is not surprising as many significant changes have taken place in that area.

Mervyn Moulder told me that his grandfather, Sam, took a great pride in looking after the upkeep of the 'Park Wall'. He guarded it fiercely, and quickly sent children on their way if they should clamber over it – 'even his own grandchildren'. After 1914, when Col. William Gregory Dawkins died, Over Norton Estate was run from Wilcote House where Mr George Dawkins lived. George Dawkins had married Mrs Sartoris, a widow, living at Wilcote House. His estate agent, Mr J.B. Lutener, came to The Mission Room, now St James' Chapel, to collect rents. One senior resident said he hated being sent by his mother to pay the rent because it was a time when the village boys' misdemeanours were reported to 'the top'.

Mr George Dawkins was joint owner of the Over Norton Estate with Major Charles G. Hereward Dawkins, both nephews of Col. William Gregory Dawkins.

A pleasant feature of Over Norton village is the dry stone walling enclosing properties throughout the village. It is likely that this will remain for future generations to enjoy as much of the village is designated as a conservation area. There have, of course, been many changes over the years. For example, the 1918 sale notice for Witts Farm included:

> At the front is a small railed-in garden, and at the side is a capital walled-in garden.

No railings exist there now (1999). The high wall surrounding Cleevestones, the old farmhouse formerly Hill View Farm, was originally much lower and passers-by could see into the garden.

Another great change is the number of entrances in the walls to allow car access.

Large stones can be seen in many parts of the village. One which is lying at the footpath entrance to the present village hall was called – forty years ago – 'Walty Webb's stone' by the village children as he was always resting on it. When the new village hall was built this stone was moved to its existing position although it had been in Choicehill Road before. Mr Bernard Aries believes it used to stand under the 'Old Shed' at the bottom of Choicehill Road.

When the Over Norton lakes were restored and extended in the 1990s a large stone embedded in the surface of the dam was found. It was very much like the King's Men of the Rollright Stones, being of shelly oolitic limestone with a covering of lichen and similar in size and weathering pattern. The Over Norton stone may be from a structure such as the Hoar stone situated at the Fulwell crossroads Enstone – a portal dolmen set in a small circular barrow. Another monolith has been re-erected in a rear garden of a house in the centre of Over Norton.

At the Chapel end of the village an important looking stone stands in the garden of a house erected in 1968. It was moved there from the Fountain Cottage property where it had been used as a gate post.

The stones protecting the grass edges to the village green were placed there by Ian Pearman, who brought them down from 'Big Field' – part of Firs Farm land – SW of the Village Hall.

In the nineteen sixties there was a great fear that part of the county was going to be excavated for ironstone; one of the places where notices against this plan were displayed was on the roadside around Great Tew. The following minute from the Over Norton Parish Council on 7th April 1960 reflects their concern:

Ironstone mining in North Oxfordshire
It was reported that the proposed ironstone workings would come near to Over Norton and the meeting agreed to recommend that the Parish Council should formally register their objections to the two applications to excavate ironstone in about 3,500 acres of the County.

Coal Survey

A search for coal was carried out in Over Norton Parish in January 1891. Borings were made about $5/6$ of a mile N.W. of Over Norton House. There were no further developments.

William Smith

It was with delight that I read the *Memoirs of William Smith – The Father of English Geology* – edited by his nephew John Phillips, in the Bodleian Library and to discover that William Smith spent a considerable amount of time in Over Norton. Dr William Smith was born at Churchill on 23rd March 1769 and he died, aged 69 years. A large memorial stone to him stands in the centre of Churchill village. He was distinguished in the field of geology; as well as being the author of the famous 'Map of the Strata of England and Wales' he was responsible for producing twenty-one geological maps and many reports on engineering projects and mineral surveying.

William Smith's close links with Over Norton began at seven years of age following his father's death.

Extract from: *Memoirs of William Smith* by his nephew and pupil John Phillips 1844:

> After his father's death and his mother's second marriage, the person to whom he [William Smith] was principally to look to for his protection was his father's eldest brother, to a portion of whose property he was heir. From this kinsman, who was but little pleased with his nephew's love of collecting "the pundibs" and "poundstones", or "quoitstones" and had no sympathy with his fancies of carving "sun-dials" on the soft brown "oven stone" of the neighbourhood, he with great difficulty wrung, by repeated entreaty, money for the purpose of a few books fit to instruct a boy in the rudiments of geometry and surveying. But the practical farmer was better satisfied when the youth manifested an intelligent interest in the processes of draining and improving land, and there is no doubt that young William profited

in after-life by the experience, if it may be so called, which he gathered in his boyhood while accompanying his relative ("Old William") over his lands in Over Norton.

Whatever he saw, was remembered for ever. To the latest hours of life he retained a clear and complete recollection of almost every event of his boyhood, and often interested young and old by his vivid pictures of what he had seen as a child. These notices would be swelled to an unreasonable degree by introducing the pleasant stories of the 'narrative old man'.

Village Stonemason

Mr and Mrs Jack Joines were well known in the village (see last Chapter). Both used their varied talents and skills for the benefit of the local inhabitants. Mr Jack Joines showed great craftsmanship as a stone mason. The following is a transcript from a tape in which Mrs Grace Joines (b. 1899) describes her husband's method of wall building and of how she assisted him. (Source: Tape made by Rosalind Garrod (née Adams) 1965/66 for a C.S.E. project.)

> My husband's speciality was dry stone walling. The stone was dug up out of local pits; some of it differed greatly. Some was flaky which didn't suit him and some was soft which didn't suit him. There were particular pits that he liked.
>
> The wall was made below, two faced, and the middle was filled up with stone. The building of it was one stone on top of two that is one stone on top of the join. Every now and then there was one put right across and held it. There was a line put along to keep it level and a plumb bob was put down as he called it, "a tingle", to keep it upright.
>
> After he retired we used to do a bit for charity and one wall was surrounding the village hall [old wooden village hall below Firs Farmhouse].
>
> When we came to one part which had fallen down over the years, we repaired it, and the stones were all black and burnt and I recall that it used to be the old blacksmith's shop and these stones came from the old fire.
>
> I didn't do the actual building. He did all that showed, but I had to fill all the middle up which meant getting all the small stones and rubble that I could find all the small broken stones. If he had to chop a stone into shape I had to pick all the bits and pieces up and I'm sure I handled far more stones than he ever did.
>
> When we built to the required heighth stones which locals sometimes called "toppers", sometimes "shuckers", had to be cemented on and that was the only wet stone which was put in and they will stand for hundreds and hundreds of years. I've only known but one fall down which my husband built and I think that was the last one he ever did and he built miles and miles of walls in the County. I've often seen one which he built and I think it is a memorial to him.

Mr Jack Joines was given a new Atlas, at his request, as a present for re-building the old village hall wall enclosure. His daughter Mrs Alma Millard still (1999) has it in her possession.

It is interesting to note that a Josiah Joines, age 25, stone mason and his wife, Jemima were listed on the 1841 census as living in Over Norton.

Water

The former poor water supply to Over Norton has caused many problems over the years and this subject has featured frequently in the minutes of the Over Norton Parish Council as follows:

24th June 1898 O.N.P.C.

... Colonel Dawkin's stated that in consequence of his intention to be much away from Over Norton he had decided upon handing over to the Parish Council, free of cost, the tank, pump, pipes and all the apparatus connected with the water supply to the village, which had cost him about £300 or £400. [Quite a difference between the two figures!]

The Council decided upon accepting the Chairman's offer, and it was agreed that a meeting ... be held ... for the purpose of receiving Colonel Dawkins' offer in writing.

Signed Col W G Dawkins
Chairman

29th June, 1898

The Clerk presented the following offer in writing from Colonel Dawkins:

"I hereby make over to the Parish Council of Over Norton the pump, pipes, tank, and taps, all relating to the water supply now taken from my land, springs, on the condition that water be not taken from springs higher up the valley than those which it is now taken.

I would undertake to keep in repair, at my own private cost, the pipes leading water from Bowen's tap [Glover's Close 1998] to Over Norton House."

Mr F. Allen proposed that Colonel Dawkins' offer to hand over the Over Norton Water supply be accepted.

Mr Henry Moulder seconded.

Colonel Dawkin's proposed that Messrs William Moulder and Joseph Jarvis be appointed a sub-committee to manage the water supply, and that they be empowered to carry out any small repairs, and that Samuel Moulder be employed to attend to the Water-Wheel at a salary of Two Pounds per annum.

Mr F. Allen seconded the proposition which was carried.
Colonel W G Dawkins
Chairman

10th August 1898
... Messrs Rowell & Sons estimate for repairs to the Water-Wheel ... it was decided ... that such tender be accepted. (No figures were given)

11th November 1898
... Mr F Allen proposed that Samuel Moulder apply to Thomas Fox for the key of the main [water] near the Park Gate.
Complaint was made of the inefficient supply of water at the public tap opposite Mr Cornish's house.
William Moulder
Vice Chairman

3rd March 1899
... A discussion took place as to the defective condition of three of the taps and the hydrant of the public water supply ...
William Moulder
Chairman

Chipping Norton had a severe water shortage too in 1899 as shown by the following notice in *Jacksons Oxford Journal* :

16 September 1899
The Water Committee of Chipping Norton
This committee met on the 19th ult and resolved that the supply of town water to Captain Daly [Over Norton House] be continued for one week only from that date ... town water to be turned on for three hours daily only and for Rock Hill one hour only ...
... it was resolved that Alderman Bowen's supply of water at his tan-yard be disconnected at the main. [Distons Lane]

O.N.P.C. 15th April 1901
... Complaint having been made of the defective state of the Fountain Pump ... Mr G Hedges, of Chipping Norton, be asked to repair the same.

30th July 1901
... Complaint having been made of the shortness of the water supply the Clerk was instructed to see [Mr] Moulder and ascertain from him if anything could be done to increase the supply.

14th November 1906 O.N.P.C.
A meeting of the Parish Council at which the following were present

– was held for the purpose of considering what means should be adopted for increasing the supply of water to the Parish:

Messrs A A Webb, P J Smith, G Harrison and J Jarvis – Several Ratepayers of the Parish were also present including Capt Daly, Mr W P Walford, and Mr E M Sanders.

An inspection of the Pumping Station, the Pond, and the Springs was made and also a spring in the Terrace Field, the ground around which had been opened, and which appeared to be then yielding a good supply. It was thought that if this could be picked up at some future time, and conveyed by means of pipes to the existing supply, it would materially add to the volume of water available for pumping.

It was eventually decided, in the hope that the springs would shortly be replenished by autumnal rains, that the further consideration of the subject should be adjourned, but it was unanimously agreed that the water wheel should be thoroughly overhauled and the necessary repairs done to the same, the work being entrusted to Messrs Rowell & Sons, engineers, Chipping Norton.

William Warne 15 April 1907

1906 November O.N.P.C.
... Capt Daly had generously offered to the Parish Council a small oil engine for pumping the spring water.

... Messrs Rowell & Sons estimate accepted. [For repairs to Water Wheel. See also two letters: Col. W.G. Dawkins to Mr Sam Moulder Chapter Six.]

And so the problem of an inadequate water supply continued for a hundred years. In the 1990s the O.N.P.C. were still receiving many complaints particularly from families living in houses on the highest ground. At last, in 1998, Thames Water Authority developed a brand new scheme throughout the village, the work being carried out by the firm, O.C. Summers.

At the Annual General Meeting of the O.N.P.C. in April 1999, there were, for the very first time, positive comments on the water supply and no complaints.

Wells

Many wells existed in the village. Dorothy and Tom Rudge recall:

There were three close to Witts Farm house and two at Hill View farm, now Cleevestones. One of the latter was near to the house and the second was on the other side of the road near the large barns now converted to homes. Home Farm had a well at the back of the house and one in the yard plus one in a field. There was also one at Firs Farm. As regards other houses and land along Main Street: Glovers' Close, Double Diamond (when farmland) and Three Chimneys each had a well. There was also a well situated under the extension to the house with the War Memorial on it.

These were the wells remembered by Dorothy and Tom Rudge. There would of course have been others too.

A few people have mentioned the existence of a 'Holy Well' at Chapel House, commemorated in the name of the garage, but to date I have been unable to find out anything about it.

CHAPTER 4

Archaeological Finds—Domesday—Cold Norton Priory—
The Steeple Aston Cope—Chapel House from 1770—Window Tax—
The Naming of Over Norton

Oxfordshire Museum's Store

The Oxfordshire Museum's Store at Witney Road, Standlake, holds very few artifacts from Over Norton. In the archaeology collections there is a small quantity of Roman and medieval pottery (deposited 1976) and a beautiful bronze age flint blade from Over Norton Park (deposited 1988). A great amount of Roman material has surfaced at Chipping Norton including a stone carving of a Roman head which can be seen in Chipping Norton Museum. This head may represent Jupiter and was probably used in a late second century shrine. Personally I prefer to think of it as God of the River Glyme.

Some traces of paving, possibly Roman, were noticed by an allotment holder at the extremity of Chipping Norton (1997).

At the Standlake store there are some human and animal bones, including an ox bone, found at Cold Norton Priory.

Other items of social history will be listed in later chapters.

Charles Kirtland (1871) stated that at Chapel House,

> an ancient chapel stood ... for the use of pilgrims.

Stone coffins were found; in one beads and a silver crucifix were discovered. In a small vault three urns were found and fragments of masonry and painted glass were retrieved. The Ashmolean Museum, Oxford, have nothing recorded of this find. No information on the whereabouts of these artifacts has materialised.

Domesday

We have firm evidence of Chipping Norton's and Over Norton's history in 1086 from the Domesday Book. It was towards the end of

William I's reign (1066-1087), in 1085, that he decided he needed a written record of all land holdings and resources in his conquered lands.

These facts were eventually written in an abbreviated form of Latin on pages of sheepskin which were sewn together to make a book – later referred to as the Domesday Book – the original of which is held at the Public Record Office, London. The commissioners were instructed to note 'whether more could be taken than is now being taken' – a significant phrase! The name Domesday may be associated with the idea of the Day of Judgement. (Chambers Dictionary: *a day of reckoning and pessimism about the future.*)

The following translated extract is taken from *Domesday Book* edited by John Morris, 14 Oxfordshire published by Phillimore 1978.

TERRA ERNVLFI DE HESDING
(Land of Arnulf of Hesdin)

Arnulf held lands in Bortone (Black Bourton) and Lvdewelle (Ludwell).
Arnulf also holds (Chipping) Norton
15 hides and 1 virgate of land.
Land for 21 ploughs. Now in lordship 10 ploughs;
15 slaves.
22 villagers with 16 smallholders have 11 ploughs.
3 mills at 62d; meadow, 60 acres; pasture 1 league
in length and width.
The value was £16; now £22.
Wilfward White and Aelfric Whelp held it.

This entry covered the area now known as Chipping Norton and Over Norton.

Some historians think that a 'hide' was an area large enough to support a peasant family over a year but possibly varying according to the quality of the soil. Many sources quote a 'hide' as being about 120 modern acres. A 'virgate' is thought to be a quarter of a hide. A league is an old measurement of length, varying, but thought to be about 3 miles.

Ballard (1893) suggests that the population of Norton in 1085 was not less than 265, and that there were about two thousand and five hundred acres of cultivated land in Chipping Norton and Over

Norton. Of these, 12 hundred (or the land of ten ploughs) were in the demesne or home farm of Arnulf de Hesdin.

At the time of 'Domesday' the common or open field system was in operation in which the lands were probably divided into two large fields on which were grown wheat, barley and oats. Some land was allowed to be fallow supposedly to enable the soil to regain its fertility. The fields were divided into strips, sometimes but not usually, divided by broad banks of turf. Tenants may have held a virgate or yardland – about thirty acres – which consisted of strips of varying sizes scattered over the fields of the parish. All could turn their cattle into the fields after harvest until seed time.

The three mills in 'Nortone' belonged to the Lord of the Manor. All tenants had to pay to use them and were not allowed to go elsewhere to get their corn ground. Two Chipping Norton mills are marked on a map dated much later, and it is possible that one mill was in Over Norton.

The labour for the Lord's land at Nortone, consisted of his fifteen slaves plus their families; the villeins (villagers) and bordars (smallholders) also had to do a certain amount.

The villein tenants did gradually manage to break free from the many duties which they had to perform for the Lord and it is thought that by 1279 in Chipping Norton

> all the work and gifts were commuted for a money payment.
> [Ballard 1893]

Dorothy Rudge relates that when her family took over Witts Farm in 1935 medieval field patterns could be seen clearly on the NE side of the road – near the apex of Choicehill Road with the 'old coaching road' – in the two fields named Top Endolls, (10 acres and 12 perches) and Lower Endolls, (10 acres 22 perches) described as pasture in a 1942 conveyance.

Many acres of medieval ridge and furrow field patterns were lost due to ploughing during the 1939-45 war as the need for greater home production increased.

On the opposite side of the road to the Endolls fields on Firs Farm land, small ridges and furrows can be seen. Don Cambray, who farmed there, pointed out that these were not medieval but were part of a drainage system made in the 1800s. He has practical knowledge of this having discovered drainage systems when tilling the land.

The 1770 Inclosure Act shows that the Over Norton Common Fields, or part of them, were in the direction of Choicehill Farm.

Mary Endoll was allotted part of this land in the 1770 Inclosure Act:

> Publick Road leading from north west end of Guys Lane in the hamlet of Over Norton ... to Long Compton ... having allotments to ... Samuel Huckvale and Mary Endoll on the north east side thereof.
>
> [and to] John Endoll in lieu of his Yard Lands [etc] and Right of Common and Property in ... Common Fields [etc] ... to be inclosed The Two Several Plotts of Ground ... Forty eight Acres One Rood and Twenty seven Perches ... Bounded [by] ... on the south west by an Allotment to the said Mary Endoll. One other plot Twenty-two acres one Rood and seventeen Perches. Bounded on the north by the Turnpike Road leading from Enstone to Long Compton ... on the north east [by Henry Dawkins' land] and on the remaining part of the north west [by Mary Endoll's allotment].
>
> Thomas Wisdom [and] John Endoll to maintain hedges ditches and fences on the first allotment and at the expence of John Endoll and other owners on the second allotment.

Fencing charges were 10 pence (5p in present currency) for every yard in length.

(Mary Endoll married William Wright, see further references chapter 7. Endoll is sometimes written as Endall).

Cold Norton Priory

As Cold Norton Priory is of great historical significance something of its history is being included in this book although the site is no longer in Over Norton parish; it was transferred to Heythrop parish, 31st March 1985. The priory was situated on the site of the present Priory Farm House and Priory Farm (1999), $1^1/_2$ miles from Chipping Norton and located off the Chapel House to Heythrop road.

During the period 1148 to 1158 Cold Norton Priory, dedicated to St. Mary and St. John the Evangelist with, at some point, a hospital dedicated to St. Giles, patron saint of cripples, was set up by Avelina, Lady of Norton. 'Cold Norton Priory hospital was the only Oxfordshire one recorded in a list drawn up by Gervase of

Canterbury c.1200.' (V.C.H. Vol. ii p.155). Avelina was the daughter of Arnulf de Hesdin, Lord of the Norton manor in 1085/86. The priory was endowed with the tithes of Avelina's demesne and with lands probably 348 acres. (Source: Mr W. Wing, of Steeple Aston, read a paper on 'Cold Norton Priory' at Chipping Norton Town Hall 1854.) It was an Augustinian Priory with the canons following the Austin rule. They wore black habits like the Benedictine monks. (Following based on V.C.H. Vol. ii p.8 & 9.) The Benedictine houses were the first of the religious houses to be founded in Oxfordshire, followed by the Austins (Hermit Friars of St. Augustine) and Cistercians. Augustinian houses were formed at St. Frideswide and Osney in Oxford, and at Dorchester, Bicester and Wroxton. It was usual for the Augustinian houses to be endowed with several churches which they looked after but this does not seem to be so with Cold Norton Priory, which was quite a small one. They did however 'maintain a chapel for the laity' at the site of the present 'Chapel House' and 'Courtyard'. (V.C.H. Vol. ii p.96) This has now disappeared.

Steeple Aston church was given to the canons in 1363 (V.C.H. Vol. ii):

... hence the wish that a connection between the famous Steeple Aston cope and Cold Norton Priory will be found one day! (See later section on this subject.)

The 'hospital' may have been used for giving out hospitality and providing shelter for travellers and not just for care and treatment of the sick. Just why that particular site was chosen is open to conjecture but in those days hospitals were often built 'out of town'. The Priory was situated in the valley of a tributary of the river Glyme.

A charter dated 1204, was granted for a fair to be held at Cold Norton for three days beginning on the Feast of SS Philip and James (1st May). Chipping Norton was granted a fair in 1205. (Ballard, *History of Chipping Norton*, p32)

The priory held land in many parishes; this was certainly necessary if the canons were to live up to the Augustinians' reputation for generous hospitality. Many of the endowments were 'to buy' prayers for the after-life.

In the late 13th and early 14th centuries there was a dispute between Bruern Abbey and Cold Norton Priory. Bruern enclosed some land but were forced to allow the priory sheep grazing rights. Bruern had agreed with Cold Norton Priory in 1187 that there would be a 'stint of 25 sheep, 2 cattle and a pig for every yardland held' [a half yardland was 12 acres]. (V.C.H. Vol. xi p.138)

Walter of Broadstone leased to Cold Norton Priory 1/2 hide land, yielding hay and corn. (V.C.H. Vol. ii p.138)

In 1229 the priory was said to hold of William of Dunthrop land in Redcombe field by 1292 1 hide. Redcombe may have been the north field of Dunthrop's 13th century two field system. The priory was granted the right to pasture 200 sheep by William of Dunthrop in the late 12th century. (V.C.H. Vol. xi p.136 & p.138)

In c1231 they were given all the Little Tew meadow said in 1279 to comprise 36 acres of John des Preaux, Lord of Great Tew. The meadow was later known as Priory Mead. (V.C.H. Vol. xi p.251)

They also acquired in the 13th century 13 acres arable land from the Broc family. (op. cit)

Other gifts included: 1250 Lady Eva de Grey gave the priory a new fulling mill in Standlake, in return for 'the recital of prayers'. Fulling was a process in the manufacture of wool. The earliest known example of an Oxfordshire fulling mill is at Cleveley in Enstone parish, which was recorded c.1190 (James Bond).

1263 The Bishop of Lincoln arranged that the priory had the tithes of Adam de Brinton (Middle Aston). (V.C.H. Vol. ii p.96)

By 1291 all their possessions worth £16 a year were in Oxfordshire, except for half the rectory at Thenford, Northants. (op. cit)

1304 The Bishop asked Bucks, Oxon and Northants to welcome representatives of the canons who asked for alms. (op. cit)

1370 They were given a manor in Rollright to support two canons who should pray for the soul of the donor.

1396 The Bishop, describing the prior Robert de Enston who had resigned says:

> that for his negligence and idleness, whereby the priory is burdened with debt, and short of vestments and books, he deserves punishment rather than

honour; but having compassion for his old age, the bishop allows that he should eat at the prior's table, unless a worthier person be present, in which case he must sit among the brethren. He is to attend all services, and shall be allowed one servant at the expense of the priory.
(op. cit)

By 1399 the Priory was so poor that the prior might hold the vicarage of Steeple Aston as well as the rectory – the church there to be served by a canon. (op. cit)

At this time when being charged with mis-management, the Prior declared that the canons were:

(i) victims of demands for hospitality on the part of intolerable crowds of wayfarers [and that]
(ii) the lands were untilled as there were no labourers,
(iii) the houses ruined by storms,
(iv) and if help was not given the canons would be obliged to wander into the world to seek food and clothing.

Excesses and crimes were also looked into some twenty years later in about Dec 1415.

Twenty-two priors are listed in V.C.H. Volume ii and the last prior, William of Wootton, died 1507. By this time the whole organisation of this 'society' at Cold Norton Priory had collapsed. There was no one left to carry on and therefore a new prior could not be elected. The king, Henry VII, claimed the priory and its lands; Sir Robert Empson had a hand in this and they were given to St. Stephen's, Westminster, 1507. Bishop Smith of Lincoln, the founder of Brasenose College offered St. Stephen's 1150 marks for it. He acquired the property in 1512 and passed it to Brasenose College in 1513. At this time lands were held in twenty-one parishes including Burford, Hoggesnorton (Hook Norton), Lyddestone, Stratford, Netenenstone (Neat Enstone) Churchill, Childston and Banbury as well as the places already mentioned. (V.C.H. Vol. ii p.96 and Vol. xi p.136 & p.137) They owned Priory Mill (Over Norton) and three other mills. (W. Wing)

It is believed that the priory was used as a place of escape when the plague was in Oxford.

Having done research on Cold Norton Priory, from original documents, at Brazenose College, Miss Elizabeth Allen gave a talk on this subject to Over Norton History Group in October 1997. This speaker and subject drew in the greatest number of members and visitors that the group had ever known. The other great interest at this meeting was the fact that Mr and Mrs Jim Wiggins, who own Priory Farm attended and brought a varied collection of masonry which they had found over the years. Mr Wiggins believes that the line of his barn follows the line of the Priory buildings. Samuel and Nathaniel Buck did an engraving of the remains of the priory in 1729 (see illustration).

During the 1990s the Wiggins family have restored several of the medieval fish ponds. (At Heythrop there were twelve well-stocked fishponds near the manor house 1679. V.C.H. Vol.xi p.137)

The Priory farmhouse, which is of the 16th and 17th centuries, probably has some medieval parts remaining. It is no longer part of Priory Farm.

Mr Pitts of Ducklington, used to visit his father's cousin, Mr Roper, who farmed at Priory Farm around the 1939-45 war years.

> When visiting I was told stories of graves being exposed in dry weather and of the remains of monks being discovered, walled up, when the farmhouse was altered.

The Steeple Aston Cope

An interesting point that comes up for discussion locally from time to time is a belief that the famous Steeple Aston Cope originated from Cold Norton Priory. Being of great importance this cope is in the care of the Victoria and Albert Museum. The cope had been cut into two pieces making an altar frontal and dossal (used at the back of an altar). The dossal is displayed in the Victoria and Albert Medieval Treasury Gallery 43 and can be seen during opening hours and the altar frontal can be viewed by appointment. In answer to a query made in September 1998, the Assistant Curator of Textiles and Dress (Victoria and Albert Museum) wrote:

> I do not know of any connection with Cold Norton Priory. As far as I am aware the only knowledge we have of its history is that it was at Steeple Aston church from "time immemorial".

The cope dates from the early XIV century when English embroidery was famous throughout Europe. It is made of delicate silk, embroidered in gold and silver thread and silks. Jesus Christ with Mary his mother, the Crucifixion and the martyrdom of many saints are depicted. The border shows angels riding on horseback including their back views; it is, apparently, very unusual to see this.

After depositing the cope with the Victoria and Albert Museum, Steeple Aston parish was able to display it in church on one occasion. (The cope was delivered from the museum in an air-conditioned vehicle.) Very strict security was in force, including a complete guard throughout the night. A telephone had to be installed to enable 'the watch' to keep in touch with the police.

Photographs of the cope and further written details can be seen in Steeple Aston church.

Chapel House from 1770

The 1770 Inclosure Map shows that Thomas Kerby (sometimes written Kirby) owned land totalling just over 78 acres. The main part of this bordered the Chipping Norton, Banbury Road opposite Hit or Miss Farm with six acres on the present (1999) Chapel House site.

At Kerby's death in 1790 he was reported as having been the owner of the Shakespeare Inn at

> Chappel on the Heath where he had converted a poor cottage on wild heath to a successful business [and a] Pile of Building perhaps not equalled by any single Road Inn in this Kingdom. (*J.O.J.* Mon. 31st May 1790)

The Executors of his Will appealed to the 'Nobility, Gentry and the Publick' to continue their support for the 'Inn [as it] will be carried on for the Benefit of his Relations, with the greatest attention;...' John Witts of Over Norton was one of the three executors of the will. They were each given ten guineas to purchase a ring.

Diarists of the late 18th century have left useful documentation on the Shakespeare Inn. William Hickey captured the flavour of the times when he wrote in his memoirs:

> I rose at break of day ... stepped into a post chaise for Reading, [from London] on my way to Chapel House near Chipping Norton to join the sportsmen ...

> Upon my arrival at Chapel House, Charlotte greeted me with extraordinary warmth ... By five o'clock, the chasseurs being all assembled at the inn, we sat down to dinner, were extraordinary merry, and kept it up until mid-night, when we separated.
> ... At ten we breakfasted, then mounted our horses, Charlotte being one of the best horsewomen I ever saw. We took a long ride towards Birmingham ... [They would have followed the old coach road – see map.]
> At Chapel House I spent four as pleasant days as ever I experienced, in the enjoyment of women, wine and admirable society.
> ... On the fourth evening ... I bid the party adieu; ordering a chaise-and-four I set off for London giving Captain Browne a passage.

Hickey took Charlotte to India where she died in 1783 aged 32 years. She had refused his offer of marriage but consented to assume his name.

The Torrington Diaries contained praise indeed for the Chapel House Inn:

> 6th July 1785
> The town of Chipping Norton stands airily, and chearfully; but all the inns are eclipsed by that of Chapel House, which is quite a principality; and surrounded by gardens and other embellishments: it being a single house, is apart from village noises; an excellent station for hunters and I should suppose for convalescents, from the dryness of the soil, and purity of air.
> Here we came at 1/2 past six o'clock; after tea we endeavoured to play at bowls in the garden; and laughed at the crowded fantastic follies of a Ranelagh, or a Vauxhall; whilst Mr R. played on his flute, to the delight of the house company ... We smoked our pipes; this sport has been decaying ... and will soon be reprobated in genteel inns.

After having an early morning ride the diarist continued,

> 7th July 1785
> In three miles I came to Long Compton, a tedious village; at the top of the descent I turned to the right to view Roll-right Stones, an antient druidical temple.

(Note. Ranelagh: a public London Pleasure Garden 1742/1813
Vauxhall: Ditto c1661 to 1859)

William Makepeace Thackeray set Chapter six of Vanity Fair (1848) in the Vauxhall Royal Gardens, London. He included details of the entertainments: a hundred thousand extra lamps; the fiddlers in cocked hats; the country dancers; pots of stout; fireworks and rack punch for the gentlemen.

In 1787 the Chapel House Inn was used by 'The Acting Magistrates' for 'their ensuing sessions'.

> [The] Ale Keepers within the Hundred of Chadlington and North Division ... [and] all Publicans [were expected to attend.] The Minister Churchwardens and principal inhabitants'... were asked to lay their objection. (*J.O.J.* 8th Sept. 1787)

Badminton Hunt supporters stayed at the Chapel House Inn when the Badminton hounds were brought (1802) to join the Heythrop hounds.

Many guide books including *The Cotswold Country* published by G.W.R. 1936, have recorded Dr. Johnson's visit to the inn in 1776 where he supposedly

> delivered his famous panegyric on inns, and which was also patronized by Queen Victoria and her mother about 1826.

Oral sources state that George IV, as Prince of Wales, also stayed at the Chapel House Inn.

A document, seventy-two pages long and covering 1632-1836 entitled: *Abstract to the Title to a freehold and leasehold Inn and premises called Chapel House the property of Mr William Bulley 1835* can be seen at Stratford-upon-Avon's Record Office. It recorded that the premises had

> 26 bays of buildings in 1783.

My visit had been arranged to study 'The Chamberlain's Accounts' for 1735. (See Dawkins, Huckvale and Clarke Chapter 14) and I was surprised to discover the Chapel House document.

Window Tax (1695-1851)

By 1695/1696 it was decided by Parliament to raise more funds for the Exchequer by imposing a Window Tax – payment to be made according to the number of windows in each house. Some of these funds were used to replace totally the damaged coinage of the realm.

It had been common for clippings to be taken from the handmade silver coins. Many counterfeit coins were also in circulation. (For the earlier Hearth Tax see Chapter 5)

Many Window Tax records have not survived to present day but it is fortunate that the records of ones paid by Over Norton's inhabitants for the period 1785 to 1796 can be seen at the Oxfordshire County Record Office. Some other taxes are included on the same sheets (see appendix). Particularly relevant to this chapter is an undated sheet, but probably 1785, showing that Thomas Kerby of Chapel House paid:

Window Old Duty	£09. 9s. 0d. }	
Do. New Duty	£10.10s.0d. }	for 93 lights
House Tax	£00. 7s.6d.	
Carriages with four wheels	£28. 0s.0d.	
Waggon Tax	£00. 4s.0d.	
Priory Window Old Duty	£00.17s.0d. }	
Do. New Duty	£00.18s.0d. }	for 12 lights
	£50. 5s.6d.	

In 1790 the Executors of the late Mr Kerby paid a total of £58.10s.6d. taxes for the year, the increase being explained by one extra carriage (£7.0s.0d.) and one male servant (£1.5s.0d.).

<blockquote>An assessment made the 11th day of June 1785 by William Huckvale and Thomas Roach Assessors for the Tything of Over Norton of monies payable to his Majesty King George the Third for an Additional Duty charged upon Houses Windows and Lights in lieu of the Taxes ...</blockquote>

... resulted in the following being collected annually at two six-monthly intervals:

	No. Lights	£	s	d
W.ᵐ Gore Langton Esq	50	6	10	0
John Austin	7	0	6	0
John Witt	6	0	3	0
W.ᵐ Wright Gent void	—			
Robt. Fletcher	6	0	3	0
W.ᵐ King	7	0	6	0
Rob.ᵗ Wheeler	7	0	6	0
Mary Witt	6	0	3	0
Tho.ˢ Roach	14	1	5	0
W.ᵐ Cecil	7	0	6	0
John Endall Junior	7	0	6	0

	No. Lights	£	s	d (continued)
Wm Huckvale	18	2	5	0
Richd Hyatt	8	0	8	0 [But 7 windows in 1786]
Richd Bucketts	8	0	8	0
John Endall Senior	6	0	3	0
John Collett	6	0	3	0
Wm Kight	8	0	8	0
Thos Wallington	12	0	18	0
Thos Kirby Chapel House	93	10	10	0
Thos Kirby Priory	12	0	18	0
Saml Huckvale Junior	16	1	15	0
Wm Carpenter	13	1	1	0
		£28	11	0

Signed the 13th day of June 1785 by us
     Wm Huckvale }
     The mark of } Assessors
     Thos Roach +

[Countersigned by
L. Rollinson and
? T. Hudgkin?]

N.B.: Inhabitants had to pay this New Duty on windows plus the Old Duty, e.g. Wm Gore Langton Esq. paid (1790) an old duty of £5.3.0. – John Austin's old duty was 9s.0d. – John Endall's was 4s.2d.

Boarding School

The 1861 census shows that there was a boarding school at Chapel House run by Henry Hamilton Hamilton, a forty-four-year-old Clergyman 'without care of Souls and Schoolmaster' (i.e. not in charge of a parish) who was born in London. Mary his wife was from Suffolk. They had three children. There were two young tutors each aged 24 years: William Chevalier from London and William Watlington from Ireland. Nine pupils were boarding, their ages ranging from eleven to fifteen years. They came from Mausbury (?Maugersbury) Gloucestershire; Stafford; Stoke Fleming (?Devon); Mickleton, Oxon; Great Rollright, Oxon; Gedding, Suffolk. The domestic staff consisted of: Emily Stockford age 21, a cook from

Swerford, Oxon; Emily Clarke age 21, a housemaid from Taston, Oxon and Anne Short age 32, a housekeeper from West Chilington.

Over Norton Estate Sale 1918

In 1918 the Over Norton Estate put all of the properties at Chapel House up for sale:

> Lot 4 Chapel House Farm including the Farm House with its 'Stately Avenue with Stone Pillared Entrance' (opposite the Banbury Road plant nursery) [plus] '86a 1r 9p' and a 'two bedroomed cottage'.
>
> Lot 5 Chapel House [former coaching inn] a two bedroomed and adjoining four bedroomed cottage facing the Oxford Road, total acreage 7a 3r 2p with stables etc.
>
> Lot 6 Seven stone built cottages, four facing the Oxford Road and three at the back. [The latter now (1999) forms the house Mo Tighe from which Wendy and David Osborn run their boarding kennels 'Paws With Inn']
>
> Lot 7 Burgess Gate [land measuring 4a 0r 33p]

Against Lot 5 was pencilled timber '153' and '630'; Lot 6 '490'; Lot 7 '80 Busby'. Presumably these figures represent pounds and indicate the prices paid.

Moving on to 1924, *Kelly's Directory* had the following entry under Commercial:

> Bayliss Capt. James William – farmer and landowner. Chapel House Farm.
> Bayliss William George – poultry farmer.

(On a personal note I recall going to Bayliss', opposite the nursery in Banbury Road, during the 1930's to collect day-old chicks. They were supplied in cardboard boxes.)

The following advertisement also appeared in *Kelly's* 1924 :

> Chapel House Hotel (temperance) family and commercial; tennis and tea parties catered for; accommodation for hunters.
>
> (Capt. W.M. Bayliss Proprietor)

No one living in Over Norton (1999) remembers this hotel.

It can be a little confusing for non-locals as the term Chapel House has two meanings: the large house built on the site of the ancient chapel (Cold Norton Priory connections) or the small geographical area around it. Just to confuse matters further the large house has in recent years been divided to form two separate residences. The one with the entrance off the Heythrop road has retained the name 'Chapel House' and the section having a gabled porch with columns facing the A3400 is named 'The Courtyard'. Chapel House Cottage is attached to The Courtyard and has full frontage to the A3400.

Other interesting facts about Chapel House can be found in the late Dennis Lewis's book *Chipping Norton Inns* published in 1986 by Chipping Norton Local History Society and obtainable from Chipping Norton Museum.

The Naming of Over Norton

There are many variations on the name Over Norton.

A 'joke-name' has been 'Peckham'. Senior residents smile as they recall 'Peckham Town Hall', the old open shed meeting place. A Chipping Norton septuagenarian recalled that Over Norton road to Chipping Norton was always called 'Peckham' in his young days. Some residents were nick-named 'Peckham' as was Wilf Harrison. Rebecca Pearman says that when building work was being carried on at Firs Farm the gang of men referred to the Over Norton man as 'Peckham'. No one seems to know how it started.

But now to serious names. According to Misses Meades the spelling of Cold Norton was Cholde in 1269 and a later deed grants lands to '*Domini hosspitali Frigide Nortune*'. The term 'The Prior of Spitalnorton' (meaning hospital) was also recorded.

In 1302 Over Norton was written as Overenorton. Burt Norton, meaning Over Norton, was used in 1641 in the Chipping Norton Estreate. Some authorities explain that Burt may mean 'near a fortified place' (Chipping Norton Castle?). When James Dawkins first came to Over Norton in 1726 the village was called Upper Norton. It was also called Parva Norton at one time. (The Rollrights were listed as Rowlright Magna and Rowlright Parva in the 1641 Estreate.)

CHAPTER 5

Taxes (1634/5, 1649 and 1650) collected by the Constable of Over Norton
—Hearth Tax and returns for 1665—Burying the Dead in Woollen Cloth—
Sheep farming restrictions—Huckvale and Busby families: their wills and
inventories—Dissenters applications—Over Norton's Protestation Return 1641

Taxes collected by the Constable of Over Norton

In the archives at County Hall, Oxford, there are, among others, three small documents relating to instructions to the Constable of Over Norton. Extracts from the earliest one included here is dated 1634 and instructs:

> ... Thomas Grott constable of Over Norton from Michaelmas 1634 to Michaelmas 1635 ... [to collect] £10.6s.10d [made up of six amounts which included] 53 yardlands at 4d ...

This tax went to the depleted Exchequer of Charles 1st.

The following two documents are again addressed to the Constable of Over Norton:

> ... to require you to Levy and collect the some of 7s.0d which is due and ought to be payd for this year: 1649 for the House of Correction maymed Souldiers and other survivors and that you bring that money soo gathered to me to the White Hart in Chipingnorton upon the first day of march next...
> Dated the 21th of february 1649. [Date as written]   Thomas Marten
>
> ... to leavy and collect fourteen shillings for this year: 1650: [as above] plus... all other somes of money in arrears for the survivors... the money so gathered you bring to me at my house in Radford upon the 21st August next...
> Dated this 13th of August 1650.   Thomas Marten

These taxes collected in 1649 and 1650 would probably have been used to support the casualties of the Civil War (1642-1646). A law passed in 1600/1 stated that a weekly sum towards the relief of

> the sick, hurt and maimed soldiers and mariners

should be paid by every parish.

Houses of Correction were, by law to be

> set up before Michaelmas 1611' for 'disorderly persons, rogues, vagabonds and sturdy beggars.

Some were put to work for a year. (*The Justice of the Peace and Parish Officer* by Richard Burn. Vol. IV M.DCC.LXXII)

Radford, the home of Thomas Marten the collector of the taxes, is in Enstone Parish. In St. Kenelm's Church, Enstone, there is a memorial plaque on the north wall stating,

> Near this Pillar Lieth the body of Mr. Benjamin Marten of Radford, son of Thomas Martin of Rowsham, Gent ... He died February 4th 1715-1716 aged 47 years.

He left £120 for Twenty Poor Parishioners of Enstone Parish – five were to be inhabitants of Radford.

Hearth Tax

The hearth tax (1662 to 1689) was imposed by Charles II. Petty Constables had to collect two shillings for each hearth – half at Lady Day and the second instalment on Michaelmas Day – unless the occupants were exempt due to poverty or for other reasons. Included in the latter were:

> Those whose houses were worth less than 20s a year
>
> Certain types of hearths; blowing houses; ovens; furnaces and kilns
>
> Almshouses with yearly income less than £100.

(Burn op.cit.)

Some problems were found in collecting the tax from direct refusal to making false returns. When it was realised that the local officers had not carried out their duties correctly Chimney Men (1664) were appointed to replace them. It would be easier to count chimneys than undisclosed hearths. By 1666 a system of 'farming out' the collection, under a seven year contract was tried, but this method was unsuccessful too and the release from the contract was given in 1668.

The collector of the hearth tax received 2d in the pound as wages. The balance was handed to the High Constable, who took 1d in the pound, and then to the sheriff. The latter did well and took 3d in the pound and a further 1d per pound was paid to the Clerk of the Peace who looked after the returns. The amount left went to the Exchequer. (Meades) This very unpopular tax did not raise the amount that was expected.

Thirty-five Over Norton residents are listed on the return for 1665. Four houses had four hearths each, three houses had three hearths, ten houses had two hearths and as would be expected the greatest number (18) had only one hearth each.

Nine inhabitants were discharged by poverty as was John Freeman whose house was uninhabited. There is only one woman listed, a widow. When transcribed from the original documents the number of hearths is shown in Roman numerals with 'j' representing the final one e.g. iiij=4. In the original the final minim was lengthened, written with a tail, rather like a modern 'j'.

It would seem that the Exchequer would have received about £48.9s.8d. from Over Norton.

<u>Hearth Tax Return 1665</u>

Overnorton

Membrane 51r.

Thomas Chamberlayne gent	iiij
Robert Gay	iij
John Busby	i
Richard Busby	i
Christopher Saacks	ij
William Times	i
Edward Piggerstaffe [?Biggerstaffe]	i
Robert Wheeler	ij
Thomas Taylor	iij
Robert Croft	i
Anthony Robins	ij
Edward Busby	ij
John Hopkins	i
Thomas Hopkins	iiij

Hearth Tax Return 1665

Overnorton (continued)

George Burbridge	i
John Buckett	ij
John Scarlett	i
Richard Hutchins	i

Membrane 52

William Picksford	i
William Times	iij
James Collins	i
John Haydon	i
Edward Gardner	i
William Kite	ij
William Ingram	iiij
	xlvj

Thomas Andrews	i }
William Busby	ij }
Samuel Mintue	ij } dis-
William Ward	i } charged by
- Welcher widdow	ij } poverty
Richard Hutchins	i }
Thomas French	i }
William Fletcher	i }
John Wellen	ij }
	xiij

John Freeman	(uninhabited)	iiij

Sources: 1. *Short Guides to Records, First Series – guides* 1-24 pages 45/46.
2. *The Local Historian's Encyclopedia*, John Richardson. Pub. Historical Publications Ltd. 1993.
3. Chipping Norton Library: Meade's typescript Hearth Tax Returns based on *Oxfordshire Record Society*. Vol. 21

As sheep farming was a very important part of Cotswold life some of the points of law connected with it have been included.

Burying the Dead in Woollen Cloth

From 1666 to 1678 there was a law in force which said that the dead must be buried in wool, a good way to boost the woollen cloth industry.

The following extract concerning this law is taken from Burn op.cit.

> Concerning burying of the dead in woollen cloth no corpse of any person (except those who shall die of the plague) shall be buried in any shirt sheet, or shroud, or any thing whatsoever made or mingled with flax, hemp, silk, hair, gold or silver, or in any stuff or thing, other than what is made of sheep's wool only; or be put into any coffin lined or faced with any sort of cloth or stuff, or any other thing whatsoever, that is made of any other material but sheep's wool only.

The minister had to keep a register of burials and within eight days after interment an affidavit had to be made. If this was not done,

> the party deceased shall be liable to the forfeiture of £5 one fourth to the king, two fourths to the poor and one fourth to him that shall inform and sue.

Sheep farming restrictions
A statute was passed:

> By the 25 Henry, 8 [1533-34] c.13
>
> For the preventing many farms being accumulated into few hands, and for the encouragement of tillage, it is enacted that no person shall have above 2000 sheep at one time, at six score to the hundred, except it be upon his own inheritance only, and except what are necessary for his houshold; on pain of forfeiting 3s.4d for every sheep above that number, half to the king, and half to him that will sue.
>
> And lambs not reckoned sheep, till the second Midsummer after they are lambed.
>
> No person shall take above two farms, with houses thereon; nor shall any person have two, except he dwell in the parish where they both are; on pain of 3s.4d a week in like manner.

No live sheep to be carried oversea or all goods taken and shared half to the king and half to him that will sue and a year's prison sentence ... and at the year's end in some open market town, in the fullness of the market, on the market day, he shall have his left hand cut off and nailed up in the openst place of the market;

... And for the second offence shall suffer death.

If any person shall in the night time maliciously and willingly kill any sheep; ... to avoid judgement of death, he may make his election to be transported for seven years.

The statutes are herein continued to the end of parliament 11 Geo. 3.

[April 3 1772]

(Burn op.cit.)

In 1783 William Bowler of Gagingwell was hanged at Oxford for stealing a sheep at Kiddington belonging to Lady Browne Mostyn and her second husband, Sir Edward Gore.

The Huckvale Family

The Huckvales were prosperous yeoman of Over Norton where they had lived since about 1500 and at one time they farmed Choicehill Farm, Over Norton, and Glyme Farm, Chipping Norton. They were effectively the founders of the Baptist Church at Chipping Norton in 1775 and Samuel Huckvale was Mayor of Chipping Norton in 1841-42. He died during his year of office. By the end of the 19th century the entire family appears to have left the district... The graves of the Huckvale family are situated in the old Baptist burying ground behind the Baptist Church, New Street, Chipping Norton...

(Revd. Ralph Mann)

Jonathan Huckvale applied to use his house as a Dissenters' Meeting House in 1722 and John Wheeler did so in 1744.

Quarter Sessions/1722
Trinity/6

The house of Jonathan Huckvale in Over Norton in the parish of Chipping Norton in this county may be registered as a meeting house for protestant Dissenters.

and at Michaelmas 1744,

To his majestys Justices of ye Peace for ye County of Oxon

The humble Petition of John Wheeler of upper norton in ye said County Desiring his house may be Licensed for Protestant Dissenters to meet according to Act of Parliament.

Extracts from John Huckvale's Deed of Gift 1594 enrolled 1606/7 (MS Wills Oxon 193/189), which includes details of provision for himself and his wife Joanne, for their old age, is followed by Cuthbeart Huckvale's will 1637 with notes by Revd. Ralph Mann. Cuthbeart Huckvale's inventory of his possessions is also included. (MS. Wills Oxon 31/4/28)

In a deed of gift (8th Dec 1594, enrolled 21 Feb 1606/7) made by John Huckvale, his son Cuthbert was to inherit:

> all manner of these my goods moveable and unmoveable Chattells, Cattells, leases, household stuffe land and tenements ...
>
> the said Cuthbert Huckvale ... will provyde and fynde unto the said John Huckvale and Joanne his wyffe mother of the said Cuthbert good and sufficient meat drink fyre candle washinge and lodginge at and in the house off the said Cuthbert wheresoever he and they shall happen to dwell And alsoe to satisfie and paie unto the said John Huckvale and Joanne mother of the said Cuthbert and to the longer lyver of either of them the somme of fyve pounds of lawfull money of England at twoe usuall Feasts ... or daies of payment in the year viz at the Feast of St. Michaell tharchangell next ensuinge the day of the Date hereof fyfty shillings and soe half yearly the somme of fyfty shillings.
>
> ... and also to either of them one half todd of wooll yearly at sheere tyme duringe their natural lyves and the longer lyver of either of them one half todd of wooll yerely at sheere tyme the which said paiement to beginne in Anno Dni 1595.

John Huckvale retained for his own and his wife's use:

> Imprimis xxxty sheep ... to geeve or to sell ... at his pleasure
>
> Three Heckfers – one each had been given to Mary Huckvale, Margaret Huckvale and Francis Huckvale (Cuthbert's children)
>
> Item: one nagge and the keeping thereof winter and summer yerely during the lyfe of the said John.
>
> Item: fower coffers will all such linen as is in them
>
> Item: two bedsteeds. Item: fower blanketts. Item: fower coverletts .Item: fower boulsters and fower pillows.   Item: six platters.   Item: fower sawcers.   Item: fower smaller such dishes.   Item: one great chest in his owne chamber

John Huckvale's (?1540 to 1606) parents were Christopher (1515 to 1577) and Anne Huckvale. John married Joanne (born? 1538) and Cuthbert their son (born? 1566) married Alice (born? 1570)

Cuthbert Huckvale's will follows (MS. Wills Oxon 31/4/28):

In dei nomine amen The foure and twenteth day of June in the Twelfe yeare of the Reigne of our / Sovereigne Lorde Charles by the grace of god of Englande Scotlande France and Ireland kinge defender / Of the Fayth &c and in the yeare of our Saviour Christe one thousande sixe hundred thirty and sixe I / Cuthberte Huckvale of Overnorton, within the parish of Chippingnorton in the County of Oxon gent beinge / Sicke in body but yett of perfett memory thanks be geven to almyghty god for the same; doe make and /Ordayne this my laste will and testamente Revockinge all Former Willes by me heretofore made In / maner and form followinge First I Commende my sowle unto Almighty god my Creator and Redemer / hopinge and assuredly trustinge to be saved, by the merites of the death and passion of his sonne our / Saviour Jesus Christe, and my bodye, I will to be buryed in suche semely sorte & maner in the Church As / By my executrixe shalbe thought fytt and convenyente Item I doe give and bequeth unto my sonne Thomas / Huckvale, all suche my goodes, that nowe I have att Brayles in the County of Warwick Item I doe give / And bequeth unto my sonne Richarde Huckvale the Some of five pounds, the which I doe stande / Joyntly bounden with hyme unto the Bayliffs and Burgesses of the burrowe of Chippingnorton, and the use / of the sayde v^{li} beinge eighte shillings att the daye I doe paye for hyme Item I doe give & bequethe / unto my sonneinlawe Richarde Busbye and to his heyres for ever, after my decease and my wyffes, all suche / parte of a certayne diche quicke sett hedge & grounds, lyinge and beinge, one the northe syde of vernehill / By the grounde, of the sayde Cuthberte Huckvale, the which I boughte of his Father John Busbye and / payde, for the same thirty shillings of lawfull monye of Englande. Item I doe give and bequeth unto my / Goddaughter Judeth Sheephyrde alias Laughton the Some of Five pounds of lawfull monye of / Englande, to be payde and sett forthe to her use, within sixe monethes, after my decease, Into sure/menes hands untill suche tyme, as she shall accomplishe, the full adge of xxith yeres, and yf that / She, shall fortune, to dye before that she be of the adge of xxith yeres, that then my mynde & will is / That the sayde some of v^{li} shall Remayne and come, to her two sisters Alice & Marye, equally to / Be devided betwne them bothe, Item my mynde and will is, And I doe give and bequethe unto my / Loving wyffe Alice Huckvale, my debts being payde, and my Funerall expencs discharged / All my goods and

Cattalles moveable and unmoveable whatsoever, Whom I doe make my sole and /Full Executrixe of this my laste will and Testamente, for her better preferment of livinge In Wyttnes / whearof I have wrytten this my presente laste will and Testamente, with my owne hande & sealed / the same the day and yeare above wrytten in the presents of

per me Cuthberte
Huckvale manu
Probatum &c apud Chipnorton &c decimo
nono die Aprilis 1637 coram &c Egidio
Sweit &c Offle &c Jurto Alicie Huckvale
relicte et Executrice &c
Inv 67^{li} 7^{s} 0^{d}

The following notes on Cuthbert Huckvale's will and inventory were written by Revd. Ralph Mann.

The will of Cuthbert Huckvale, proved 19th April 1637.

"As was the custom, Cuthbert Huckvale made his will when he saw death approaching in fact he had only six weeks to live. In these circumstances, his calligraphy is superb, and he makes the point (twice) that the will is written in his own hand. The wording also is precise and in the correct contemporary style, which suggests that he was well acquainted with the niceties of testamentary conventions. He describes himself as 'Gentleman' as did his father and grandfather before him; subsequent generations will prefer the appellation 'yeoman'. Of his eight known children (Mary, Margaret, Francis, William, Richard, Thomas, Mark and Judith) only four (Mary, Richard, Thomas and Judith) are referred to in his testamentary dispositions. The omissions may be significant. It is likely that Margaret and Francis died in infancy, but his eldest son, William, is passed over in silence. William Huckvale will have inherited the copyholding in Over Norton without the need for mention in the will, although one would have expected there to have been some reference to him. Richard (born 1600) may have been well established in a trade or profession which would explain the bond of £5 made to obtain the freedom of the Borough of Chipping Norton. Thomas inherits goods at Brailes, and disappears from history in Chipping Norton; it is unlikely that this also included freehold property since ownership of land in more than one county would have led to Cuthbert's will being proved in the Principal Probate Court at Canterbury. If Mark Huckvale (born 1605) is to be identified with the Mark Huckvale, innholder, who died at Enstone in 1666, he too may have been already adequately provided for. Cuthbert's 'goddaughter' Judith was his eldest granddaughter, daughter of Judith and John Laughton alias Shepherd who are not mentioned in the will. Laughton would appear to be the preferred spelling (alternatively spelt 'Lathan'); there was a family of yeomen by that name in Stonesfield. Cuthbert Huckvale specifically expected to be buried within the church, rather than (as was normal) in the churchyard; this also is an indication of his superior social status."

Cuthbeart Huckvale's Inventory (MS Wills Oxon 31/4/28)

The Inventory of the goods and Cattalls of Cuthbeart Huckvale of Overnorton in the parishe of Cheppingnorton / in the County of Oxon Gent late deceased as hearafter Followeth, vewed seene & prayssed by Wm Fletcher / & Ric Busbye of Overnorton aforesayde, the 25 days of the month of March in the yeare of our lord god one Thousand / six hundred & thirtie seven, and in the yeare of the Reigne of our Sovereigne lord Charles by the grace of god kinge / of England France & Ireland defender of the faith &c

	£		
Inprimis three horsses prayssed att	7	0	0
Item five kine prayssed att	10	0	0
It three heayfors prayssed att	4	0	0
It five Akars & a land of Wheate prayssed att	5	0	0
It five akars of Barlye prayssed att	2	10	0
It fowre akars Peaese att	2	0	0
It three akers & three yeards of Oats prayssed att	1	5	0
It three quarters of Barlye & a halfe for seeds prayssed att	3	10	0
It grist Corne prayssed att	1	6	8
It one yron bound Carte one ploughe three harrowes & horsegeares & one donge Carte & other Implements prayssed att	2	10	0
It haye prayssed att	2	13	0
It one Sowe & piggs & fowre flichings of Backon prayssed att	2	0	0
It fire woode & Cart timbber & plough timber prayssed att	1	0	0
It one Scaffoulde with a littell fearne onit prayssed att	0	6	8
It one furnes one malte mill & other Implements att	1	13	4
It in the Chamber over the Buttrie one olde garner one dowghe kiver & one spininge wheele & olde yron & other Implements	1	0	0
It one morter & pestell & other brase prayssed att	1	10	0
It two poots & three posnets prayssed att	1	0	0
It one Basson & kawer & other pewter prayssed att	0	5	0
It three silver spoones prayssed att	0	15	0
It two peare of flaxen sheets & pillowes prayssed att	0	13	0
It eight peare of Coase sheets & halfe a dossen of napkins & two table Clothes prayssed att	1	10	0

		£		
It one Cubberd in the hall one table one Cheyer one form & two stooles with other Implements prayssed at		1	6	8
It one yron barr & one olde yron beame for weight three Spitts andirons & other Implements prayssed att		0	10	0
It Cooperie ware prayssed att		0	6	0
It two fether Bedes two floxbeds fowre pillowes fowre bowsters with Coverlids blanckets & two bedsteeds prayssed att		5	0	0
It two Chests two Coffers & a warmeinge pann att		0	10	0
It his wearinge aparrell & books & other Implements att		6	0	0
It att Brayles one table borde one bench & waynescott & two joyne stooles one littell kettell & one shelfe & other Implements prayssed att		0	6	8
	Some is	67^{li}	7^s	0^d

Exhibitum erat huius Inventorium apud
Chippton in visitatione ibiden tent decimo
nono die Aprilis 1637 per
Aliciam Huckvale Relictam et Executricem &c
pro vero et pleno Inve10 &c sub protestatione
tamen de addendo &c quid &c si &c

For probate of a will to be granted a detailed inventory of possessions had to be produced. It will be noticed from the Over Norton ones that two or three villagers checked and priced these items. One wonders how much expertise they had. In the case of **Cuthbeart Huckvale 1637**, William Fletcher and Richard Busbye of Overnorton 'vewed seene and praysed' [priced] his 'goods and Cattalls' [chattels]. The farm animals listed include horses, kine [cow] heafors and piggs plus foure flitching [side of salted and cured pig] of Backon – an important food source.

Wheat is shown to be more valuable than barley except for the barley seed crop. Grist corn [for grinding] and haye are also featured as are pease and oats.

Included in the farm implements is a donge cart showing that manuring of the land was practised.

The timber list shows that they expected to make or repair carts and ploughs.

The Inventory seems to suggest that the things stored in the Chamber over the Butterie were not in current use.

The modern version of the useful morter and pestell [mortar and pestle] continues to this day in Delia Smith influenced kitchens but the posnets – probably a three legged cooking pot for standing in the fire – are more likely nowadays to be interpreted as plant containers for the garden.

The materials used for equipment within the kitchen included iron, brass and pewter and one would imagine that it was with great pride that three silver spoons valued at 15s.0d. were recorded.

The recording of spits is a reminder of how meat was roasted in front of the fire.

Sheets were in good supply, two pairs flaxen [linen] and eight pairs coarse. Perhaps the finer ones were kept for special guests. Four beds are listed but only two bedsteads.

It is sometimes possible to work out the size of a house from an inventory. In this case only two rooms are mentioned.

Cuthbeart owned some books, unusual for this period, but not unexpected as we already know he was proud to have written his own will.

There was ample storage for that time – one cubberd, two chests and two coffers – and a warming pan [a long-handled covered pan for containing hot coals] ensured a comforting warm bed could be prepared.

Very little was listed for Thomas Huckvale to inherit from Brailes but one interesting item was the waynescott which may have been a removable wooden panelled lining to a room.

In William Busby's Inventory of 1678 (see later pages) sheep and pullin [poultry] were kept as well as the animals mentioned in Cuthbeart Huckvale's list. William also had more farm equipment but very little furniture. Four rooms: Hall Chamber; Old Chamber; Hall House; and Low Chamber were mentioned.

The Busby Family

The Busby family were very important in the history of Over Norton and records of them can be found at least from 1543 and the name was still much to the fore in 1898 when there was a bitter disagreement between Col. William Gregory Dawkins of Over Norton House and Farmer Busby. Mr Busby had rented two farms from Col. W. G. Dawkins for over ten years – Priory Farm and Hillside Farm (formerly 'The Folly'). The 'Explanation' of the problem was displayed on a public poster by the Colonel. Strong words were used and Mr Busby was accused of 'outragious and prolonged insolence'. The poster was dated April 13th 1898 (see illustration).

The following has been taken with permission, from *Oxford Church Courts Depositions* 1542-1550 written by Jack Howard-Drake. (Page 5)

> 14 Tithes: sheep [c1543] ff 32.32V
> Parties: Hawll v John Busby of Bicester, formerly of Over Norton
> Others: Busby's shepherd; two of Busby's brothers
> Substance: Busby, his shepherd and brothers, had 140 plus sheep between them in Over Norton in 1542 and had offered tithe on them according to custom. Had he paid wool tithe it would have been worth 6d.

The four wills following, and inventories, give a sample flavour of what was happening in Over Norton's Busby farming families in the 1600s. All transcriptions were provided by Revd. Ralph Mann. Included are:

1. Richard Busby's will 1602/3 (MS Wills Oxon 3/5/49).
   His sons Rychard and John were Executors.
2. John Busby's will 1613 (MS Wills Oxon 4/3/9).
   Kathren, his wife Executrix
   (son Richard and daughter Mary mentioned).
3. Nicholas Busby's will 1648. Extract only (MS Wills Oxon 115/4/46).
   Sarah, his wife Executrix.
4. William Busby the elder's will 1680 and his inventory 1678 (MS Wills Oxon 7/2/6).
   Sonne William & Sonne John   Executors
   John is not to be a beneficiary if he should marry Ann Gardner
   – a warning which is repeated twice in the will.
5. Mary Busby's will 1710 (MS Wills Oxon 8/4/3).

Richard Busbye of Over Norton - 10 January 1602/3

In the name of god Amen the tenth daye of Januarye in the fyve and Fortyth yeare of the Raigne of oure Soveraigne Ladye Elizabeth by the grace of god of England Frannce & Irelande Queene defender of the fayth et al I Rychard busbye of Overnorton in the countye of Oxon husband theldre being Sycke in bodye but of good & perfett remembrannce praysed bee god doe ordayne and make this my Last wyll & testament in maner & forme folowing Fyrst I comend my Sowle to allmyghtye god & my bodye to be buryed in the Churche of Chippingnorton Itm I geve unto the poore of Overnorton vi^s viij^d Itm I geve unto preost of Fencot tenne of the best wethers that I have for Nathanyell my Sonnes deptes Itm I geve & bequeth unto Sysleye busbye my daughter in Lawe vi^{li} xiij^s iiij^d Itm I geve unto Margerat Brayne xx^s & one shepe Itm I geve unto Rychard Brayne one sheppe Itm I geve unto Blance busbye one sheppe Itm I geve unto Emme bastyne one sheppe Itm I geve unto Thomas cowlyng one Sheppe Itm I geve unto Ales Rowland of Chippingnorton one Sheppe Itm I geve unto Wyllyam hethecot vi^s viij^d Itm I geve unto Jamne hyet iij^s iiij^d Item I geve unto Sara iij Sheppe And all the rest of my goods moveable & unmovable I geve & bequeth unto Rychard busbye & John busbye my sonnes whome I make my whole executors of this my last wyll and testament / Overseers of this my last wyll & testament I make John Lancaster vicar Wylyam busbye & to have for theyre oaynes v^s a peece

        wytnes here unto John Lancaster clark

	Rochard	busbye
Rychard	geves	his hand
his	marke	

    Probatum erat hoc testamentum Coram nobis Johnne
     Stone Archin viro substitut venlis viri Anthonij
     Blincowe Legum &c Apud Oxon vid septimo
   die mensis Januarij Anno Dm 1603 Ac per nos approbatu
    et insiuat ac &c Executoribus in eodem nomti
     in forma juris jurat salvo iure cuiuscumq

    Invent Summa /

John Busby of Over Norton 1613

In the name of god Amen: the xxth day of march in the yeare of our Lord god one thousand six hundred and twelfe I John Busby of Overnorton in the County of Oxford husbandman beinge sicke of body but of good and perect memory thanks be given to god doe make this my last will and testament in manner and forme followinge viz:

Imprimis, I give and bequeath my soule into the hands of Allmighty god my maker and redeemer trustinge by the merits of Christ Jesus my soule to be saved & my body to be buried in the Church of Chippingnorton and my goodes that god hath blessed me withall in manner and forme followinge.

Item I give unto my daughter Mary Busby her heires or ass[ignes] for ever my two houses and the Closse there unto adjoyninge lyinge in Overnorton afforsayd or els thyrtie poundes of good and lawfull Englisshe mony at the Choysse of my sonne Richard Busby to be payd at Michaelmas next ensuing after the date hereof.

Item I give unto my sonnes wife Mary Busby my daughter in Lawe and unto her two Chilldren two sheepp apeece

Item I give to William Horsman vj^d

Item I give to William Baffin a Chilver sheepp

Item I give unto John Miles vj^d

Item I give unto Thomas Busby a Chilver sheep

Item I give unto Richard Huchins vj^d

Item I give unto James Busby xij^d

Item I give unto the poore of Overnorton vj^s viij^d

The rest of my goodes moveable & unmoveable my debts legacies and funerall discharged I give and bequeath unto Kathren Busby my wife whome I make my sole and whole Executrix Inwitnes hereof I sett my hand

Witnessess

Edward Allaway
& Edward Chadwell

Probatum coram doctore Blincowe...
... apud Chippingnorton...

... vicesimo secundo die mensis Aprilis
Anno dni 1613...

Inven summa   67^{li} 7^s 8^d

Extract from the Will of:
Nicholas Busby of Over Norton 1648

First I doe bequeath my soule into the hands of almightie god my Creator & unto Jesus Christ my lord & only Saviour with sole confidence by his meritts to attaine eternall Salvacion. And my body I bequeath unto the earth to bee buried in Christian Buriall at the discretion of my friends and executors. And as for my worldly estate I doe give & dispose of it as followeth First I doe give & bequeath unto Sarah my now wiffe all those houshold goods which shee brought unto mee at her marriage of what sort soever. & which were formerly her owne before shee became my wiffe

Item I doe give unto my Grandchilde Nicholas Kite my Bible.

Item Forasmuch as I have given unto all my Children severall portions in marraige with them already I doe now by this my will only bequeath unto them two shillings Six pence Apeece

Item I doe give unto my brother Thomas Busbie Twentie shillings

Item I doe give and dispose to the poore of Overnorton Tenn shillings to be divided amongst them by my executrix upon the day of my Fnerall

Item I doe make Constitute & ordaine Sarah my now wiffe to bee the sole executrix of this my will & testament

Item I doe give & my will is that yf my Grandchild Nicholas Busbie of Churchill shall survive & overlive my wiffe Sarah That then the two presses in my Chamber shalbee & remaine unto him after her decease

In witnesse heereof I have heereunto put my hande & Seale the day & yeare abovewritten

Sealed & subsccibed   sig Nicholai
in the presence of   Busbie
John Norgrove

William Busby of Over Norton 1680

In the name of god Amen the Tenth Day of August in the Thirtyth Yeare of the Raigne of our Soveraigne Lord Charles the second by the grace of God King over England &c Annoque dni 1678 / I William Busby thelder of Overnorton in the County of Oxon yeoman being of sound and disposing memory doe / make this my last Will and Testament conteyning therein my last Will and Testament in manner and form following / First I Committ my selfe to God and his grace in an humble hope of eternall life and I will that my body be decently interred according to the discrecion of my Executors in a manner befitting the respects due to humane / nature And as for and concerneinge my Reall & personall Estate I dispose of in manner as Followeth

Item I give / & devise to me sonne William Busby his heires & assignes for ever All my Messuage or Tenement & homestall / thereunto adjoyneing and one Yardland of arrable meadowe & pasture ground and three acres of arrable / and halfe a Common with all thappurtenances thereunto belonginge Upon this Condicion following (that is to say) That / my sonne William shall well and truely pay or cause to be payd unto my sonne John Busby the summe of One hundred / Pounds of lawfull English money to be payd unto him within sixe moneths next after my sonne John shall marry / and take to wife any other woman Excepting Ann Gardner the daughter of Edward Gardner of Overnorton / aforesaid or within Sixe moneths next after the said Ann Gardner shalbe marryed to any other man Excepting / my sonne John

Item my will is that if my sonne William doe Refuse and will not pay the said Summe of One / hundred pounds of lawfull English money to my sonne John Busby as aforesaid then I give and devise to my sonne / John Busby his heires & assignes for ever the moity or one halfe of my Messuage or Tenement & homestall and the / moity or one halfe part of my Yardland and three acres of land and the moity or one halfe part of all / thappurtenances thereunto belonging.

Item my Will is that if my sonne John Busby doe marry and take to wife the said Ann Gardner the daughter of Edward Gardner of Overnorton aforesaid That then his / Legacy of One hundred Pounds or the moity or one halfe part of my Messuage or Tenement & homestall and / the moity or one halfe part of my Yardland and three acres of land and the moity or one halfe part of / all thappurtenances thereunto belonging shalbe absolutely voyd and of one effect Then I give and devise / to my sonne John Busby the summe of Five Pounds of lawfull English money and no more.

Item I give / & devise to my Grandson William Coldicott one Ewe and lambe Item I give and devise to the Overseers / of this my Will two shillings and sixpence a peice to buy each of them a paire of Gloves.

Item all the / rest of my Goods Cattle Chattells and personall Estate undevised I give and devise to my Two sonnes / William Busby and John Busby whome I doe make my whole Executors of this my last Will and / Testament

But if my sonne John Busby doe marry and take to wife the said Anne Gardner then my / sonne John Busby shall have nothing to doe with the Executorshipp nor to have any profitt thereby.

I doe / intreate my lovinge Friends John Smith of Chippingnorton Gent and William Timms the younger / of Overnorton aforesaid Yeoman to be the Overseers of this my Will to see the same performed according / to the true intent and meaneing thereof IN WITNES whereof I the said William Busby / thelder have hereunto sett my hand and seale the day & Yeare first above written

Signed Sealed and Published	William Busby thelder
in the presence of	his marke
Wm Huckvale Ju.	Probat &c apud Chippingnorton 27th die
John Wheeler Ju	Aprilis Anno Dni 1680 ... Gul et Johis Busby ...

William Busby of Over Norton Inventory 1678

A true Inventory of all singuler the Goods Chattells and Credits of William Busby thelder of Overnorton in the County of Oxon yeoman deceased praised at Overnorton aforesaid the Second day of February Anno dni 1679 by John Wheeler thelder Thomas Hopkins & John Scott as followeth

	£	s	d
Imprimis his purse & apparell	02	00	0
Item one Joyne Bedsted and Bedding lying on it, one Chest, & all other goods lying in the Hall Chamber	02	10	0
Item one Bedsted & bedding & all other goods lying in the Old Chamber	01	00	0
Item One Table Board & frame, one Cubberd, one Chaire and all other goods lying & being in the Hall house	00	15	0
Item one Bested & bedding lying on it, and all other goods lying & being in the Low Chamber	00	10	0
Item Brass, and Pewter	02	00	0
Item for Whitmeate	01	00	0
Item all Coopery Ware, and Woodden goods not praised before lying & being in the dwelling house	00	10	0
Item Five horses, Two Colts, and horse harness	15	00	0
Item one Waggon, Carts, Plowes, harrowes and all implements of husbandry	10	00	0
Item Twelve Cowes Young & Old	18	00	0
Item One Hundred Sixety & sixe sheepe & lambes	27	00	0
Item Two hoggs and Three store piggs	03	00	0
Item all the Cropp of Wheate, barley, pease, Oates, & hay and all Corne & pease about the house and Wheate and masling now growing	45	00	0
Item for Pullin	00	02	0
Item Wood and all Lumber within doores and without not praised	01	00	0

	li	s	d
The whole Summe is	129	07	0

        John Wheeler thelder
         his   marke
        Thomas Hopkins
         his   marke
        John Scott

The Will of Mary Busby 12th January 1710

Memorandum this Twelfth day of January one thousand seaven hundred and tenn That Mary Busby widd this last night deceased being in sound and perfect mind and memory Did yesterday between the hours of one and two in the afternoon of that day in the presence and heareing of us Sarah Timms the wife of William Timms of Over Norton in the County of Oxon Yeoman Alice the wife of Edward Gardiner of Over Norton aforesaid laborer and of Mary Crossley of Over Norton aforesaid spinster make and declare her nuncupative Will in these words or words to the effect following (that is to say) First I make and appoint Mary Scott the wife of John Scott and Elisabeth the wife of William Busby my full and sole Executrix's. Then she did give and bequeath to each and every of the Children of the said John Scott and William Busby and also of John Busby one shilling apeece and also to all her poor kindred one shilling apeece and Did will and desire her poor kindred should have some of her cloaths In testimony whereof wee the said Sarah Timms Alice Gardiner and Mary Crossley have hereunto sett our hands the day and yeare firdt above written

In presence of	Sarah Timms
	her marke
John Scott	Alice Gardiner
Stephen Biggarstaf	her marke
his marke	Mary Crossley
Wm Busby	her marke

Protestation Returns 1641-1642
Men, and some women, throughout England were asked to sign the protestation returns promising to

> maintaine and defend ... ye true Reformed Protestant Religion expressed in the doctrine of the Church of England ... the power and Priviledges of Parliament. The Lawfull Rights & Liberties of ye subject ...

As will be seen there is a mixture of two elements — firstly, they were opposing popery and maintaining protestant unity and secondly King Charles I was no longer to be allowed to rule by divine right. Charles was very unpopular due to his taxation of the population without the approval of parliament. This was the cause of the opposition to the ship money writs which he issued. He persuaded his judges to rule that he could make such charges when 'danger lurking' and 'His Majesty [to be] the only judge'.

Over Norton Feb 24 1641 Protestation Return
(List compiled for this book by Robert Moulder in 1999)

Nicholas Busbie	Roger Profit	John Busbie
Richard Brame	George Turner	Samuel Minton
Anthony Robins	John Hawkes jun	William Busby labourer
John Buckett sen	William Dier	Robert Wheeler sen
Richard Busby	William Huckvale	John Wheeler
Edward Bickerstaffe	William Hopkins sen	John Meeks jun
Charles Braine	Walter Chawney	Thomas Ingraham
William Fletcher	John Meekes sen	Richard Ingraham
Thomas Scott	Richard Shelfox	Robert Wheeler jun
John Hutchins - taylor	Richard Buckett	Thomas Tymes
William Gardner	William Hopkins jun	William Times
Edward Hopkins	Thomas Taylor	George Wesbury
John Miles	William Watson	William Busby sen
Richard Braye - taylor	Richard Nicholls	William Busby
John Hawkes	Edmond Braine	Thomas Smith
John Hutchins - shepherd	*Thomas Hind	Thomas Neatson
William French	Richard Hutchins	Thamas Titmas
Thomas Kite	George Durbridg	George Greame
Thomas Harris	Richard Fletcher	John Coper
William Braine - shepherd	Richard Hopkins	Christofar Scott
Nathaniell Busbie	William Greenhill	William Neale
John Buckett jun	John Freeman - Constable	

William Fletcher   }
Richard Bickerstaffe   } collectors for the poor

There is not any ... that hath refused to take the protestacon.
                                                          John Freeman

NB   *Thomas Hind was probably brother to Captain James Hind, the Chipping Norton Highwayman. (O.M. Meades and M.G. Meades)

William Sheffield, a sergeant in the Oxford & Bucks, was stationed in Cologne during the army of occupation.

William Sheffield worked at The Hub Ironworks during the 1939-45 war.

William (Bill) Sheffield served in 1914-18 war.

Coronation tea 1953 Amelia (née Eley of Enstone) and William Sheffield in charge of the teapot.

Eight Moulder brothers (left to right back row) Jim, Walter, William, Frank, John, (front row left to right) Tom, Bob, Fred. Their parents were Henry and Susan; they had four daughters and lived at No.34 Over Norton. Fred was killed in the 1914-18 war. The sons played at the Primitive Chapel, Distons Lane, Chipping Norton. Moulders were in the village from the early 1800s.

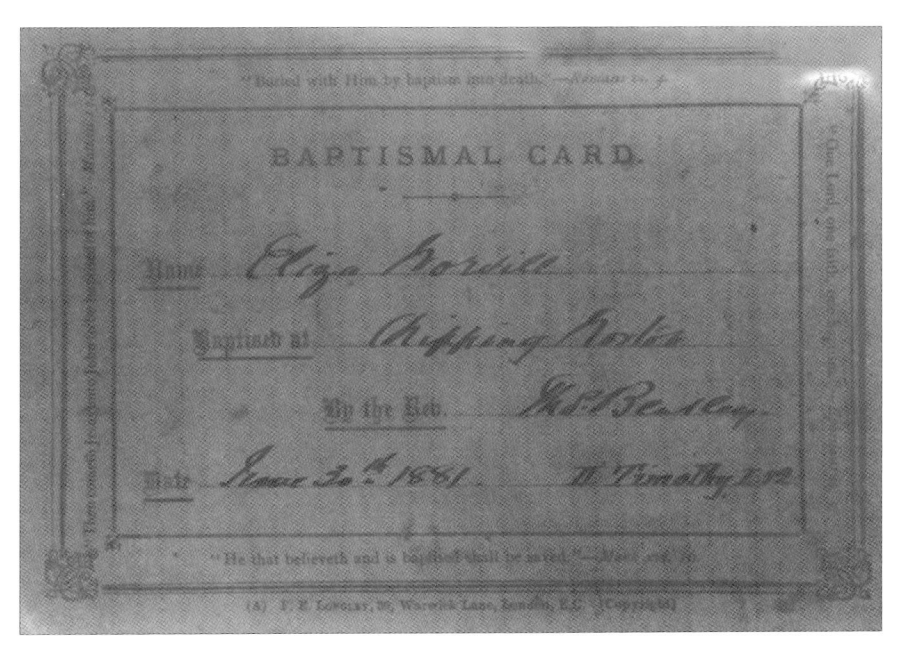

Eliza Worvill's (of Over Norton) Baptismal card 1881. (Roy Worvill's grandmother). The Worvill name has been known in Over Norton for many years.

Mrs Ivy Moulder with baby Mervyn. Photo taken in Over Norton House gardens. ?1935

Above: Over Norton Public Elementary School (now St. James' Chapel), The Old School House and former laundry. The estate donkey lived in the foreground (now Pony Close).

Below: James Harrison's Certificate of School Attendance 1st February 1898 covering 1890 to 1894.

ELEMENTARY EDUCATION ACT, 1876.   Education Department Form No. 144.

CERTIFICATE OF SCHOOL ATTENDANCE.

Over Norton Public Elementary *School.

I hereby certify that the following particulars with respect to the Attendances made by the Child named below, at this School after attaining the age of 5 years, are correctly taken from the Registers of the School.

Name in full, and Residence of Child	Number of Attendances made within the 12 months ending the 31st December.	
James Harrison Over Norton	1890	301
	1891	306
	1892	241
	1893	301
	1894	306

Signed this 1st day of February 1898

William S. Foote

Principal Teacher of the above named School.

* Enter name in full, and state whether a Public Elementary, or Certified Efficient School.

Above: Pupils at the old school (now St. James' Chapel).

Below: Pupils at the old school (now St. James' Chapel), showing what a wide age range had to be catered for in one classroom. The school in Choicehill Road opened 1901.

Pupils at Over Norton School, Choicehill Road. Mrs Joines, born 1899 marked with X.

Choicehill Road school. Mrs Meredith, Head Teacher (right); gentleman unknown; Miss Burtonshaw (m Padbury) pupil teacher 1920/21 (left).

Mrs Joyce Thomson (née Moulder) fondly recalls being chosen to hold the board 1925.

May Day at Choicehill Road school.

Empire Day celebrations.

May Day 1922 Over Norton.

May Day 1925 centre of Over Norton village.

An example of a pupil's arithmetic 1931.

CHAPTER 6

The Dawkins Family

James Dawkins bought Upper Norton House 1726 was labelled a Jacobite—
Dawkins connection with Penrhyn Castle—Census Returns Over Norton House—
The Memorial Fountain—William Gregory Dawkins (1825-1914)—
Oxfordshire Yeomanry 1887 at Over Norton Park—Chipping Norton Church
Faculty 1877—Subscriptions 1838/39 for repairs to church
—Receipts of Four Days Bazaar at Chapel House 1839

The Dawkins family have owned property in Over Norton for almost three hundred years and the family line continues living in the village to this day. The present family, Mr and Mrs Clinton John Dawkins with their two children, Sarah and Richard, left Africa and came to live at Over Norton Park in January 1950. Their two grandsons, Nicholas and Peter Kettlewell – Sarah's sons – and five great grandchildren live in the village too. To see the young children crossing the park with their parents, in the early morning – often before 8am – gives a great feeling of continuity and calls to mind Walt Whitman's (1819-1892) poem:

> There was a child went forth every day,
> And the first object he looked upon, that object he became,
> And that object became part of him for the day or a certain part of the day,
> Or for many years or stretching cycles of years ...
>
> And the third month lambs and the sow's pink faint litter,
> and the mare's foal and the cow's calf ...
>
> And the water-plants with their graceful flat heads,
> all became part of him.

James Dawkins of Rusley, Bishopstone, Wilts, bought the late 17th century Over Norton (then Upper Norton) House and estate from William Busby gent, of Over Norton, in June 1726. James was born in Jamaica in 1696 and died, unmarried, in 1766. He was buried at Chipping Norton Church. The Dawkins' Family memorial tablets are on the north wall of the church and the memorial to James Dawkins takes the form of a white marble urn designed by N. Revett. The inscription reads:

> To the Memory of James Dawkins Esquire
> of Upper Norton
> who died
> May 11 1766
> Aged 70

The Dawkins' family mausoleum was built against the north wall by Henry (m Juliana) Dawkins in 1800.

James Dawkins was the second son of Col. Richard Dawkins of Jamaica by his second wife Mrs Elizabeth Masters. He gained matriculation at Magdalen College, Oxford in March 1713 aged 16 and was a member of parliament for Woodstock from 1734 to 1747.

Colonel Richard Dawkins and his brother William were among the first settlers on the Island of Jamaica which had been formally ceded to England by the Treaty of Madrid in 1670. Jamaica was discovered in 1494 by Columbus. The Spaniards took possession of it in 1509, but in 1655 a British expedition, sent out by Oliver Cromwell under Penn and Venables attacked the island which surrendered to them. William Dawkins, Lieutenant in the Militia was killed fighting against the French invasion, 1694. He left a son William, who died without issue. Col. Richard Dawkins, who died 1705, was married twice, secondly to Elizabeth Masters (died 1702) in 1693 with whom he had James, already mentioned, and Henry Dawkins born 1698 (died 1744) who married in 1719 Elizabeth, daughter of Edward Pennant (see Penrhyn Castle later).

The Pennants and the Dawkins lives were intertwined. In one matter James Dawkins and Edward Pennant held opposing views. Edward Pennant was a sheriff of London from 1744 to 1745 during the second Jacobite rebellion, and for his contribution and his loyalty to the Hanoverian cause he was knighted by George II in 1745. James of Over Norton and his nephew also James were labelled Jacobites along with many others in North Oxfordshire showing support for the Pretender, Prince Charles Edward, against George of the House of Hanover. James planted many Scots pine trees in Over Norton to show that he was a follower of Charles. The present (1999) Dawkins family refer to the remaining ones as Charley Trees. Scots pine are growing at three entrances to the village.

The planting of Scots pine was not an idiosyncrasy peculiar to James Dawkins but is believed to be a recognised sign of Jacobite support although I have found no original documentary proof of this; secondary evidence comes from Canon Michael Hayter who writes of Steeple Aston:

> About 1749 Rector Eaton ... being of Jacobite sympathies planted the Scotch Firs which give Fir Lane its name.

James Dawkins of Over Norton was included in a list of twenty names (including Sir James Dashwood Bart. M.P. for Oxfordshire) of those who refused to support an association formed in Oxford in 1745 when they were asked to pledge men and money to support the Church and State, should it be necessary, against Prince Charles. This seems to reinforce other information that James was a Jacobite. Cornbury Park, Charlbury, was used as a meeting place for the Jacobites of this area and it is thought that refugees from the 1745 rebellion took shelter there. Chastleton House was also used.

The book *Burford Papers* written by William Hutton in 1905 has a chapter about Oxfordshire Jacobites, and has provided the following Dawkins' references, which are mainly to the younger James (1722-57) – the one who 'discovered' Palmyra (see later) – nephew of the earlier mentioned James.

> "Jemmy" Dawkins, a Jamaica planter, of the Oxfordshire family, and bred at the Jacobite college of S. John's in Oxford ... already famous for his expedition to Palmyra, was now deep in Charles's interest. As early as 1751 we find Charles sending compliments to him. He [Jemmy] assisted in the published books on Palmyra in 1753 and on Baalbek in 1757; and, while to the world he might seem a rich and leisurely antiquary he was really deep in plots for the return of the Stewarts ... Burford Papers.

In 1753 it was reported that 'Dawkins went lately over [to France] and brought money for the Prince. Pickle [the Spy] believes upwards of £4,000'.

Dawkins, with other English representatives, had discussions with Frederick the Great in Berlin – Frederick being more than ready to make use of the plotters. The English Government was aware of what was happening and Lord Albemarle's report to the Secretary of State stated:

> Mr Dawkins, as well as his uncle, who lives in Oxfordshire is warmly attached to the Pretenders interest. [The uncle being James who had bought Upper Norton House]. The younger James, having been watched from his arrival in Paris in the Spring of 1753, subsequently had a warrant issued for his arrest.

According to the Burford Papers Jemmy Dawkins

> became reconciled to the Hanoverian government

because he had found out that

> Charles could not be depended on.

However there is a tradition that includes details of a Jacobite meeting at Burford about 1780 at which one of the Dawkins family was supposedly present. News of this reached the Crown and Dawkins and fellow Jacobites fled the country.

Henry Dawkins, nephew and brother respectively of the two already mentioned Jameses, was married in 1759 to the Lady Juliana Colyear, daughter of the 2nd Earl Portmore. He had come back from Jamaica and lived at Dunstan Park near Chippenham (now disappeared). In 1766 he inherited Over Norton Park on the death of his Uncle James, but in the same year bought Standlynch House near Salisbury and moved there.

He often let Over Norton House. In 1766 the following advertisement was placed in *Jackson's Oxford Journal*:

> Sat Sept 28th 1766 [Over Norton House]
> To be lett, ready furnished for a term of six years ...
> Late in the occupation of Thomas Foley.

(Thomas Foley, later Lord Foley, I believe, had relatives at Kingham where Robert Foley was rector for thirty-three years to 1776. The Foley family were manufacturers of iron in the Midlands.)

Another advertisement, in 1783, gives a very good picture of the size of the house and number of outbuildings and is a reminder of a very different style of life. From *Jackson's Oxford Journal* Saturday 12th July 1783 and Saturday 27th Sept 1783:

> To be Lett unfurnished, and entered upon immediately – The MANSION HOUSE at Over Norton, in the County of Oxford, (pleasantly situated in a good Neighbourhood, and a fine Sporting Country) consisting of a good Hall, three parlours, six Bed-Chambers, with Closets, and good Lodging-Rooms over them, a good Kitchen, Servant's Hall, Butler's Pantry, exceeding good vaults, and other proper Conveniences; very good Gardens, Fish ponds, an Ice House, Coach House, Dog-Kennel, and excellent stabling for twenty-eight horses with Rooms for Servants over them; together with the Manors of Over Norton and Bartletts, and four inclosed Pasture Grounds, lying contiguous to the said House. Any person taking the House may have the furniture of the late Tenant at a fair Appraisement.
>
> For particulars enquire of Mr Bulley, Apothecary, at Chipping Norton, Oxfordshire.
>
> **N.B.** There being a very extensive Manor, with Plenty of Game, this is a most desirable object to any Gentleman who wishes to keep Hounds.
>
> Any unqualified Person killing Game or Shooting on the said Manor will be prosecuted.

The fishponds mentioned were held behind a series of dams built by the monks of the nearby Cold Norton Priory (Source: Mr C.J. Dawkins). Clinton John and Jean Dawkins in 1950 found all three fishponds reeded and silted up, and had the two upper ones dug out and enlarged into mini-lakes.

Ice houses were the fore-runners of refrigerators. They were built deep down in the ground and ice was stored from the winter months.

> The remains of the Over Norton ice house can still be located near the stream below the old Village Hall. It was underground like a stone-arched cellar about 12 feet by 8. Nearby is what is left of a low dam which spread the stream's water for ice formation. (Mr C.J. Dawkins)

Famous Paintings

Henry (m Juliana) commissioned two enormous paintings from important artists: described in Sothebys News as

> one of the greatest of all Scottish paintings of the mid 18th century

is the work commissioned in 1757 from Gavin Hamilton 1723-98, an outstanding Scottish artist, which depicts James Dawkins (Henry's brother) and the architect Robert Wood, guarded by turbaned Turkish horsemen, looking at the Roman Ruins of Palmyra in Syria.

It is an oil on canvas 3.1m by 3.9m and is entitled *Wood and Dawkins entering Palmyra* and now hangs in the National Gallery of Scotland, Edinburgh. Hamilton chose to paint the travellers wearing Roman dress.

In 1753 Robert Wood had published a folio-size tome entitled *The Ruins of Palmyra* full of architectural drawings of the ancient buildings.

Of this James, Boswell's *Life of Johnson* has it: 'The only great instance that I have ever known of the enjoyment of wealth was that of Jamaica Dawkins who, going to visit Palmyra and hearing that the way was infested by robbers, hired a troup of Turkish horsemen to guard him!' According to another quotation it was seldom fewer than three hundred Turks at a time.

The second, yet larger painting (3.2m by 5.1m) was of Henry and Juliana and their ten surviving children, painted at Standlynch by Richard Brompton in 1775, shortly before he was appointed Official Artist to the Tzars of Russia. It shows their tenth (unborn) child as a miniature on Juliana's wrist.

Both these pictures were hung in Standlynch House, but were transferred to Over Norton at Henry's (m Juliana) death in 1814 when Standlynch was sold.

Soon after Clinton John Dawkins inherited Over Norton Park in 1949 he acted on requests to pass both pictures for public view, on semi-permanent loan; the Gavin Hamilton went to Glasgow University and was later sold to the National Gallery of Scotland at Edinburgh, as mentioned above; the Brompton went to the National Trust at Penrhyn Castle in North Wales. George Hay Dawkins, second son in the picture, later inherited and largely rebuilt Penrhyn Castle, see later. Tenants of one of the Over Norton flats had the good fortune to 'live' with this painting for some time before it went to Penrhyn and imagined that in a certain light they could see a Cavalier type figure showing through the painting!

Both paintings were too large for the old Over Norton House walls and it has been suggested that the full-height two-storey addition to the three-storey old house, visible in a 1864 photograph, was built to accommodate them after 1814.

Henry (m Juliana) died in 1814, leaving Over Norton and neighbouring Manors of Bartletts and Salford by entail to his eldest son (another James), who later (1831) added Colyear to his name, on inheriting the property of Juliana's brother, the 3rd Earl Portmore.

This James had been M.P. for Chippenham or Hastings or Wilton from 1784 to 1831. He died in 1843, Over Norton then passing to Henry (m Augusta). There is no record of this James having ever lived at Over Norton, though his mother Juliana did, and from 1831 his nephew Henry (m Emma). Henry (m Juliana) had been M.P. variously between 1760 and 1780 for Southampton, Chippenham and Hindon. At his death, the Standlynch and neighbouring Wiltshire properties were directed to be sold and the proceeds added to his large pecuniary legacies – though not so large as his second son, George Hay's legacy

> being most handsomely provided for by our late cousin, The Right Honourable Richard Lord Penrhyn.

Standlynch was bought by the Nation and given to the Nelson family and became known as Trafalgar House.

The Dawkins' connection with the Penrhyn Estates North Wales
George Hay Dawkins (1764-1840) second son of Henry Dawkins and Juliana inherited the Penrhyn Estate – which included huge North Wales slate quarries – from his father's cousin, Lord Penrhyn [a Pennant] in 1808, but Lady Penrhyn had been left the income of the slate quarries for her lifetime. To meet the requirements of the will George Hay Dawkins had to take the Pennant arms and name. He was the great great grandson of Gifford Pennant of Jamaica.

Penrhyn Castle was extended by George Hay Dawkins Pennant over many years in the 1830s.

> The Castle of Penrhyn is a magnificent structure ... and occupying the site of the Palace of Roderic Molwynog, Prince of Wales in 720 ... the ebony

room is lined with silk velvet, on panels of ebony ... Penrhyn slate quarry ... about 2000 persons are employed ... slate taken from the quarry amounts to 200 tons [daily] ... shipped ... even to the United States of America

[Parliamentary Gazetteer Pub. 1840].

In 1951 Penrhyn Castle was transferred to the National Trust and they advertise it in their guide book as:
> Penrhyn in Gwynedd is perhaps the most extraordinary fantasy castle of the 19th century – a gigantic neo-Norman building.

George Hay Dawkins Pennant was buried in the family vault at Chipping Norton just one mile from the Dawkins family home at Over Norton Park. His memorial tablet reads as follows:
> George Hay Dawkins Pennant Esq
> of Penrhyn Castle North Wales
> Second son of Henry Dawkins Esq
> and the Right Honourable Lady Juliana Dawkins
> Died December 17 MDCCCXL Aged LXXVII years

his wife's memorial reads:
> Elizabeth, widow of George Hay Dawkins Pennant Esq
> of Penrhyn Castle North Wales
> Eldest daughter of the Honourable
> William Henry Bouverie and the Lady Bridget Bouverie
> Died July VII MDCCCLIX Aged LXXVIII years

George Dawkins Pennant had two daughters, Juliana Isabella Mary (1808-1842) who inherited Penrhyn and Emma Elizabeth Alicia born two years afterwards (1810-88). These two daughters were known as 'The Slate Queens' – the 'Queen of Diamonds' and the 'Queen of Hearts'.

Henry and Juliana's third son was also Henry (1765-1852). He married in 1788 Augusta Clinton, daughter of Sir Henry Clinton who had been the last Governor of the American Colonies, and General Officer Commanding the British Forces in the War of American Independence (1775/6).

> He lost the American Colonies –
>
> Dawkins family quote.

It seems though that Henry Dawkins could not get the approval of the General – then of Portland Place, London – to marry his daughter, Augusta, so

> hiring a brigade of hackney carriages he stationed one at each of the eight exits out of Portland Place and gave them strict orders to gallop like ... each in its direction the moment Henry was seen to emerge from No.39 and jump into the nearest one with his ladylove. The Jehus were with him to a man, and the General was non-plussed!
> (Quote from a contemporary book review. C.J.D.)

They did not drive to Gretna Green however but to Marylebone Church.

It seems also that this Henry was equally disapproved of by his own father Henry (m Juliana) because at the latter's death in 1814 Henry and Augusta received £2000

> to enable them more comfortably to remove from Over Norton together with all their possessions and effects to wherever else in England they wanted to go!

They went to Encombe, near Folkestone, where they built a 'charming' house and lived there till Henry died in 1852, despite having inherited Over Norton by entail from James (Colyear) in 1843. This story is recorded (handwritten) by their son Henry (m Emma) in his manuscript book (see later).

Henry's (m Augusta) career was Commissioner of Woods and Forests and Land Revenues, and was elected M.P. for Aldborough, Yorkshire in 1812. They had six sons and four daughters; the eldest was Henry (m Emma – see later); the sixth was Clinton George Augustus (1806-1871) who was British Consul in Venice, and narrowly missed losing his life (or worse) during the Austro/Italian war of 1848/49,

> when an Austrian cannon ball fell through his roof at 5.15am and between his knees on to his bed and down through the floor.

This cannon ball and C.G.A. Dawkins' official report (in French) are still preserved at Over Norton.

Henry and Augusta's eldest son was Henry (m Emma) 1788-1864. His army career in the Coldstream Guards began in 1804, at the age of 16. He served under the Duke of Wellington in The Peninsular War, and at Waterloo (as Colonel) finally retiring in 1846 having been on half pay since 1826. He banqueted with Wellington and other officers to celebrate the Waterloo victory, annually on twenty-two occasions.

Many of Col. Henry's letters from the battlefields are preserved; in one describing the battle of Waterloo:

> ... our cavalry, *entre nous*, behaved so ...

He was elected M.P. for Boroughbridge in Yorkshire in 1820 and again in 1826, and married his Yorkshire wife, Emma Duncombe, in 1821. They lived in London at first but came to Over Norton in 1831 and stayed till their deaths in 1864. This Henry kept a copious Memorandum book, with minute details of personal and topical events in his life. The following are some examples.

At the death of his father in 1852 he received silver, wine, furniture and pictures from Encombe which are all listed in his Memorandum.

Memorandum of various Effects sent from Encombe after my Father's Decease in 1852

Wine from Encombe	Furniture from Encombe
62 bottles of Madeira	Mahogany Circular Table
2 " " Hock	Long Oak Table
2 " " Sauterne	Mahogany Wardrobe
1 " " Hollands	Dark Mahogany Table
2 " " Brandy	Mahogany Escritoire
17 " " Constantine	Weighing Machine
4 " " ?	Book Door

Left me by my Mother
Pictures from Encombe
My Mother Lady
Juliana Dawkins
Picture in fraym of my Grandfather
Print of Duke of Wellington & Officers
Pictures of Harriett & Emma

90

Left me by my Father

Memorandum of Plate sent from Encombe after my Father Decease in 1852

Silver	Plated
Four large Silver Candlesticks	4 Wine Cooler Left me
and other Branches	4 Side Dishes
(The above 'left me by my mother')	1 Epergne
Four Silver Sauce Boats	1 Waiter
One Silver Tea Pot	1 pair Decanter Stands
One Silver Punch Ladle	3 pair Nut ?
One Silver Soup Ladle	
One Silver Salad Tool	
One Silver Cruet Stand	
Two Silver Sauce Ladles	
Two Silver Gravy Spoons	
One Silver Waiter	
8 Silver Tea Spoons	
8 Silver Desert Spoons [as written]	
14 Table Spoons	
12 Table Forks	
1 Silver Butter Knife	
1 pair of Grape ? Scissors	

Henry (m Emma) Dawkins kept meticulous details of all household expenses:

Memoranda
The Expence for our House at Over Norton for the first three years averaged £270 per annum ... House and Window Tax £24. [The house in Montague Square had averaged £310 per annum]

The Average expense of our <u>wine</u> for ten years from 1822 to 1831 has been about £26 per Annum. We then had drunk about eleven dozen a year but we had lived scarcely more than eight months of each year at home until 1831 and have had wine given to us. [approx. 20p per bottle]

Average of our yearly Expences for Ten Years from 1822 to 1831 both inclusive (in London):

	£	s	d
Living and travelling	400	0	0
Grocery	40	0	0
Wine	26	0	0
Coals	33	0	0
Washing	78	0	0

Servants wages	98	0 0
Servants Liveries	18	0 0
House Rent expences and Taxes	238	0 0
Physician	86	0 0
Children's Clothes	32	0 0
?- ?-	200	0 0
	1249	0 0

The average Expence of our Coals for ten years from 1822 to 1831 has been about £33 per annum.

Average consumed yearly fifteen tons (only eight months of the year at home).

			£	s	d
1831	twenty-three	tons	39	0	0
1832	forty-seven	"	72	0	0
1833	fifty	"	71	0	0
1834	forty-four	"	70	0	0
1835	forty-six	"	69	0	0
1836	fifty-eight	"	84	0	0
1837	fifty-nine	"	91	0	0

Expence of Horse keeping at Over Norton including Shoeing Veterinary Surgeon

	£	s	d
1832	46	1	0
1833	32	1	0
1834	43	2	0
1835	35	7	0
1836	49	12	6
1837	50	7	0

Expences of Job Horses – claim during eight years residence in London average about £36 per annum. [Job-master, one who lets out horses and carriages, *Nuttall's Dictionary* 1919]

Our consumption of Beer, has been more than double the quantity consumed in London and maybe reckoned at about £25 per Annum. I endeavour to brew twice in the year namely in March and October – Two Hogsheads of 108 gallons each of Ale, allowing 14 bushels of Malt to each Hogshead. [One Hogshead = 54 gallons. One Bushel = a dry measure of 8 gallons]

Our Malt has varied from 7s. to 7s.6d. a bushel, and hops from 1s.6d. to 1s.8d. per lb.

Our Ale brewed at home has averaged 10d. a Gallon and our Beer has averaged 3d. a Gallon. Some Table Beer brewed at home in 1836 was 8d. a gallon. [In 1837 7½d. a gallon and down to 6½d. in 1838]

From Henry (m Emma) Dawkins' Memoranda

A new greenhouse was erected in 1852/53. The total cost of this was £130.19s.6d. It was begun in May 1852 and completed in October 1853.

Items from the record of account include:

3220 bricks from Mr Tilley	cost	£5. 11s. 3d.
Lead		£20. 12s. 9d.
Hiatt for slating and plastering		£23. 0s. 0d.
From Bicester drawing mortar bricks and stone		£3. 16s. 6d.
Dozen labr at Old Pitts digging stone		£0. 14s. 0d.
Carriage of wood from Banbury		£1. 4s. 0d.
Joyner for working and setting two steps		£0. 7s. 6d.

This 'hot-house' was converted by C. John Dawkins in 1960 to be a dwelling house for his parents, and became known as 'The Orangery'.

Census Returns

Extracts from the census returns record who was living in the original Over Norton House in the years 1841, 1851, 1861 and 1871 – the first three dates being Henry's and Emma's family. By 1881 the new Over Norton House appeared on the census. This had been built by William Gregory Dawkins 1875 to 1887 who had demolished the original one in 1874.

Over Norton House 1841 (adults ages shown to the nearest five)

	Age	
Henry Dawkins	50	army
Emma	40	wife
William	15	son
Clinton	14	son
James	13	son
Harriett	11	daughter
Emma Augusta	6	daughter
Catherine Bent	20	Governiss

They had one male servant and four female servants living in and one male servant living in a room over the stables.

Over Norton House 1851

		Age	
Henry Dawkins		62	
Emma	wife	52	
Clinton	son	23	Lieutenant in Army unm
Harriett	daughter	20	unm
Emma	"	16	unm

They had a footman, a groom, and five female servants living in.

Over Norton House 1861

			Age			Born
Henry Dawkins	Head		72	Col. in the army	Middlesex London
Emma	"	Wife	61	Gentlewoman	Yorks Thurcroft
Harriett	"	Daughter	30	unm "	Middlesex London
Emma	"	"	25	unm "	Oxon Over Norton

They had a butler, housekeeper, Lady's maid, two housemaids and a kitchen maid all living in.

Over Norton House 1871

		Age		Born
Hawkins Charles	Head	53	Land owner	
	Tenant		Major in Militia	Middlesex London
Thomasina	Wife	51		Norfolk Lynn
Emily	Daughter	20	unm	Wilts? Keynes

They had three general servants

Over Norton House 1881

			Age	
Edward Dawkins	Head	M	43	Landed Propri [as listed]
Louisa "	Wife	M	39	Lady
Ethel	Daughter	U	13	Lady
Augusta? Jumd. A	Visitor	U	24	Governess Frankfurt Germany
James Bishop	Butler	U	33	Butler
Walter Dixey	Servant	U	17	Footman
Maria Price	"		39	Housekeeper

Sarah James	"	30	Cook
Debrach Ebbom	"	18	Kitchen maid
Mary Laskins	"	17	Schoolroom? Maid

None of the domestic staff was born in Over Norton but two were from Oxfordshire. Edward Dawkins was of Moggerhanger a JP and High Sheriff, Beds b. 1837 m. 1859 Louisa Maria Barnett of Stratton Park, Beds.

The Mansion   1891

			Age		Born
William Gregory <u>Dawkins</u>	Head	Single	66	Landowner	London
Edward Clack	Servant	"	?44		Over Norton Oxon
Francis Fennell	"	Widow	36	Cook	Cheltenham Glos
Elizabeth Haynes	"	Single	22	Housemaid	Twyford Bucks

At the time of Henry and Emma's death in 1864, two diamond-shaped wooden hatchments placed above the front door can be seen in a contemporary photograph of the original Over Norton House. It was customary, following a death, for the hatchments – which had the family coat of arms painted on them – to be displayed on the house and then to be hung in the church. The final resting place of the Dawkins' family hatchments is unknown. If the man was married the left half of the hatchment would be black, and for a married woman the right half, with variations to denote a bachelor, widow or widower. Other interesting hatchments can be seen in the churches at Great Tew and at Sandford St. Martin.

Henry and Emma's four surviving children, William, James, Harriett and Emma were responsible for having a memorial fountain erected to their parents, who both died in the same year, 1864. This memorial still stands in the centre of Over Norton village and was extensively restored in 1985. At this time, Mr and Mrs Michael Barfield were living in Fountain Cottage and owned the memorial and the ground on which it stood. By 1st July 1985 transfer of ownership was made to the Over Norton Parish Council who agreed to

> undertake responsibility and liability for the monument.

Mr C J Dawkins provided three new pillars but the centre one remained. The work was expertly completed by Mr Robert Warner,

Builder, of Over Norton, and he contracted Mr John Mann (Mann Restorations) of Witney to clean the memorial.

The fountain and attached railings are listed Grade II, being of architectural and historical interest. It may appear to be of an unusual design for the centre of a small edge-of-the-Cotswolds village, particularly as the centre pillar is of Cornish serpentine marble as had been the three outer pillars. However at this time, 1864, there were many examples of Monumental Drinking Fountains – some using marble – being erected all over the country.

The *Illustrated London News* (July to Dec 1869 edition) was provided by Miss Dawkins for the village reading room, now St. James' Chapel, in Over Norton. In that magazine a 'Public Drinking Fountain Association' is mentioned and

> ample proof that in one day at a city fountain – more than eighteen thousand individuals assuaged their thirst and three hundred and seventy horses drank at the troughs.

Chipping Norton had a fountain on Bottom Side complete with cast iron cups on chains for use by the public. Did they not worry about infections? It is likely that Over Norton inhabitants were well pleased with their fountain. On an old photograph a woman can be seen carrying her black iron kettle for re-filling.

William Gregory Dawkins (1825-1914), Henry and Emma's eldest surviving son, (the first born Henry Thomas having died in 1835, just before his twelfth birthday) is recorded in his father's Memorandum as having

> entered the 49th Regiment 2nd August 1894, exchanged with the Coldstream 16th September 1844 ... [and was] ... appointed Captain Lieutenant Colonel in December 1854.

He served in the Crimean War and was awarded the Crimean Legion d'honneur. He left an album of pencil sketches and watercolours of Crimean Scenes.

He inherited Over Norton with Bartletts and Salford on his father's death in 1864. By 1873 he was listed as owning 2512 acres 16 perches with a gross estimated rental of £4017.17s.0d. (Source: *The Return of Owners of Land*, 1873 Oxfordshire OFHS)

'The Bartletts', a deserted hamlet, was mentioned several times in the Chipping Norton Salford Inclosure Act of 1770. It was situated between Over Norton and Salford and seems to have been included as part of Over Norton. Henry Dawkins was Lord of the Manor of Over Norton, The Bartletts and Salford. He paid £60.4s.5¼d. to the proprietors for

> obtaining passing and Executing the said Act ...

There was an

> allotment to Margaret Bradley for land in the Hamlet or Tything of Bartletts.

The description of Over Norton parish boundary included

> and the boundary or Extent of the Hamlet of Over Norton and Bartletts beginneth at the north east corner of an allotment to the Poor of Over Norton ...

A further reference states:

> The said Hamlet of Over Norton and Bartletts and be and remain chargeable and rateable in respect of church rates to the parish church of Chipping Norton, [A George Draper paid 9d. to the proprietors of the act for 'a little close in Bartletts'.]

Samuel Huckvale was the lessee in lieu of Tyths for Bartletts. One hundred and seven acres one rood and thirty perches of land were allocated to the Dean and Chapter (Gloucester) from which Samuel Huckvale received the tyths.

William Gregory's birth, 26th April 1825, is recorded in his father's Memoranda and also that he was baptized on 9th May 1825, christened on the 6th July 'by my brother Edward' and vaccinated 6th June when six weeks old. Clinton Francis Bevens was born 1826 and christened by the Dean of Carlisle. James Annesley the fourth son born 1828 and Harriet Elizabeth Georgiana the first daughter born 1830 were christened 'by my brother Edward'.

Emma Augusta Juliana born 1834 was baptized by Revd. R.S. Skillern vicar of Chipping Norton. The first three children were first baptized and then christened between two to three months afterwards.

Clinton Francis Bevens Dawkins died of yellow fever in Trinidad in 1859.

William Gregory Dawkins is always referred to as 'the Colonel' by the senior inhabitants of Over Norton. He was listed as being resident at Over Norton House, 'The Mansion' on the 1891 census, but not in 1881. He rented it out for most of his ownership, and more or less permanently to the Daly's from 1899. The Colonel lived variously in London, Eastbourne and Brighton after leaving the army.

William Gregory had disliked the original house so much – believing it to be haunted – that he had it demolished and built the present Over Norton House between 1875 and 1879.

In my opinion the house is situated in a beautiful position but is not attractive in itself. The present day sees it divided into several flats. The Daly family (chapter 7) found it too small for their needs and built a large extension on the N.E. side. They also had a portable bungalow constructed near the kitchen to accommodate two members of staff, later sold to Mr Weale, a local farmer, who used it as a garage (see Firs Farm Chapter 14). The bungalow had disappeared before 1949.

It is almost impossible to find photographs of village people who lived in Over Norton in the late 1890s but it is fortunate that the Colonel, an accomplished artist, painted oil portraits of many of them. Fred Moulder's father, Samuel, as a boy was one of these. Sam was depicted wearing a fur cap which was supposed to have been worn by the Colonel in the Crimean War. Sam handed this cap on to Fred, his son, who still lives in Over Norton.

There is a painting of Roy Worvill's father as a boy and of Ernest Moulder and his wife Sarah Ann (neé Compton). This couple died of tuberculosis at a very early age – leaving a young family – Ernest in 1898, followed by Sarah in 1899; Sarah had lived in West Street, Chipping Norton before her marriage. A full length portrait of Lizzie Saunders has survived in good condition despite the fact that at one time it was used by her family to cover a hole in their pantry door. Lizzie was George Harris' grandmother and much of the record of the oral history of this village has come through them; they often sat talking by the fire-side in the long winter evenings.

I first heard of the existence of these paintings from Mr Dennis Lewis; he and his wife owned one of Bill Giles. They were given it by Bill's son-in-law, John Philips, coach proprietor at Charlbury. After Dennis' death Mrs Lewis kindly allowed me to have it photographed. Dennis had said that at one time Bill Giles dealt with the funerals for the Chipping Norton workhouse and that he could remember seeing Bill sitting on a black-covered box, on the long horse drawn carriage.

Each painting was signed with the Colonel's initials, W.G.D., the year e.g. 1887 was added and above these details the Colonel painted his crest – which included a dexter arm couped at the shoulder holding a battle-axe. (couped = cut off evenly, dexter = turning to the right.)

Mrs Beck, during her childhood, lived in a cottage just below the fountain. Later it became part of present-day Haven Cottage. She recalls that her grandmother told her that the Colonel used to sit painting on the Village Green and that the children used to gather round.

Mr Nicholas Kettlewell now manager of the Dawkins' estate farm said that the Colonel was also fond of painting flowers.

Another example of the Colonel's gentle, artistic side is shown in the 'story' from Mrs Jean Dawkins about the snowdrops which he brought back from the Crimean War for his garden. During January and February a sheet of white snowdrops can be seen across the far side of the lakes and also at the main entrance to Over Norton Park. Mrs Dawkins has been instrumental in extending the planting of these.

During the Colonel's many absences, he relied on the services of William and later Samuel Moulder, his estate foremen, to attend to matters. Some of his letters to Sam Moulder have been preserved by Fred, his son, and Robert Moulder, his grandson. They include instructions, or rather requests, to attend to the water supply and other problems:

> 36 Ceylon Place Sept 27th 1906
> Could not you and Frank in this splendid dry season repair the several leak places at head of bridge pond and cut a clear water way for it thro' the two ponds below it? ...

> Yrs of Sept 3 duly received – you have taken a capital and spirited step in closing the taps from the shameful abuse practised on my supply and if you see no objection I think it may be well to add to the notice on each tap: "by order of William Dawkins the owner". Then they will know who they have to fight.
>
> ... The Daly servants used to get splendid supply by water cart from the Cherry Orchard spring. I hope they are not failing ...

and with reference to some building repairs he wrote:

> ... Taylor from Long Compton I should like to employ really, a famous chap that, both in time, quality and price – I tried to get him to settle with us, but unluckily I forgot entirely to apply to the wife [Mrs Taylor].

An interesting example of social history was included in a letter dated Sept 4th 1906 from Eastbourne.

> What a terrible heat! I never suffered more from it in Jamaica – Today it seems a little diminished.
>
> The street cryers here seem mad with the heat, and I am distracted by their howling, screaming row quite unintelligible to sell fish or a banana.
>
> I wish I could have a gun and return fire loaded with dust shot! or rain water.

Over Norton Park has been the scene of some dramatic events. The *Oxfordshire Weekly News* carried a paragraph about the Oxfordshire Yeomanry who were going to assemble at Chipping Norton for annual training on 7th May 1887. After a parade in the Market Place they were to march to Over Norton Park,

> where, through the kindness of Colonel Dawkins and Mr John Busby, the drills will take place.

Their military sports were to include 'clearing the Turk's head, tilting the ring, tent pegging, lemon cutting, single sticks, cockade fight, ... tug-of-war etc'.

In 1890, Colonel Dawkins had recorded that Mr Busby was renting from him 90 acres of the park for 15s.0d. an acre. Later there was trouble between these two men and the Colonel had a poster printed and displayed to show his side of the story (see photograph).

At one time, horse racing took place in Over Norton Park. Chipping Norton held two-day race meetings in some years between 1734 and 1753 when three-day fixtures began to be arranged. Prizes from 30 to 50 guineas were awarded. In 1741 an offer of 80 guineas encouraged only six starters; it is believed that the race took place in Over Norton Park, or possibly Heythrop Park.

In 1784 a cup worth 100 guineas was offered at Oxford and was later called 'the Gold Cup'. It was the main prize in 1816 when Mr Dawkins entered a horse for this race; of the seventeen entries seven were from outside Oxfordshire.(V.C.H. Vol.ii)

Chipping Norton Church – Faculty 1877
Application by the Reverend Francis Harris, Vicar of Chipping Norton and others, was made to the Bishop of Oxford for permission to take down the gallery and to make changes in the seating arrangements in Chipping Norton Church. William Gregory Dawkins was very much involved in trying to prevent any changes.

The Vicar in his statement explaining his request included the following points:

> That he has for the last eleven years been vicar of this parish, and therefore has had ample time for acquiring an accurate knowledge of the spiritual wants of the people.
>
> That from his first coming he called attention to the unsightliness of the present pews.
>
> ... a few monopolise the greater part of the best portion of the church and shut out those who have not pews, compelling them to sit round the outside in the free benches.
>
> ... That the present state of things, making so great a distinction between classes ... is utterly opposed to the whole spirit of Christianity ...

Formal objections to this plan were sent to the Diocesan Registry by George Henry Saunders of Chipping Norton, Solicitor, on behalf of Lieutenant Colonel William Gregory Dawkins and others.

All ratepayers and churchmen were invited to a vestry meeting to be held in the Town Hall, Thursday 26th April 1877 at 8pm, to oppose the scheme proposed by the Vicar and Churchwardens.

Mr J. Farwell, solicitor, former representative of the parish, spoke of his recollections 'of forty years ago' when:

> ... the church was in a very disgraceful state, the pews were scattered about in all directions.

At that time, he reminded the audience, Col. Dawkins and Mrs Dawkins (Henry and Emma, parents of William Gregory Dawkins) came into the parish:

> They said, "Well, this must not be".
> They did all they could amongst their friends to find the money, to make the necessary improvements, the town co-operating with them. The work was then carried out all being unanimous. There was no quarrelling, no ill-will, but all was done in the quietest possible manner.
> [See end of this chapter for records from Henry Dawkins' 'Memoranda 1838 and 1839 Receipts of money raising'.]

Part of the proof to answer objections was as follows:

> To prove that Lieutenant Colonel William Gregory Dawkins is a non-resident land owner living in London, but who for some years past has been building a House in Over Norton Park in the Ecclesiastical Parish of Chipping Norton, though the former mansion was, (like the Pews) not worn out, but only (also like the Pews) un-sightly: that he has not attended service in the Church half a dozen times since Witness has been Vicar of the Parish ...

Prior to the Poll arranged for Friday 27th April the following two statements were posted throughout the town:

First the opponents issued:

> The Parish Church: Vote with Mr Farwell, the old representative of the parish, for no alteration in the Parish Church, vote against Mr Rawlinson's proposition. (This group represented by Mr Saunders.)

The Vicar and his supporters replied with the following:

> The Parish Church: If you want sitting in the Parish Church equally and fairly allotted to all, vote for Mr Rawlinson's motion for altering the pews etc.

Vote for destroying the monopoly of large empty pews, and giving the poor as well as the rich, a decent sitting in their Parish Church. Notice. The alterations of the Parish Church will be paid for by voluntary subscriptions, not by rate.

The Vicar presided at the Poll, and the two opposing groups were represented by Mr Rawlinson (for alterations) and Mr Saunders (objector to alterations).

The Vicar and Churchwardens won by a majority of 47 and so a faculty for 'Re-pewing of the Church' was obtained dated 28 August 1877.

Colonel W G Dawkins had issued the following statement prior to the Town Hall meeting:

TO THE RATEPAYERS. – It depends upon yourselves to check the progress of Roman Catholic doctrine and practice at Chipping Norton. Open pews, open space for processions, niches for images, bright robes for clergy, flowers on Communion Tables, musical services, would be harmless but they mean worship through use of objects, instead of through the spirit, they being outward forms of ceremonies, in place of inward penitence and prayer: They mean a repeated offering and repeated sacrifice on the altar, instead of the Protestant belief of only a commemoration of a sacrifice made once for all. They are followed by nearly inaudible prayer, erroneously made for the people instead of by them. They are accompanied by sermons about obedience to the Church, instead of about proper conduct of life in the world. Ritualists consider the clergy the Church, but the Apostles included the congregations as well. Such changes, making the church building itself more important, bring with them an undue prominence of the clergy and of their office. We may all see that no countries are so wretched as those governed by the clergy. These manifest public facts deter me from supporting any change. It is to be hoped that all the resident ratepayers may be able to attend the vestry meeting on Thursday evening, for I believe the majority are for the Protestant religion. If the majority vote the change to be worth the danger, the church repairs of 1840 might be completed by placing oak pews, for which funds were then wanting. Do not rebuild niches designed for images which do not belong to the Protestant religion. Do not allow yourselves to be crowded together by narrowing the seats and removing the galleries, to embellish and magnify a church which is for the people. ... Although as Spirits all are equal, it cannot advance Religion to assume an equality of men which does not exist. To mix up classes is a mock humility, it is desired by none, and it is a hindrance to the Religious Services of all. Some of the best parts of the church should be allotted to the poor as well as the rich, and let us preserve that privacy and ownership of pews and seats which is consistent with our customs, and which is destroyed by changing pews with doors, for open seats.

William Dawkins April 24th 1877

Throughout the 1890s, Lt. Col. W.G. Dawkins was supporting the Chipping Norton Churchyard Fund by donating ten shillings and five shillings on alternate years.

[From Henry (m Emma) Dawkins' Memoranda] "Subscription from our Family for the Repair of our Church at Chipping Norton" [Probably 1838/39]

			£	s	d
James Colyear Dawkins Esq		Eldest of Henry & Juliana	100	0	0
George Hay Dawkins Pennant Esq	2nd	" " "	50	0	0
Henry Dawkins Esq (m Augusta)	3rd	" " "	10	0	0
Richard Dawkins Esq	4th	" " "	5	0	0
John Dawkins Esq	7th	" " "	10	0	0
Miss Dawkins			10	0	0
Miss Colyear Dawkins		d. of James above	10	0	0
Colonel Dawkins		Eldest of Henry above	10	0	0
Mrs H Dawkins		Emma	10	0	0
* Master William Gregory Dawkins			1	0	0
* Master Clinton F.B. Dawkins			1	0	0
* Master James Annesley Dawkins			1	0	0
* Miss Harriett Dawkins			1	0	0
* Miss Emma Dawkins			1	0	0
Revd. Edward H Dawkins		5th of Henry & Juliana	5	0	0
Mrs Edward Dawkins			5	0	0
Colonel Serjeantson }	Henry & Juliana's daughter, Elizabeth,		5	0	0
George Serjeantson Esq }	married a Serjeantson		1	0	0
Thomas Duncombe Esq }	Parents of Emma		5	0	0
Mrs Thomas Duncombe }			1	0	0
Revd. Henry Duncombe			1	10	0
Mrs Vadef [unclear]				10	0
			244	0	0

*Henry and Emma's children

1839

"Receipts of Four Days Bazaar at Chapel House"
[For alterations in the Church; St. Mary's Chipping Norton]

	£	s	d
Entrance Money	46	18	0
Revd. E.B. Weare's Stall [unclear]	41	18	6
Mrs H. Dawkins Stall	114	4	0
Mrs Rawlinsons "	32	13	6
Mrs Hitchmans "	40	1	0
Mrs Fau and Mrs Ben Stall [unclear]	31	3	0
Miss Kingdon Stall	19	13	0
Miss Sotham "	8	0	0
Mr Matthews Cake Stall	2	19	6
	£347	10	6

"Expenses of Four Days Bazaar at Chapel House"

	£	s	d
Expenses of Band	7	10	0
Oxford Tent	2	5	0
Forest Tent		13	6
Bicester Tent	6	6	0
Turnpike Expenses for Tents		8	6
Man with Bicester Tent	1	15	0
Meals for Village [unclear]		10	0
Smith stationers Bill	8	0	0
Mr Wilmot's Bill	7	6	0
Baughan Carpenters Bill	1	0	0
Police Men	1	0	0
	£36	14	0

	£	s	d	
From	347	10	6	
Take	36	14	0	
	£310	16	6	Balance

[It is interesting to note the turnpike tolls and the cost of policemen!]

CHAPTER 7

The Laws of Settlement—Over Norton's Workhouse Agreement—
Workhouse conditions—Speenhamland System 1795-1834—
Wages and Cost of Food 1795—William Wright's Charity—Dawkins' Charity—
O.N.P.C.'s fight to have a say in distribution of charities—
Captain Daly's donation 1901

The Laws of Settlement

By a statute made in 1388-99 in the Reign of Richard II,

> the poor were to repair, in order to be maintained, to the places where they were born.

The conditions were changed in 1491- 92 by Henry VII when they were

> to repair to the place where they last dwelled, or were best known, or were born

and by 1503/04 (Henry VII)

> or made last their abode by the space of three years

were added. The regulations were adjusted as time passed but there were always two ruling elements 'by birth' or 'by inhabitancy'.

A very lengthy description of a case between Salford and Over Norton was used in *The Justice of the Peace and Parish Officer* Vol. III by Richard Burn, published in 1772, to explain

> That a purchase under the value of 30 pounds shall not gain a settlement.

A removal order was given to Peter White's pauper son telling him he must return to Over Norton from Salford.

Peter White was settled in Over Norton in 1726 and he bought a tenement for 29 pounds at Salford from John Lardner. Peter White lived at Salford for thirty-six years and was still there at the time of the removal of his son. The pauper son, had lived with his father until marriage, eight years previously, and then lived in a separate tenement in Salford – but, never gained any settlement but what he derived from his father.

An appeal against the 'removal order' which had been presented to the son was made, and the sessions cancelled that order, but Lord Mansfield was called to give his judgement in court on the case and he explained ...

> that the only settlement which the son could derive from his father was at Over Norton' and that ... 'he can have acquired no settlement in Salford by virtue of his father's purchase.

The order of sessions was quashed and the original order affirmed.

There are many 'Orders of Removal' recorded by the Chipping Norton Churchwardens and Overseers of the poor including the following:

> 16 Sept 1773 The order of removal of Joseph Holloway and his wife and John their son from Chipping Norton aforesaid to Over Norton aforesaid

and earlier in Dec 1759 Susanna Smith was ordered to remove from Chipping Norton to Over Norton.

Settlement certificates were given on 22 Feb 1779 to John Somersby and Hannah his wife from the Parish of Over Norton to Chipping Norton and:

> 28 Feb 1781 Richard Provost, Sarah his wife and William their child from Over Norton to Chipping Norton
>
> 6 April 1741 Mary Kirby and three children from Over Norton to Chipping Norton.

Dr Plot's (1676) account of a traveller giving birth to a child in a hollow elm tree on Bletchington Green is repeated in V.C.H. Vol.ii. No one would provide shelter for her in the parish so as 'to prevent her bringing a charge on it' for maintenance.

Workhouses

Single parishes were given the power to erect workhouses for the poor by the General Workhouse Act 1723 (Knatchhill's Act). Over Norton certainly had one by 1780. It was probably in the centre of the village in the location of Workhouse Row. On a 1770 map, showing the Dawkins estate at that time, the area by the War Memorial was labelled as farm buildings. Perhaps a conversion was done to house the poor.

Over Norton's Workhouse Agreement 1780 (PAR 64/5/L1/1)

Articles of Agreement made and agreed on the twenty-fourth day of November 1780 Between the Churchwarden and Overseers of the Hamlet of Over Norton in the County of Oxford on the one part and John Hodgson of Comb in the said County (Victuallor) on the other part Wittnesseth that the said Churchwarden and Overseers do set and to farm let unto the said John Hodgson the Work-House at Over Norton aforesaid for the term of two years (to commence or begin on the 27th day of November next ensuing the date hereof) at the Yearly Rent of eighty Pounds to be paid monthly in the following manner (that is to say) the first Month, pay to be made on the 27th day of March next ensuing the date hereof and so to continue to be paid monthly during the aforesaid term And at the expiration of the said term to be paid for the other months omitted at the beginning of the said term And he the said John Hodgson agrees to find and provide the Poor belonging to the said Work-House hot Victuals four times weekly and every week during the said term and at all times good and sufficient Meat, Drink, washing, Lodging, Cloathing and proper Fires And Also all nessessaries for lying-in Women if required likewise to be at the expence of Christnings, Burials, and sicknesses of all sorts (except the small Pox, broken Bones, or what may be properly called a putrid Fever) And it is also agreed between the said parties that if any poor Men (or Boys of fourteen years of Age) want only employment then such poor Men (or Boys) shall be sent round the Parish to work by the Yard Land and if their Wages is not sufficient to maintain them and their Families (if any) then the said John Hodgson shall support them with what more they stand in need of (if required) Also the said John Hodgson doth engage that no Person or Persons in the said Work-House shall cut any Gause or Furze from off the Poor's Plot during the said term And the said John Hodgson agrees to pay to Jane Fletcher (Widdow) the sum of two shillings weekly and every week so long (within the said term) as she can subsist with that pay and if she happen to die within the said term the said John Hodgson agrees to be at the expence of her Funeral And further the said John Hodgson agrees to permit the said Churchwarden, Overseers, or any of the principal Inhabitants at any time or times to go into the said Work-House in order to enquire of the poor People as to their maintainance, cloathing, Fires etc. And Also the said Churchwarden and Overseers do covenant promise and agree to be at the expence of the carriage of four Tuns of Coals each Year from any place not exceeding the distance between Over Norton and Evesham the said John Hodgson to pay for the coals at the place and for the loading and Turnpikes and the Churchwardens and Overseers agree to be at the expence of the carriage of two loads of Wood each year not exceeding the distance between Over Norton and the Forrest of Whichwood the said John Hodgson to be at the expence of loading and Turnpikes (if any) and the Churchwarden and Overseers agree to find and provide a sufficient Garden for the said Work-House in the most proper place on the said premises Also the said Churchwarden and Overseers agree to keep the said Work-House in tenantable repair (except the Windows) and to provide all nessessary Household Goods the same to remain and be left on the premises at the expiration of the said term and the said John Hodgson agrees to find and provide Wheels or other Implements or Tools whatever that may be wanted in the employment of the poor People in the said Work-House Also it is further agreed between the said parties that if any Man or Men shall go away and leave a Bastard Child or a Family chargeable to the said Parish the Churchwardens and Overseers shall assist the said John Hodgson in endeavouring to bring him or them as soon as can be to their Parish And further it is agreed that the said John Hodgson shall be exempt from all costs and charges of Law suits (respecting settlements) and Order of removal etc. And it is also agreed that each partie to those presents shall be at an equal expence in the payment of those written Agreements and lastly if either of the parties neglect to fulfil and perform those covenants and Agreements they engage to forfeit the sum of twenty Pounds to the other In Witness whereof the parties to those presents have interchangeably set their Hands and Seals the day and Year first above written: II:

Signed sealed and delivered (being first legaly stampt) in the presence of

	Jos Slatter	
	Sam Wheeler	
Thos Wallington	Wm Carpenter	John Hodgson
Churchwarden &	Overseer	
Overseer		

When John Hodgson's term of office as Over Norton's Workhouse Governor was completed the following advertisement was placed in the press.

1782 Sat. 2nd Nov J.O.J.

Wanted – A Governor to undertake, at a certain yearly sum, as shall be agreed on, the Care, Maintenance, Cloathing, and Relief of the Parish of

Over Norton, in the County of Oxford. All such Persons who are inclined to engage in the same, are desired to send their Terms and Proposals under Seal, to Mr William Huckvale, of the said Parish, on or before the 20th Day of this instant November; and in the mean Time may have such Information as is necessary, by applying to the Overseers of the Poor.

Workhouse Conditions

No details of the actual conditions in Over Norton's Workhouse have come to my notice but a great deal of information about workhouses in this country can be found in Eden's, *The State of the Poor*. Eden says that it was due to the exceptionally high prices of 1794 and 1795 that he began his survey published in 1797.

> At Lichfield Staffordshire
> ... On meat days the Poor generally endeavour to save a little meat, to add to their dinner the succeeding day ... [How did they store it?]
> ... The war [with France] has added very considerably to the number of the Out-Poor. [The allowances ranged from 6d to 1s per head. A considerable number in 1794 were for soldiers' children.]
> ... There are eight or ten beds in each room, chiefly flocks [the waste of cotton and wool] and consequently retentive of scents and very productive of vermin [when illness strikes] the mortality rate is very high.
>
> At Sheffield
> ... Two, three and sometimes even four paupers sleep in a bed... [as if the company of bugs and vermin were not enough!]
>
> Leeds
> ... the bedclothes are scoured once a year [and at Leicester] ... much infested with bugs ...

Oxford workhouse had a bad report too:

> ...The house in general dirty, unsweet, and in a miserable state of repair without a single rule or order established for the regulation and government of its numerous family who were in general idle, riotous and disorderly. [and then, not surprisingly] ... a notice that all applicants for relief would be sent to the Workhouse reduced the number by half.

The Settlement Act 1697 said that Paupers were to wear a capital P on their clothing followed by a letter indicating the name of their parish so at Newark, Nottinghamshire, Eden recorded:

The badge ... is worn by paupers in this parish. It was laid aside a few years ago, but the Poor having increased very much, it was resumed in 1794, and in consequence several persons who had before made regular applications to the parish have now declined asking for relief [despite the fact that:] The Workhouse here is one of the very best in England. It is sufficiently capacious and well aired. The men are lodged on one side the women on the other ... beds [are] mostly of feathers ... well supplied with vegetables ... it exhibits a degree of comfort, and cleanliness that is seldom met with.

At Suffolk Melton
All paupers, whether in the house or receiving quarterly allowances to wear a badge P.L.W. [P for Pauper LW for the hundreds of Loes and Wilford].

The Badge Man was an official responsible for ensuring that all paupers in receipt of 'Parish Relief' wore their badges. 'Badging the Poor' was supposed to have reduced the Poor Rates. By Gilbert's act of 1782 paupers of good character were excused from wearing the pauper's badge.

At Deddington July 1795
There were 18 inmates [and] ... Out pensioners are often supported by the Parish, 40 or 50, in winter; the parish employs them in stone quarries.

The Poor are farmed in the Parish Workhouse for £1000 a year.

At Oxford July 1755
... the inmates earnings were about £300 a year from working in a sacking factory and sweeping the streets.
The Banbury Poor were employed in 'spinning and twisting' ... Their earnings amount to about £40 a year.

At Bradford, Wiltshire
... The Poor are kept clean and well fed, but are made to work or are punished. ...

It is reasonable to suppose that the poor in Over Norton were set to work in horticulture or agriculture.

The Over Norton Workhouse agreement with John Hodgson (1780) stated that he was to provide hot victuals four times weekly and at all times good and sufficient meat and drink . No doubt the diet would have been something along the lines of the menu shown on the chart for the inmates of the Banbury and Oxford Workhouses.

This chart shows the diet of the Workhouse inmates at Banbury and Oxford 1795

	Sunday	Monday	Tuesday	Wednesday	Thursday	Friday	Saturday
Banbury							
Breakfast	Bread and broth	Bread and broth	Bread and cheese	Bread and broth	Bread and cheese with beer	Bread and broth	Bread and broth
Dinner	Meat and vegetables	Cold meat	Meat and Vegetables	Cold meat	Bread cheese and beer	Meat and vegetables	
Supper	Bread cheese and beer every day						
Oxford							
Breakfast	Milk potage and bread or broth every day						
Dinner	Butcher's meat and roots or vegetables	Bread and cheese	Butcher's meat and roots or vegetables	Bread and cheese	Butcher's meat and roots or vegetables	Suet pudding	Bread and cheese or pease soup
Supper	Potatoes with lard	Broth or milk potage	Potatoes with lard	Broth or milk potage	Potatoes with lard	Bread and cheese	Bread and cheese

Speenhamland System 1795 to 1834

Great difficulties were being experienced in the 1790s due to high prices and low wages, and to try to solve this imbalance a group of county magistrates met at Speen near Newbury, Berkshire intending to fix a minimum wage. This idea was howled down by employers and a different scheme was presented whereby labourers would have their wages made up by the parish rates. This scheme was known as the Speenhamland System 1795: the name derived from the meeting place. It proved to be disastrous as employers reduced wages and so even greater numbers applied for poor relief. The Speenhamland scheme was abolished in 1834.

Examples of wages and cost of food (1795) in Oxford, Deddington and Banbury:

Oxford
Common labourers paid (men)
    15d to 18d a day in Winter
    18d to 20d in hay/harvest
    10s a week corn harvest
(women) 8d a day corn weeders without victuals

Deddington
Common labourers paid (men)
    7s a week in Winter
    8s in Spring
    12s in corn harves
(women) 6d a day for weeding corn
    8d for haymaking
    1s in corn harvest without victuals

Banbury
Common labourers paid
    8s to 9s a week during whole year

Women and children in the manufactories about 3s a week
(Principally worsted, hair-shagg or plush manufacturers)
Weavers in full business 8s to 30s a week and some even earn 40s a week

Currency values at decimalisation:
New Pence (p)		Old Pence (d)
½p	=	1d
50p	=	10 shillings
100p	=	£1 (240d)

The Prices of Provisions 1795

	Beef	Mutton	Veal	Bacon	Milk	Bread	Butter	Eggs
Banbury	5d per lb	5d per lb	No figures available	10d per lb	1d per pint	1s.10d. ½ peck loaf	Not available	Not available
Deddington	ditto	ditto	No figures available	ditto	ditto	ditto	9d and 10d per lb	Not available
Oxford	5½d per lb	5d per lb	5d to 6d per lb	9d to 10d per lb	ditto	1s8d ½ peck loaf	10½d per lb	6 for 4d

113

Chipping Norton Union was formed in 1835 with room for 230 paupers. This became redundant following the Welfare State System 1948 and the premises were later used as the Cotshill Hospital.

William Wright's Charity

One hundred pounds was left for the poor of Over Norton, in 1786, by William Wright of Over Norton. He may have lived at Home Farm but his wife was also connected with Endolls Farm and Witts Farm. If a school had been founded the interest on the money was to be paid to the schoolmaster. Failing that, bread was to be bought and given out to the poor on the day before Christmas day – St Thomas' day. According to the Charity Commissioners' Report of 1826, for which information gathered in 1824 and 1825 was published, £3.18s. was spent in 1824 on shilling and sixpenny loaves. These were distributed to the poor of Over Norton, at Chipping Norton Church, according to the size of their families and the report states that about 70 families received this gift. Due to the expenses of a new trust deed that had been set up, only £1.19s.2d. was available in 1825 and Joseph Austin wished to use it to erect an inscription board in St Mary's Church to record the charity. If this was done it may have been removed when the Church Wardens recorded:

> Inscriptions removed from walls of Chipping Norton Church on its undergoing repairs.

It was also recorded in their accounts that £3.12s.0d. was spent each year from 1895 to 1900 inclusive on bread for the Over Norton Poor. Bakers named Marshall (1896) and Dolphin (1899 and 1900) were mentioned as supplying the loaves.

In 1895 the O.N.P.C. appointed

> ... Mr A.H. Baughan as Overseer of the Poor for the coming year
> ... resolved that Mr W.A. Fawdry be also appointed ... and for 1896.

Messrs F.Allen and F. Marshall served in this capacity in 1897, with William Giles and Joseph Jarvis filling the role in 1898.

William Wright, who was buried at Cogges, also left money for the poor of Hailey and Cogges. There are commemoration boards to him in both of these churches. The first information about these charities which came to my attention was due to a chance viewing of Hailey church.

William Wright married Mary Endoll (see Chapter 4) and in his will left the

> Rectory or Parsonage of Coggs to Mary my wife.

William Hollands (son of Ann Hollands late of Swerford deceased), Joiner and Cabinet Maker, was left Wright's

> Messuage or Tenement in Over Norton with Close Orchard Garden... that which [he] lately purchased from Thomas Edwards of the Lime Kiln Inn of Great Rollright.

William Hollands was also to have

> all my plate and my working Tools and Implements and household goods and furniture.

William Wright also left Estate and premises at Aston and money to many members of his family.

Samuel Colleth [?Collett] an Over Norton Tailor, received

> £30 and my Fiddle

and Mary, wife of John Austin had

> £30 and my snuff box

– but she died before receiving her legacy.

Thomas Edwards of the Lime Kiln Inn, received

> my Pointer Dog called Ponto and my Gun.

Thirty pounds went to Thomas Taylor, and John Austin received

> £30 and my wearing Apparel.

The balance of the money was to go to William Hollands. Included in the final clause was £20 left to the

> Parish Clerk of Coggs and his successors to keep the Chancel and monumental inscriptions at all times neat and clean. (MS Wills Oxon 75/1/24)

The will was witnessed by John Collett, Saml. Wheeler Sen. and Saml. Wheeler Jnr.

Sat 29th Sept 1787 (*J.O.J.*)

> Over Norton Messuage or tenement to be lett, late in the occupation of Wm Wright gent decd. together with acre of land.
>
> Enq. Tho. Taylor of Witney

Sat Feb 14th 1789 (*J.O.J.*)

> All persons who stand indebted to the Estate of Mrs Mary Wright, late of Over Norton, in the County of Oxford, Widow deceased, are desired to pay their respective Debts to Mr Richard Gibbs of Chipping Norton aforesaid, one of the Executors of the Last Will of the said Deceased; or to Mr Winter of Chipping Norton, Attorney-at-Law ...

A second entry Sat March 7th 1789 was signed by:

Richard Gibbs	)	Executors of
Henry Colborn	)	the said
William Endall	)	Mary Wright

Sat 29 Sept 1796 (*J.O.J.*)

> To be Lett, and Entered upon immediately, a New-erected Messuage or Tenement, pleasantly situated in Over Norton, near Chipping Norton, in the County of Oxford, late in the occupation of William Wright Gent. deceased; containing a neat Parlour and Kitchen in Front, four Bed Chambers on the First floor, with Rooms over: a very good cellar and Brew House, Pantry, etc. with Out Buildings: a neat Garden and Orchard fronting the said Messuage, containing pear [trees] an Acre of rich land, the Orchard planted with choice Fruit Trees. The Whole being an Eligible Situation either for a small genteel family, or a single Gentleman for the Hunting Season, there being a Pack of excellent Harriers kept and likely to remain in the Village, and several Packs of Fox Hounds in the Neighbourhood.
>
> The Proprietor will erect any additional Buildings that may be thought necessary on having Interest paid him for the Money laid out.
>
> Further Particulars may be known by applying on the Premises, or to Mr Thomas Taylor, of Witney, in the said County of Oxford.

Mr Richard Woolliams, of Home Farm, has discussed this advertisement and it is thought that the description may fit his house. Pear trees are growing in front of his house in 1999!

Dawkins' Charity

The St. Mary's Church, Chipping Norton Churchwardens recorded:

> 1894 December
> Dawkins to the poor of Over Norton £24. 15. 0. (Jan Apl Jul and Oct four quarter dividends on stock = £24. 15s. 0d.)

The Dawkins' charity appears to be the richest one recorded at the church at that time.

The same figures were given for 1895 to 1900 inclusive but in 1904, 1905 and 1906 this charity was reduced to £22.10.0.

H. Rider Haggard explains in 1898 how the great interest in the formation of the new Parish Councils waned.

> ... to judge from this village [Ditchingham, Norfolk] and others that I know of, interest in Parish Councils is practically dead. In the beginning there was a great excitement about them – I never remember seeing so many men in the Ditchingham schoolroom together as on the occasion of the election after the passing of the Act; but now it is a very different story. For the first two years I was chairman of our Parish Council but I cannot say we accomplished anything exciting ... the parish charities were a burning question. I did not again stand ... it seemed to me the amount of time spent in discussion was disproportionate to the result achieved.

Over Norton's fight to have a say in the distribution of charities

For many years the parish charities became 'a burning question' in Over Norton too. The Over Norton Parish Council having formed in December 1894 was soon discussing the parish charities and in April 1895 recorded that:

> Councillor Allen stated that with reference to the Over Norton Fuel Allotment Charity, the Clerk ... would be willing to meet the members of the Council and explain how the funds of the Charity were disbursed.
>
> The Clerk produced a detailed statement as to the distribution of Wright's Bread Charity and Miss Dawkins' Charity, together with a list of recipients ... having been furnished by the Vicar and Churchwardens of the Ecclesiastical Parish of Chipping Norton.
>
>   Wm Dawkins
>   Chairman

In November 1911 the Over Norton Parish Council wrote to the Charity Commissioners stating that:

> in accordance with the provisions of the Local Government Act, 1894, they [the O.N.P.C.] should appoint Trustees to act with the Vicar of the Parish of Chipping Norton, in the place of the Churchwardens to administer the Charities [Dawkins' and Wright's].

They complained that the accounts which they had received from the Vicar were

> neither complete nor submitted on the form issued by the Commission.

In reply, the Commissioners promised

> a further communication ... when the investigations have been completed. [Jan. 1912]

Mr H. Burden Clerk O.N.P.C. sent another letter making the same points:

> ... the Parish Council is entitled to appoint three representatives on the body of Trustees in place of the Churchwardens ...

A reply dated February 1912 came from the Charity Commission saying that the appointments did not come within the provisions of the 1894 act.

The Over Norton Parish Council was determined to continue with the struggle and in April 1912 recorded in their minutes:

> Ref. Dawkins' and Wright's Charities for 1911 and accounts of the Over Norton Allotments.
>
> After considering the List of Beneficiaries the following resolution was proposed by Mr Walford, and agreed to: That in the opinion of the Parish Council of Over Norton the present basis of distribution by the Trustees of the Dawkins' and Wright's Charities is not in the best interest of the poor and deserving inhabitants of the Parish.

A public enquiry was held into the local charities at the Chipping Norton town hall on 5th November 1912. The Chairman and Clerk of O.N.P.C. were instructed

> that it to be represented to the commissioner that in the opinion of the Parish Council that body should be allowed to assist in the distribution of the Dawkins' and Wright's Charities .

Unfortunately for local historians when the Chairman reported back to Over Norton no details were recorded in the minutes.

> 1913 21st April
> The councillors studied accounts of the Over Norton Allotments Charity, the Dawkins' and the Wright's Charity – to be published at the Mission Room [now St James' Chapel 1999] and on the Public Notice Board in the village.

Two and a half years after the Public Enquiry nothing appeared to have changed concerning O.N.P.C.'s representation on the charities committee. Mr W.P. Walford put forward a motion resulting in the following entry:

> 1913 April 21st
> The Clerk was instructed to write to the Charity Commissioners to enquire what steps had been taken with regard to a scheme for the Charities of Over Norton.

There were no entries in the Minute Book for the years 1918 and 1919. The minutes for 1917 April 19th were signed by Austin Webb on 21st May 1920. No explanation was given for the loss of minuted records.

> 1920 May 31
> The following were appointed Representative Trustees of the Over Norton Allotment Charity: Capt. Daly, Capt. Bayliss, Messrs J, Blencow, R. Hall, J. Harrison. G.R.Lamb, G. Sandles, A. Saunders and A. Webb.
>
> 21st Dec 1937   [As above] the following trustees were appointed: Mrs Bennett, E.J. Joines, Walter Webb, — Rudge, J.P. Shephard, H. Knight, F.C. Lord, J. Benfield and Miss Daly.

From Kelly's Directory 1939

> The rents of the poor's allotment of 50 acres awarded in 1770, are devoted to the purchase of clothes, linen, bedding, fuel, tools, medical or other aid in sickness, food or other articles in kind, and other charitable purposes. Wright's Charity of £3.12s. is for bread, and Miss Dawkins' Charity is given in money, both being disbursed by the vicar and churchwardens of Chipping Norton.

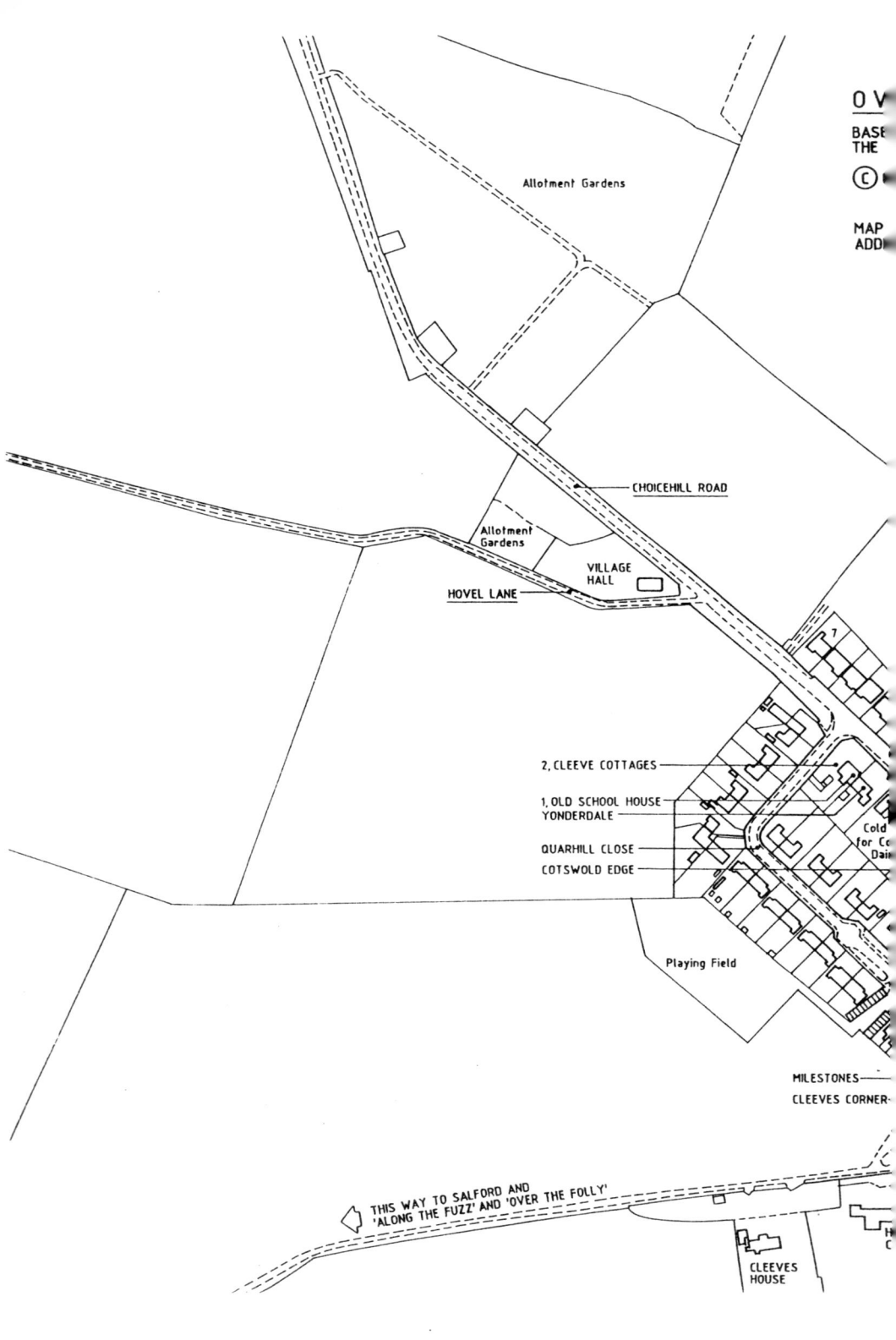

Allotment Gardens

CHOICEHILL ROAD

Allotment Gardens

VILLAGE HALL

HOVEL LANE

2, CLEEVE COTTAGES
1, OLD SCHOOL HOUSE
YONDERDALE
QUARHILL CLOSE
COTSWOLD EDGE

Playing Field

MILESTONES
CLEEVES CORNER

◁ THIS WAY TO SALFORD AND 'ALONG THE FUZZ' AND 'OVER THE FOLLY'

CLEEVES HOUSE

RTON

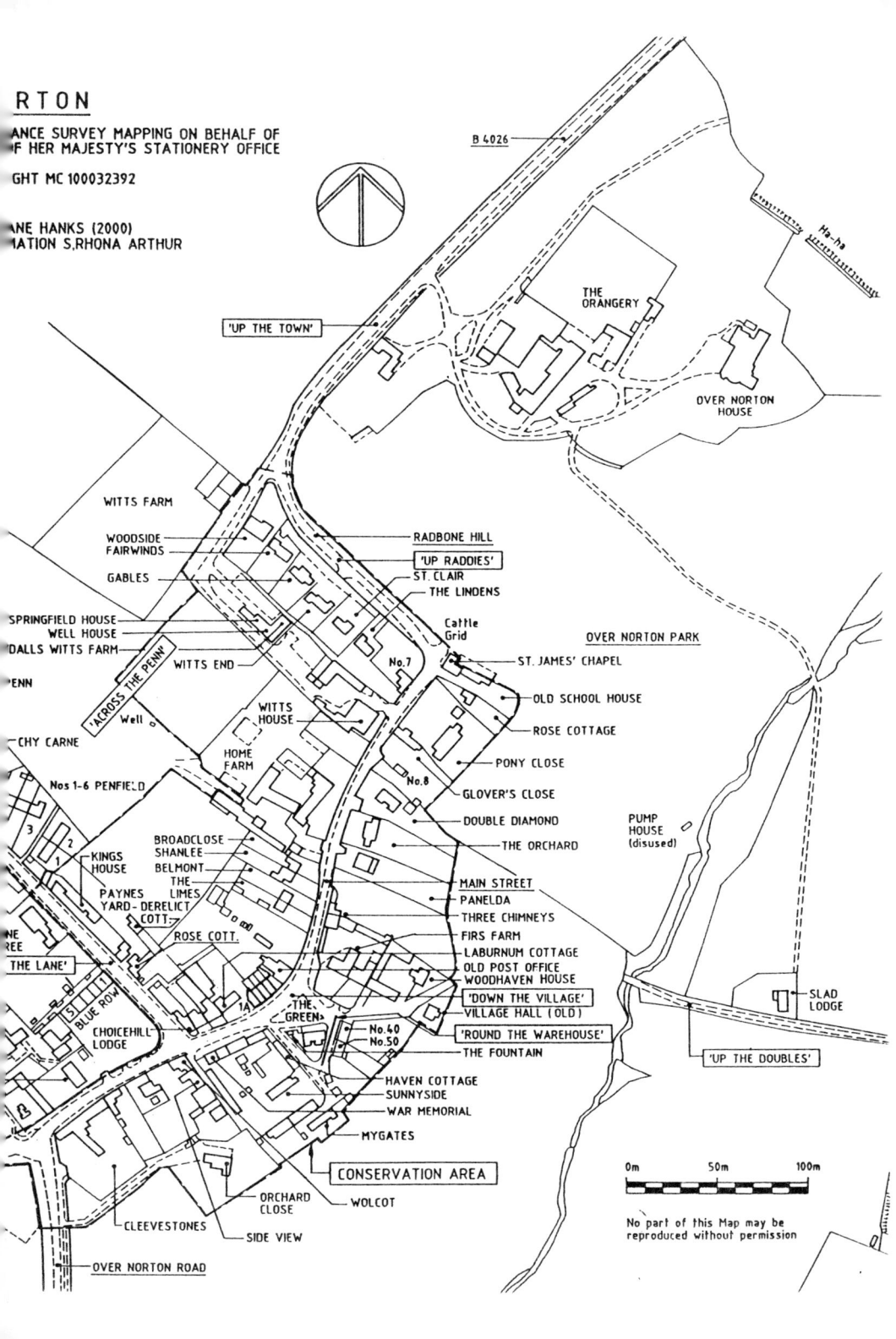

ANCE SURVEY MAPPING ON BEHALF OF
F HER MAJESTY'S STATIONERY OFFICE

GHT MC 100032392

NE HANKS (2000)
ATION S. RHONA ARTHUR

B 4026

Ha-ha

THE ORANGERY

'UP THE TOWN'

OVER NORTON HOUSE

WITTS FARM
WOODSIDE
FAIRWINDS
GABLES
RADBONE HILL
'UP RADDIES'
ST. CLAIR
THE LINDENS

SPRINGFIELD HOUSE
WELL HOUSE
DALLS WITTS FARM
ENN
'ACROSS THE PENN'
WITTS END
No. 7
Cattle Grid

OVER NORTON PARK

ST. JAMES' CHAPEL
OLD SCHOOL HOUSE
ROSE COTTAGE
PONY CLOSE
GLOVER'S CLOSE
DOUBLE DIAMOND
THE ORCHARD

CHY CARNE
Nos 1-6 PENFIELD
KINGS HOUSE
PAYNES YARD- DERELICT COTT.
ROSE COTT.
WITTS HOUSE
HOME FARM
No. 8
BROADCLOSE
SHANLEE
BELMONT
THE LIMES

Well

MAIN STREET
PANELDA
THREE CHIMNEYS
FIRS FARM
LABURNUM COTTAGE
OLD POST OFFICE
WOODHAVEN HOUSE
'DOWN THE VILLAGE'
VILLAGE HALL (OLD)
'ROUND THE WAREHOUSE'
THE FOUNTAIN

PUMP HOUSE (disused)

SLAD LODGE

'UP THE DOUBLES'

'THE LANE'
BLUE ROW
CHOICEHILL LODGE
THE GREEN
No. 40
No. 50

HAVEN COTTAGE
SUNNYSIDE
WAR MEMORIAL
MYGATES

CONSERVATION AREA

CLEEVESTONES
ORCHARD CLOSE
SIDE VIEW
WOLCOT

OVER NORTON ROAD

0m 50m 100m

No part of this Map may be reproduced without permission

30 May 1949
The Clerk raised the question of the appointment of Representative Trustees on the Over Norton coal charity necessary to appoint nine new members ... appointed Mr J.W. Benfield, Mr E.J. Joines, Mr J. Shepherd, Mr W. Webb, Mr D.G. Harrison, Mr J.W. Roughton, Mr H.A. Bennett, Mr David Pearman and Mr A. Barrett.

In 1999 the existing charity is named 'Over Norton Welfare Trust' – an amalgamation of former charities I believe. It is run under the chairmanship of Mr Simon Jennings with Mrs McCrae acting as secretary. No written applications for support are needed but applicants of pensionable age, or a person in need, should make their request to a committee member. At one time applicants needed to apply to Farrant & Sinden Solicitors and when the Saunders family ran the old post office they had application forms there.

The Daly family were always generous benefactors and the following item was taken from the St Mary's Church accounts.

1899-1900
Captain Daly of Over Norton Park donated £10.00 to the 'Sick & Needy Fund'. [He gave £1.0.0. in 1900 to the Church Ventilation Fund.]

At Christmas 1901 he gave £30.0.0. which was used as follows:

	£	s	d
District Visitor	12	10	0
Rev. B. Barford	1	0	0
Rev. C. Page	1	0	0
Vicar	1	5	0
For additional tickets Maternity Soc.	1	0	0
For Mrs Saunders' Club towards clothes	1	0	0
Club bonuses	2	5	0
Towards Phillips' Coal Charity	5	0	0
Special cases per Vicar	5	0	0
	30	0	0

CHAPTER 8

Agricultural Development in Over Norton 1770s to 1900—1770 Plan with Photographs—Field Names—Robert Fowler—Arthur Young—Rowells—Swing Riots 1830, Heythrop—Home Farm, County Fire Mark—Joseph Arch—The Ascott Women—O.N.P. Councillors 1894—Henry Dawkins Farming Notes mid-1800s—Extracts from Cropredy Farm Ledgers 1818 to 1912 (Mr W. Anker)—Agricultural Wages Scale 1899—Farm Workers and Farmers from Census Returns 1841 to 1891

To obtain an Enclosure Act owners of at least four-fifths of the land had to petition Parliament. This is what happened (1769) in this area with Henry Dawkins, of Over Norton Park, being one of the applicants. A copy of the Enclosure Map 1770 showing all of the 'allotments' made which supported the written text can be seen at Chipping Norton Museum but it does not show all of Over Norton Parish. However, Mr Dawkins has allowed me to photograph his '1770 Plan of Over Norton Estate' which was surveyed for Henry Dawkins Esq by P. Bell.

Plan of Over Norton Estate in the County of Oxford belonging to Henry Dawkins Esq
Survey'd by P. Bell 1770. (See map photograph No.1)

		a	r	p
A	**Great House**, yard, stable gardens	1	3	34
B	Scot's Close	1	0	14
C	Cherry Orchard	1	1	37
D		0	0	4
E	Lower Garden	0	1	24
F	Meads Close	0	1	1
G	Grafan Close (with Hse)	0	0	32
H	Broad Croft	3	2	28
I	Fish Ponds	2	0	22
K	Tims Close	1	1	37
L	Malt House	0	0	10
		12	3	3

L, The Malt House, was situated in Choicehill Road whereas all other areas listed above were close to the Great House.

$30_{1/4}$ sq yds = sq perch
40 sq perches = 1 rood
4 roods = 1 acre

2. New Farm

		a	r	p
a	Picket Stone Field	29	3	25
b	Long head Land	63	0	1
c	Salisbury Plain	17	2	15
d	Lather Land Bank	19	3	25
e	Hull hill field	38	3	33
f	Mill ditch piece	22	2	30
g	Richey Lays	32	3	24
h	Coppice at the Wells	1	3	11
i	Wells head Ground	182	0	31
		408	3	35

3. West Farm

		a	r	p
k	House Barns Yard and orchard	1	1	6
l	House Barn and yard	0	1	16
m	Guys house, Barns and Close	1	3	29
n	Dixons house Barns and Close	1	1	15
o	The Layes	5	1	29
p	Dixons Piece	6	1	10
q	Green way Piece	24	0	10
r	Standiup Piece	22	3	10
s	Smart way hedge piece	23	3	38
t	Over Mill way piece	21	3	12
u	Prims Down piece	32	3	25
v	Fletchels Close	9	1	6
x	Furnill Piece	30	1	28
		181	3	34
y	Tainsham	4	0	24
z	Cutlays Piece	62	3	34
	Long Hole	14	3	38

1	Upper Mill way Close		3 1 32
2	Lower Mill way Close		8 1 3
3	Between Lake		19 0 0
4	Mill way Coppice		1 15
5	Hedges Bushes		23 2 20
6	Drinit		19 0 35
7	Smart Coppice		0 0 29
			156 0 30
		Total	1051 3 27

4.	Middle Farm		a r p
M	House Barns Yard and Gardens		0 3 5
N	Orchard		0 2 12
O	Tyte Close		1 2 28
P	Dogs kannal		3 1 25
Q	Galls		21 2 3
R	New Close		10 1 16
S	Boar Lands		20 3 23
T	Rond hill field		41 2 7
U	North Wells		38 3 20
V	Cherry Orchard End		19 1 26
W	Melking hedge piece		27 3 14
X	Broad Close		1 3 31
Y	Mill Way piece		31 1 24
Z	Farmer Furz		2 0 36
	Eight Acres field		69 2 15
			292 0 5

The Dawkins Estate was divided into four main areas. 1) The Great House and grounds, 2) New Farm (now Hull Farm), 3) West Farm (now the Cleeves) and 4) Middle Farm (now Witts Farm). There was no indiciaton of a house at New Farm. The Middle Farm land was shown as stretching up to Chapel House but in recent time Witts Farm has had no land east of Main Street. (See photograph of 1770 map No.1)

As part of West Farm it will be noticed that there were two houses plus barns on the opposite side of the road to the farmhouse: Guys House situated right in the corner of the ground where Choicehill Road branches from Main Street at the bottom of Mr John West's garden (Blue Row) and Dixons House appears to have followed the line of the present day No. 6 Cleeves Corner where Mrs Connie Ward lives. (See photograph No.3A)

Map photograph (No. 4) shows a substantial track, no longer in existence, which was located from Middle Farm (now Witts Farm) south through to the bottom of the garden of cottage No 8. which then linked up with the centre of the village. A branch from this track went directly to the stream. The two closes each side of this track, Tyte Close and Dogs Kannal, both have meanings to do with water. Tyte means spring or fountain and Dogs Kannal, I think, is connected with Dogdyke (E. Ekwall) a ditch where the water lilies grow and Kenn (E. Ekwall) is explained as 'a place on streams'. Nuttalls Dictionary 1919 states Kennel: the watercourse of a street; a little channel (canal) and in Chambers, 'Kennel': a street gutter. That Dogs Kannal is to do with wet land seems more likely than a local explanation that hounds were kept there. Across the valley on higher ground adjacent to The Layes and Dogs Kannal was the Galls. Water-gall is explained in Nuttalls as a cavity, made in the earth by a torrent of water. In 1890 Col. W.G. Dawkins labelled another field 'Dogs Kennel'. This was enclosure 359 (10 acres approx) in Chipping Norton Parish next to the 'Barn Field'.

Middle Farm's 'Melking Hedge Piece' reminds us of the days when the cows were tied up outside for milking. This field has had many changes of name: Field Above Town, Squires Close and Square Ground (1999).

Names of some of the West Farm fields (photograph No.3B) may have the following meanings:

Standiup Piece is most likely to be connected with stone derived from stan.O.E.

Long Hole is possibly from holh hol O.E.; a hollow which may be a deep hole in a stream.

Cutlays Piece may mean a cut, or a share of land, but probably connected with cuttele M.E. with stream connections. There are still springs in this area so the second explanation seems more likely. Fields named Between Lake, Upper Millway Close, Lower Millway Close and Between Lake reinforce this suggestion.

Furnill (?furze) Piece was situated in the area named 'Over the Fuzz' mentioned in Chapter 2.

At New Farm (1770), 'Picket Stone Field's' shape does not fit the usual explanation of an angular piece of ground but perhaps it was 'squared up' for enclosure. The farm buildings are in this field. In modern times Hull Farm does have a 'Picket' triangular field 30° 60° 90° – just fitting a set-square – but in a different location. (See map photograph No.5)

After the allotments were made in 1770 the new hedges were planted – mainly hawthorn – to enclose the land. It would be a worthwhile project to do a survey of the local hedges when 'Hoopers Rule' could be tried out whereby the number of species in a certain length of hedge, usually thirty yards, is counted. It is suggested that the number of species gives the age of the hedge in centuries.

The main street used to continue through the park and this was bordered by buildings on the north side. It made a 90° turn north just before reaching the 'Great House'. Numerous buildings and gardens are shown situated in the park – all have disappeared leaving only the rise and fall of the land to show where they existed. The stable block which has survived (1999) now provides living accommodation and workshops. After 1770 the Main Street was diverted to form Radbone Hill and two separate buildings following the line of No. 7, Chesterton's Cottage, must have been demolished. (See photograph map No.2)

The house marked at F, Meads Close with 1 pole 1 perch of land, no longer exists but it was advertised for letting on:

21 March 1761 [J.O.J.]
To be Lett
And entered upon at Lady - Day next, if required.
   A New-built Slated House, Two rooms on a Floor, fit for a small Family; pleasantly situated opposite Squire Dawkins's; with a good Brewhouse and Garden.

To understand what was happening to the agricultural development in Over Norton from the 1770s onwards the national picture needs to be considered.

Great improvements were going on in agriculture even before Jethro Tull (1674-1741), Lord 'Turnip' Townsend (1674-1738) and Thomas Coke made their marks but it was these men whose names and doings were taught to us in our schooldays. They became the figure heads of the day but there must have been many un-recognised contributors who had devoted their time and talents to experimenting and improving agricultural practice of that time.

Jethro Tull is remembered for his invention of a corn drill and a horse-drawn hoe. His book *The New Horse-Hoeing Husbandry* (1731) influenced farmers over a long period of time. The term 'husbandry' means careful management of the land. Prior to the use of corn drills grain was planted by the hand broadcast method.

> Sow four grains in a row
> One for the pigeon, one for the crow,
> One to rot and one to grow.
>
> Quoted by Arthur Young
>
> My step-grandfather, as a boy of nine years in 1858, did crow scaring in the Leafield area, his sustenance for the day being dry bread and a raw onion. He graduated to running a farm at Churchill, Oxon.

Fred Lambert, at Cropredy, was paid.

> 35 days keeping off crows 17s.0d. in 1887.

The Marquis of Blandford, in the early 19th century stated that,

> corn should be sown broadcast or dibbled especially considering that employment was required for the poor. (V.C.H. Vol.ii p.282)

Children have always enjoyed using the nickname of Lord Townsend – Turnip Townsend – and because of this found it easy to remember that he grew turnips successfully having improved his marshy and sandy land in Norfolk by marling (clay and lime) it. He drilled and horse-hoed it as Tull had advised. The Norfolk four-fold course rotation of wheat, turnips, barley and clover, was practised on his farm. Further encouragement came from King George III whose model farm at Windsor earned him the title of 'Farmer George'.

The Choicehill Road school closed in April 1933. These children moved to Chipping Norton Schools. Freddie Watson, George Harrison, Nancy Shepard, Pat West, Betty Goodman, Ken Harris, Douglas Sheffield, Geoff Barrett, Connie Harris, Rose Harrison, Joyce Shepard, Jack Harrison, Margaret Silman, Rosie Watson, Peter Flick, ? , Joan Bennett, Alma Joines, Charlie Barrett, Bernard Aries.

Pupils of St. Cecilia's School, Chipping Norton performing a pantomime – Cinderella and the Prince – at Chipping Norton Town Hall 1936.

Practising their school dances at home. L to R Tom Rudge, Audrey Woolliams, Richard Woolliams, Dorothy Rudge. Note the dolls' tea party.

Dorothy Rudge and brother Tom in their school panto costumes.

Over Norton Council School, Choicehill road.

Major Daly unveils the Great War Memorial at Over Norton.

Over Norton War Memorial 1914-1918 (Gnr Philip Lionel Bernard Hiatt was killed in action in 1944. His name has been added to the Over Norton War Memorial).

Pte Murrell of Lidstone (left) and L/Cpl Knight (of Over Norton) were employed as coachmen to Major Daly of Over Norton Park. L/Cpl Knight was killed in the 1914-18 war and remembered by Harry Barnes in Chapter 9. (By courtesy of Chipping Norton Museum)

Major Daly opening the new wooden village hall 1934.

May Day 1934 at the Old Shed.

May Day 1937.

Planting the Coronation tree 1937.

Over Norton's entry for Chipping Norton's Hospital Carnival 1937. L/R Don Cambray, Pat Cambray, Dorothy Rudge, Audrey Woolliams, Mrs K.V. Cambray.

May Day 1938.

Watching May Day celebrations 1938.

May Day 1939.

Drawn by a young evacuee, Dennis Hudson. Collecting water from a spring following the pollution of Over Norton's water supply by the American Forces.

Pat Cambray (now Mrs Randall) collecting salvage for the war effort. (Artist Dennis Hudson)

Having commandeered the Village Hall the W.I. equipment was moved out. Escorting the W.I. banner to a temporary home. (Artist Dennis Hudson)

Thomas Coke (1750-1842) also a Norfolk man, made great improvements to his livestock. He did this by improving his pasture land having appreciated the fact that good animal food would produce good stock. As an aide-mémoire 'Coke to rhyme with Norfolk' was practised by students, although I believe 'Coke' should be pronounced as 'Cook'. The 'Holkham Gatherings' (1778-1821) which Coke arranged were a mecca for agriculturalists where farming methods were discussed – seven thousand people were supposed to have been present in 1821. (*Economic History of England*, Briggs & Jordan. Pub. University Tutorial Press Ltd. reprint 1945.)

Having perhaps felt that these Norfolk men were a considerable distance from Over Norton, and wondering what influence they may have had on the lives of people in this village, it is very satisfying to find a direct link with another well known name in the field of agriculture, that of Robert Bakewell (1725-1795) from Dishley, near Loughborough. His fame was due to his improved breeding of sheep the Leicester breed – and of cattle – the Longhorn. Through selective breeding he was able to double the weight of the animals for the meat market. We know of the influence of Bakewell's work in Over Norton through Robert Fowler, who farmed at Little Rollright – just a mile from the centre of Over Norton. Fowler became well known for his breeding stock of sheep and cattle and at his death his animals were sold over three days in 1791. The animals fetched extraordinary high prices:

The Oxford Journal April 2nd 1791

> At the sale of the Breeding Stock of the late Mr Robert Fowler of Rollright ... there were indisputably more People assembled than have ever been collected on a like occasion:
> ... The first three Lots (three young Bulls) fetched the amazing sum of Six Hundred and Twenty Guineas.

Extracts from the auctioneer's description of the sale follow:

> Mr Fowler on his first setting out ... began with two cows, purchased at what was then thought to be a great price from Mr Webster's flock, of Canly...Warwick; these he hired a Bull called Twopenny, of Mr Bakewell... from them he had two Cows called Old Long Horn and Old Nell. He had

several Bulls of Mr Bakewell afterwards, but since the Bull called D, Sire of Shakespeare, which he had of him about the year 1778, he kept entirely to his own flock ...

The merit of his sheep appears to have been derived also ... from the flock of Mr Bakewell ...

Two Over Norton men bought animals at Fowler's Sale. An incorrect purchaser's name seems to have been given for two lots – it should, I believe, be Huckvale (See chapter 5) and not Huckfield.

Lot 45 Blue Heifer four years old by Shakespeare Purchased by Mr Samuel Huckfield [?Huckvale] and	£110. 5s. 0d.
Lot 49 Cow Calf	£ 32 11s. 0d.
Lot 69 Six ewes Purchased by Mr Samuel Huckvale Choicehill, Over Norton	£ 55. 10s. 0d.
... a daughter of Old Nell, a White Backed Broken Horn Heifer sold for	£ 52. 10s. 0d.
... Young Nell sold for	£126. 0s. 0d.

... Above one thousand guineas have been made of Nell and her stock in eight years.

From Nell, a daughter of Old Nell (which was a daughter of Twopenny) more was made than by any one cow in the Kingdom ...

The auctioneer was R. Parry of Shipston upon Stower.

Arthur Young, (1741-1820) who made a detailed study of agriculture in many parts of England, Ireland and Europe, supported the enclosure of the land as the 'open field' system was not compatible with his expectations of how a farm should be organised. The following list of expected improvements to be found after enclosure is based on Young's views.

1. Previously everyone had to follow the same procedures but now crops and animals could be matched to suitable land.
2. Too much time had been wasted travelling to scattered pieces of land time saved.
3. Cattle had all been mixed together spreading diseases – now will be healthier cattle.
4. Supervision easier for farmers.
5. Drainage of land easier to arrange – will help prevent sheep rot.
6. Trespass of cattle and ploughing away from next persons strip had caused acrimony – quarrels should be prevented.

Arthur Young sought the opinion of local farmers on enclosures and Mr Dawkins of Over Norton Park replied

> ... Enclosures all around Chipping Norton, have, unquestionably added greatly to the food of mankind; and the county has been in consequence of them much improved.

Mr Davis of Bloxham told Arthur Young:

> Rents have increased by the enclosures [and] enclosures have made very little difference to the poor; but not so much pilfering; far better for their morals; they never had means of keeping cows, but when they had cottage common; the allotment much better, and the people in a better situation from the enclosure ...

The poorer inhabitants actually suffered greatly as they could no longer support themselves by keeping a cow and poultry when their rights to the commons and wastelands were taken away from them.

> Tis bad enough in man or woman
> to steal a goose from off a common.
> But surely he's without excuse
> who steals the common from the goose.
> quoted by Arthur Young

Another slight worry about the poor is reflected by Young:

> Potatoes have been a good deal cultivated in Deddington by the poor people ... The enclosure will do away with all this business.

Young commented that of all the counties he had visited, Oxfordshire possessed the fewest implements.

> There may be horse hoes in the county but I did not see one [they are] so much wanting in their bean culture ... there are some drills ... scarifiers and scufflers, on which so much in modern tillage depends, are very rare indeed.
> Thrashing mills are spreading in Oxfordshire.

By about the year 1813 the bishop of Durham, who then farmed in Oxfordshire had a thrashing mill worked by only two horses and that this thrashed five quarters in a day of eight hours ... Lord Maclesfield had a similar machine erected at a cost of £120. (V.C.H. Vol.ii p. 288)

Young:
> The ploughs most generally used are the two-wheel one – beam high and the one-wheeled plough – beam low. At Crowmarsh double ploughs drawn by oxen plough one acre and a half in six hours.

(In 1999 massive machines – six or seven reversible ploughs – can do twenty acres in a day. Source: Anthony Hobbs)

Arthur Young recorded the rotation of crops grown in Over Norton and Salford – the details were published in 1813.

1. Turnips
2. Barley
3. Seeds mown the first year, fed the second
4. Wheat
5. Oats

But on the low land:

1. Fallow
2. Wheat
3. Beans
4. Barley or oats; and half the land sown with barley or oats must be sown in seeds; and being once mown, is considered as a fallow, and ploughed for wheat.

He commented that in this 'Stonebrash District' the
> soil is dry enough for feeding turnips where they grow, and fertile enough for wheat. Rape is little cultivated in Oxfordshire [not true of 1999] ... cabbages are uncommon too .

Sanfoin (Fr. sain; wholesome and foin; hay) was grown for fodder on all the stonebrash lands –
> from Chipping Norton in all directions. It lasts ten years, and on new ground would last fifteen

but it was not successful where land was reclaimed from furze –
> it presently goes off and is lost.

There was a great deal of furze growing in the Over Norton area and remnants can be seen on Priory Farm.

Young:

> The town dunghills of Chipping Norton are sold by auction ... parcels have been sold for as high as 20 shillings a cart load on the spot.

Banbury was an important centre for the production of farm machinery. 'The Britannia Works' there was founded in the mid-1800s. Sir Bernard Samuelson, who had been building railways in France, had to return to England due to the French Revolution and he bought Mr James Gardner's small factory. One successful line of Gardner's had been his 'Banbury Turnip Cutter' made to his own design. Samuelson when starting up employed twenty-seven men – the wage bill being £32 a week. (V.C.H. Vol.ii.) In 1872 eight thousand reaping machines were produced there. (Banbury Guardian 11 May 1905 and recorded in V.C.H. Vol.ii p.268 and 269)

Mr W. Anker, a farmer at Cropredy, had an auction sale of farming stock and implements in 1891. Included in the sale were four of Gardner's 'turnip cutters' and two of Samuelson's machines: a 'Mowing Machine' and an 'Eclipse Reaper' – Samuelson's patent.

The Oxfordshire Steam Ploughing Company at Oxford started their business in 1868 during the prosperous farming years. (V.C.H. Vol.ii p.270)

On the door-step of Over Norton were Rowell and Sons at High Street and Albion Street, Chipping Norton. In 1899 they were advertising for work: repairs to steam engines and agricultural machinery. They, at that time, also manufactured drills, rollers, water barrels and drags, held agencies for Jarman's Swath Turner and were contractors for steam sawing, threshing and road rolling.

Rowell's were agents for the main bicycle manufacturers: 'Rudge', 'Whitworth', 'Star' and 'Royal Enfield'. A 'Special to Cyclists' message produced in J.O.J. September 1899 said,

> Don't keep your machine in the Hall. Have a bicycle house .

Political and Economic Background 1793 to 1900

During the French Wars (1793-1815) farmers in Britain were paid high prices for their corn. No foreign corn was imported at this time due to Napoleon's blockade. The large landowners had bought most of the freehold land. They had great influence in parliament and forced the Corn Laws (1815) through so that they would be protected from imports which were not to be allowed until the home prices of grain reached war-time prices – £4 to £5 a quarter. But at least one tenant farmer in this area seemed to prosper. That was John Busby at Dunthrop who left about £5,000 at his death (1815). (V.C.H. Vol.xi p.139)

A number of Anti-Corn Law Societies were started, their purpose being to get rid of the Corn Laws. A Reform Act (passed June 1832) helped to make representation to parliament a fairer system. The landowners were against reform as they would lose their power. Once the middle classes obtained a fair share of representatives following the reform they were able to use their new-found power to get the corn laws abolished in 1846.

The agricultural depression after the peace of 1815 meant that the working classes had a very tough time due to unemployment and low wages. At this time 72 per cent of Oxfordshire families received Parish Relief showing just how low the wages were.

The date 1830 is very significant as that is when the labourers' revolt took place. They were finally pushed into this by a major worry that the new machines would reduce their employment: for example the new threshing machines would take away their winter work. Threshing machines became a target for destruction.

The first one was destroyed in Kent during August 1830. Threatening letters signed 'Captain Swing' were widespread although it is thought that there was no such person. By November 1830 the troubles came very close to Over Norton when at Heythrop a large group of men under the leadership of Thomas Hollis, a ploughman, smashed machines. (*Captain Swing*: E.J. Hobsbawn and George Rudé)

Estimates of the number of men involved at Heythrop range from 70 to 200. One account says that Henry Somerset, Duke of Beaufort was assaulted and that

> of 24 men later tried, possibly one, John West, was a Heythrop man .
> (V.C.H. Vol.xi p.133)

Yarnton prepared themselves for the possibility of Swing attacks by ordering twenty-five staves at the cost of one guinea and Steeple Aston's farmers formed a Fire Engine company. (*Barracuda Guide to County History* Vol.II, Geoffrey Stevenson ref. to B. Stapleton pub. 1869 and D. McClatchey pub. 1960)

Through November and December 1830 threshing machines were destroyed at eleven other locations in Oxfordshire, including ones at Neithrop and Tadmarton. There were political riots at Banbury and several other places. In Oxfordshire seventy-five cases of damage and riots were tried in court and out of this number thirty-four were acquitted, five were fined, twenty-three were jailed and thirteen sentenced to transportation, of whom eleven arrived in Tasmania. (Hobsbawn and Rudé: ibid)

Mr Richard Woolliams of Home Farm, Over Norton, has a 'County Fire Mark' on his house. (1999) This insurance company which operated between 1807 to 1906, found that up to 1853 40 per cent of all fire losses which they had underwritten were classified as incendiary fires. There is no doubt that in other counties the rioters did burn down houses and at least on one occasion a landowner's dog was poisoned. There was no public fire service as we know it today and so people who could afford to, paid their premiums to gain cover and displayed their fire marks on the front of their houses. Occupiers of Home Farm must have gained a feeling of security once their fire mark was displayed.

Heythrop Mansion was destroyed by fire 23rd February 1831. The flames could be seen for forty miles. (V.C.H. Vol.xi p.135) There is no information to suggest that it was a deliberate act of destruction as it was supposed to have been caused by a domestic accident – coals falling on to a mattress which was being aired. Henry Charles Somerset, duke of Beaufort (d.1835) had rented Heythrop House from 1820. (ibid p.134)

Heythrop Mansion remained derelict for forty years when it was rebuilt by the Brassey family who sold it in 1920. (See Rose Daly chapter 9.)

(Joseph Dixon, an eleven-year old chimney sweep was suffocated whilst cleaning a conservatory flue at Heythrop Mansion. His burial was recorded as 28th April 1812. Source: Enstone Parish Council.)

The 'Swing Riots' may have hastened both the reform of the 'Speenhamland System' (see chapter 7) of poor relief and of the passing of the 'Reform Act' but the punishments were harsh. The agricultural workers rose again, briefly, under the leadership of Joseph Arch. (See later)

The large farmers experienced some very prosperous times from 1846 to 1873 often described as 'The Golden Age of Farming' but this prosperity did not extend to the poor.

The population in the towns had doubled and therefore a greater demand for food had arisen and that coupled with the fact that industrial workers had more money to spend on food, helped to create the 'Golden Age'. In 1801 there were only five towns in England and Wales with a population of over 50,000: Leeds, Liverpool, Manchester, Birmingham and Bristol (London was over 95,000). By 1851 Leeds, Bradford, Sheffield and Bristol had populations of between 100,000 to 200,000; Liverpool, Manchester and Birmingham between 200,000 and 500,000; London 2,362,236. (Pergamon General Historical Atlas pub. 1970)

There was no competition from foreign imports – but that was to come! All the new farming techniques had come to fruition. There was a greater knowledge of the use of fertilisers, a more advanced understanding of land drainage, seed quality had improved and together with more machinery and better transport, the scene was set for prosperity for the farmers.

English cattle were sought after throughout the world so the arrival of 'rinderpest' (cattle plague) in 1862-66 was a shattering blow. It spread through thirty-six counties in six months. Foot and Mouth disease had arrived in 1839. Later some control was managed by following the instructions of a 'Diseases of Animals Act' of 1890. (*Economic History of England part 2* Briggs & Jordan reprint 1945.)

The farmers Golden Years came to an end when difficult times befell them after 1875. There was some bad weather with only two good seasons between 1874 and 1882. Free trade was back in operation and allowed the market to be flooded with foreign grain. Frozen mutton was coming in from Australia and corned beef from Argentina. Rents dropped by 30 per cent to 50 per cent. Huge numbers of farmers went out of business and many acres of arable land were not cultivated. A grave agricultural depression was taking place. Industry as well as agriculture was in difficulties and the problems were worldwide. (Briggs & Jordan op.cit.)

Tenant farmers had been paying tithes – 10 per cent of everything they produced to the Church – but some relief was given to them by the changing of the terms and making the owner of the land responsible for paying these charges.

Joseph Arch

In 1872 an 'Agricultural Labourers' Union' had been founded. Joseph Arch, a travelling hedge-cutter and Non-conformist Preacher was instrumental in its foundation and he worked towards trying to get better conditions for land workers and campaigned for 16s.0d. a week pay and a nine-and-a-half hours working day. When this was refused the men went on strike in 1874 and trouble spread all over England. In some places a wage of 14s.0d. a week was paid and in others 15s.0d., but in 1875 when the great farming depression descended, wages fell and men found that they had to take what they could get. Ten years later 'The Union' was almost defunct as the men, when facing starvation, had had to give up the fight. (Briggs & Jordan op.cit.)

The Ascott Women

An event in April 1873 at Ascott-u-Wychwood, seven miles from Over Norton, ended in a prison sentence for sixteen women after they had been tried at Chipping Norton by two Church of England clergymen magistrates. Their crime had been to try to persuade two men from working at Hambridge's Farm after they had been hired to replace men on strike. Seventeen women gathered but neither threatened nor used force, although some carried sticks. Seven women were each given ten days' hard labour and nine, seven days' hard labour. There was rioting in Chipping Norton that night and police reinforcements were brought from Oxford early the next morning to transport the women to Oxford Gaol. The group of nine returned home by train after serving their sentence and the rest were driven home in a drag drawn by four thoroughbred horses. There was cheering on route and a great welcome was given to them at Ascott and Joseph Arch presented each woman with £5 and a silk dress in the Union colours. (Paraphrased from *Sharpen the Sickle* Reg Groves. Pub. The Porcupine Press.)

The clergy usually came out in support of the landowners and farmers. Reg Groves (op.cit.) mentions that these sections of society usually controlled the parish and rural councils, the village charities, the land and employment, and the magistrates' bench. Parish Councils and Rural District Councils as known today, were not formed until 1894. A cross section of the public has always been represented on O.N.P.C. In 1894 William Moulder, age 56, a shepherd living at Blue Row, was a councillor and in time became vice-chairman. He resigned in 1904 due to ill health. George Harrison of the Village, born at Salford, filled the vacancy. In 1891 George was a woollen spinner, Rhoda his wife, a weaver, their son, William George, an agricultural labourer and Frank, age twelve, Harry ten, James eight and Albert, were scholars.

In 1999 the Harrison family is still represented on the O.N.P.C. by Glen Pashley, his maternal grandfather being a Harrison. Oliver Harrison (Mrs Doris Pashley's brother) gave service to O.N.P.C. over a long period – he was mentioned as chairman in 1937. In September 1963,

> the chairman (O.N.P.C.) [Mr J. Roughton] spoke of the loyal service given to the council over a number of years by the late Mr Oliver Harrison. His valuable experience and wide knowledge of Local Government will be sadly missed .

Oliver Harrison was a J.P., a Rural District Councillor and a County Councillor.

Other Parish Councillors in 1894 were:

> **William Jarvis** aged 65 from The Village, a farm labourer, with a wife and three children working in the 'Tweed Mill' and a 12-year-old son, James, a farm labourer.

Frederick Allen lived at No. 34, was a dealer and employed one servant. He was made vice-chairman.

Henry Sandells age 62, an agricultural labourer living at No. 28, had three daughters, Rachel, Esther and Clara, working in the wool trade and a son Charles, aged 17, an agricultural labourer.

Colonel W.G. Dawkins was appointed Chairman of O.N.P.C., a position he held for many years. This was not a fait accompli as Mr Frederick Scholfield, Land Agent, had been approached first

> ... it was unanimously resolved that Colonel William Gregory Dawkins be elected a member of the Parish Council to fill the vacancy caused by the non-acceptance of office by Mr Frederick W. Scholfield.

Henry (m Emma) Dawkins was well versed in crop rotation as can be seen in his notes written between 1845 and 1860 – the 'good practice' news had travelled to Over Norton from Norfolk – in which he mentioned the growing of turnips, swedes, barley, clover and vetches. By growing so much animal fodder they could keep the stock going through the winter, consequently being able to have fresh meat at any time. In earlier years stock would have been slaughtered and salted before winter set in.

Henry Dawkins' farming pattern was described in his 'Observation on the Mode of Cultivation'.

> To begin with the Turnip Crops in October – The Lambs should be penned on the Course Turnips after some of the largest are taken for the Cows Stocks. The Turnips should be cut and with a little Hay the Lambs will do well. The Swedes about the early part of November will be better pulled and topped and put into heaps of half a Cart load sack then covered with soil, in which manner they will be kept from Frost or other injury until May, if required. The Tops may be given to the Sheep or Cattle [as] convenient. As the Turnips are cleared off the Land should be ploughed (if not too wet) that none of the mound [soil] be lost, it will also work better for the Barley and Clover, it being very essential to those Crops that a fine Tilth should be made when sown, which should not be done in Wet Weather, as it cannot be left too light for Barley. When this Crop is harvested a few lambs may be turned on the Seeds. ... In the Spring when the Lambs/or I should now call them Tegs, and other Lambs will be dropped have finished the Turnips and Swedes, they may be penned on the Clover Seeds always having a

space first cut for them which they will eat from ... the best will be made of the crops and the Land Manured. When the Pen is moved which will be about every other day, the Whole shall be moved together that the Roots may grow again which they soon will do – This will last the Sheep until there is room on the Grass Land by which time the Lambs will be Weaned and may follow the Tegs on the Clover, which will have grown again, and will do the lambs and probably after a few Ewes (as well) until it is time to put them on Turnips in the manner before mentioned. The Field will then be sown with Wheat in the Usual Manner.

At Harvest if the Ground is clear it will be better to cut it with a broad Hook, the Advantage of which is that the whole of the Straw is saved ... and it will cost less per Acre than the old manner of Cutting it with Sickles as it can be done much quicker – ... The Wheat being harvested the Ewes will have a good feed over it for some time.

The Field should be manured and ploughed deep and well any time before Xmas and without doing anything more the Land may be sown with Beans which should when high enough should be Hoed. This should be done twice at least to keep the weeds down. When this Crop is harvested the Field should be ploughed and sown with Vetches, on which the Ewes and Lambs may be penned early in the Spring so as to get the Ground cleared to prepare it for the Swedes and Turnips the former may be sown in May, and the last the first week in July.

The number of Ewes kept in this manner may be Eighty; which will produce as many lambs or thereabout. Sixty of which should be fed [on] the seeds with twenty old Ewes, and twenty young ones put into their places to keep good the Flock; by this manner none of the Ewes will be more than four years old.

The Cow Stock may be either of Cows brought into Feed, or purchased young; and put to Bull in the Spring; so that by the end of November they will be forward in Calf. ... Then those that have not fed well at grass must be put into the Stalls.

The Team may be left as much as possible in the Stable and what with chaff Corn and a few Vetches in the Summers, will feed much with the other Stocks. ... I forgot to mention a rick of hay should be placed ...

Henry Dawkins kept meticulous accounts of the sale of his wool and butter and it is from these that the following details were extracted:

'Memoranda of Wool'

Henry Dawkins sold 40 fleeces in 1832 rising to 224 in 1855 this being the greatest number sold between the years 1832 to 1864. In 1847 119 fleeces were sold for £22.5s.0.d but by 1864 this price had been more than doubled when 118 fleeces sold for £47.0s.0d. – this increase being during the 'Golden Age' of farming.

Henry Dawkins recorded every detail of his 'Sheep Expences for the years 1854 to 1863 on My Farm of One hundred and Sixty acres of Grass land'. e.g. 1854 sheep expences £4.13s.2d.

'Memoranda of Butter made on my Farm in Following Years' – under this heading were listed the butter sales for each year from 1833 to 1856.

	lbs	sold for	£. s. d.
1833	1003		46. 12. 0. [approx.. 11d. per lb]
1841	917		50. 12. 5.
1856	1542 [Maximum]		87. 2. 7. [approx. is 1s.1½d. per lb]

The butter prices for 1856 show an increase of almost 23 per cent over 1833.

In 1853 Hay-making expenses were £22.13s.0d. for 354 acres. The wages bill for that year was £44.0s.0d. and extra labour £17.10s.0d. There is no indication as to how many men were employed.

Eighteen acres of land was purchased by Henry Dawkins in Salford October 1845 which resulted in a profit on it from 1846 to 1848 of £115.2s.2d. Interest at ½ per cent was paid on a £1000 mortgage. A loss of £117.5s.6d. was incurred on eighty-nine acres of land taken for arable from Michaelmas 1852 to 1853. Receipts included 18½ tons of hay at £1.10s.0d. and eighteen acres of turnips at £20.0s.0d.

In March 1843 his father's first half-yearly accounts were

> diminished by an allowance of £370 made to his tenants for their supposed losses in a hail storm.

This seems rather a large sum but not if they suffered as did Enstone's villagers from storms in August 1843 when:

> ... high hailstones fell (circumference 6 inches weighing eight to a pound) twelve hares dead, cut through kettles on the fires, stonework broken, slates off, chimneys damaged, shutter pins halved, doors torn from hinges, all crocks destroyed and clothes singed ... [Paraphrased: *A Parochial History of Enstone* Rev. John Jordan 1857.]

In later years – 1866 – two cows were killed in Over Norton during a storm.

Continuing with 1843,

> Some other heavy extra expences were increased [by] Mr Woodward's account for valuing and re-letting the estate £212. At this time too a New Barn and two new Cottages [were built] on Mr Coldicott's Farm £500. [Probably Folly Farm later known as Hill-side] and Draining Close on Mr Coldicott's Farm £132. £70 [was paid] for similar work on Mr Radford's Farm. [Hull Farm]

In 1851 William Coldicott was at Manor Farm, Over Norton, farming 350 acres.

If my assumption about the new barn and cottages is correct then 'Manor Farm' must have been the '1770 West Farm' with the farm house being what is now 'Cleevestones' at the top of Over Norton Hill.

It is with the approval of Mr Graham Anker, Estate Agent at Banbury (1999) that I am including some details about his forebears who in the past farmed at Cropredy and West Farm, Great Bourton. It should supplement and also make an interesting comparison with Over Norton. Graham Anker told me that the family still own a field in Cropredy which they keep for nostalgic reasons and he reminded me that in 1897 a stained glass window (artist Westlake) was erected in Cropredy church by William Anker in memory of his parents, William and Kezia Anker. (At that time there were thirty lines describing it in a local paper.) I possess four of William Anker's farm ledgers covering sales receipts and wages from 1818 to 1902 with writing styles indicating the changes in the generations.

This humorous little rhyme – a newspaper cutting – was stuck inside a ledger cover:

> To be Happy
> To make life easy to the end
> A man should have, I say,
> Some cash to spend
> and some to lend
> And some to throw away.

From the Anker ledger: A James Pargeter was employed from 25th Fby. 1853 on a very complicated scale of pay –

> til hay time at 9 shillings per week
> and then 10 shillings per week till harvest
> and then 12 shillings a week for a month
> and then 9 shillings a week till
> Michaelmas

A Ths. Pargeter was paid 10s.0d. for five days work in July of that year (1853) but in 1818 James Dunn was paid 9s.2d. for six days work.

In 1853 the mowing was finished by 29th July – 31 acres at 2s.0d. per acre. Mr Anker in generous mood that same year

> Payed the women for fifteen days work ... and gave them 1d. each over and one girl at 6d. a day.

The women working in the fields were not normally named in the ledger except in the following: (shock: a pile of sheaves; the number of sixteen, Nuttalls Dictionary 1919)

8th Sept. 1854 [paid out for]		
Reaping	shocks	
John Atkins	240	£1. 16s. 0d.
Kitcher & Pargeter	227	£1. 14s. 0d.
Thos Pargeter	205	£1. 13s. 6d.
Mary Pargeter	19	£0. 2s.10d.
		£5. 6s. 4d.

Hurdles could be bought at the rate of 13s. 8d. for 'four dozen and five hurdles' in 1854. In 1857 French, the mole-catcher was paid 5 shillings a year – but not until he had completed a year's work. French, or his ancestors, were catching moles in 1817 and 1819.

The Anker domestic servants were hired from Michaelmas to Michaelmas for the year's work 1856 to 1857

> Dinah Honer recd. £3.10s.0d. and if a good girl 10 shillings more.

In 1860 on the receipts side was recorded

> Mr Dickson paid £46.6s.3d. for 19 tods 7lbs wool at £2.5s.0d. per tod

but by July 1864 the price had risen to £3.5s.0d. per tod.

June 1860
Hawtin Checkly sheep wt at 80 lbs at 4s.8d. per stone £2. 6s. 8d.
one calf at 5s.2d. stone £3. 12s. 4d.

April 17th 1885
Finished swedes [at] Bourton brought sheep to Cropredy 126 tegs 5 barren ewes 4 Tup Tegs. [See Glossary]

April 19th 1886
Finished swedes had tegs off.

Dec 27th 1860
Commenced a banking account at the Old Bank.

1860
Receipts
15 qrs wheat at 64/- a quarter	£48. 0s. 0d.
8 qrs barley at 40/- a quarter	£16. 0s. 0d.
7 sheep at 51/- each	£17. 17s. 0d.

[Note: 1841 Henry Dawkins of Over Norton expected to get 30/- a quarter for barley, 60/- for wheat.]

The cows having calved in the spring would be giving a good milk supply – the new grass also helping – and this cycle is reflected in the amount of butter produced at different months of the year.

1864 **(Anker, Cropredy)**
Butter cheque		
	Feb	£ 3. 10s. 7d.
	Ap	£ 8. 12s. 1d.
	June	£13. 3s. 7d.
	July	£16. 3s. 9d.
	Aug	£20. 9s.11d.
	Sept	£18. 5s. 6d.
	Oct	£15. 1s. 0d.
	Nov	£14. 18s. 3d.
	Dec	£ 9. 0s. 4d.
	Jan (1865)	£ 4. 12s. 0d.
	Total for the year	£123. 17s. 0d.

Henry Dawkins sold butter to the value of £87.2s.7d. in 1856. This quantity is comparable with his sales for 1864-1865. Butter prices had risen over the ten years from 1856-1866.

On the Cropredy farm receipts side for 1853

Thos Kitchen had 5 lbs. mutton at 4½ per lb = 1s.. 10½d. ... a sheep's head [was] sold for 8d.

In 1861 a side of mutton 22 lbs [sold] at 6½d. = 11s. 11d.

In 1864 there was no celebratory 'Harvest Home' at Cropredy when the work was finished but on

24th September Paid men 2s.6d. each and Boys 1s.0d. each in leiu (sic) of Harvest home – 12s. 0d.

That may have been four men (10s.0d.) and two boys. Which would they have preferred: a good supper with beer and music, or money in their pockets?

The farm bank account showed a balance of £183.7s.0d. at the end of 1864.

1891 to 1899 found Mr Anker buying butter from E. Borton – 1½ lbs each week. Prices fell in summer e.g. 1897 from 2s.0d. for 1½ lbs in January but only 1s.3d. for the same quantity in June. Prices were slightly higher in 1891 than in 1899 – a difference of ½d. on half a pound.

The prices paid for Mr Anker's horses at his sale Oct. 12th 1891 are recorded in the ledger and I am including them partly due to the pleasure their names give!

Boxer	6 years old	£39
Dumpling	5 years old	£42
Jolly	3 years old	£46
Punch	3 years old	£37
Poppet	6 years old	£37
Flower	8 years old	£33
Bowler		£14. 10s. 0d.
Diamond		£ 5. 0s. 0d.
Filly sucker		£13. 10s. 0d.
Grey cob		£15. 10s. 0d.

It must have been a sad occasion to watch these horses go to new owners — farm sales are always distressing whatever the reason. Perhaps the sale was due to partial retirement.

This is William Anker's seed order for 1891. Note that seed for permanent pasture was on order. Many farmers looking for a way out of their difficulties during the farming depression were putting down more permanent pasture.

	s. d.
4 gallons best English rye grass	1. 6
3 lbs hard fescue	2. 3
3 lbs meadow fescue	2. 6
6 lbs Dutch clover (white)	6. 0
4 lbs Broad clover	2. 4
2 lbs Cocksfoot	2. 0
2 lbs Trefoil	8
1 lb Timothy Mixture permanent pasture	<u>6</u>
	<u>17. 9</u>

The Anker ledger closed September 1902.

It was suggested in J.O.J. 16th Sept 1899 that the following scale of wages should be paid to their

> labourers who do – and prefer to – work by piecework, and it is often a great convenience indeed for an employer ...
> Nothing makes a man look more foolish than paying more than he ought to pay .

carting dung	1s a ton per mile
raising carrots	20s to 25s per acre
digging turf	80s
digging garden soil	50s
drilling corn	2/6
harrowing	1/-
harvesting (men)	10s - 12s
haymaking (men)	5s - 10s
hedge-trimming (both sides)	4d per chain
hedge-laying	6d to 8d per pole
hedge-setting quicks	1s 1d per pole
hoeing wheat	5s to 6s per acre
hoeing turnips (first time)	6s to 10s per acre
hoeing turnips (second time)	4s to 7s " "
mangold raising	6s " "
ploughing	12s " "
potato raising by hand	30s " "
potato raising by digger	10s " "
reaping by hand	3s to 3s.6d per acre

reaping by machine	1s to 1s.6d. " "
rolling	9d per acre
sowing seed by hand	2½d per acre
sowing grass seed (barrow)	6s " "
stacking grain	5s " "
ditto hay	3s.6d. per acre
thrashing	1s.8d. per qtr
raising turnips and swedes	6s to 9s per acre

(Note: 1999 Farm Workers basic weekly wage £200.
1999 Contractors charge £12 an hour for hedge-cutting using a flail.
Source: Anthony Hobbs)

At the end of the 19th century there was great discussion as to what was causing the de-population of the villages. (Note the drop in population of Over Norton between 1881 and 1891) This national trend was one of the main items on the agenda at the Ruri-Decanal Conference held at Banbury on 24th October 1901. Poor housing, low wages and lack of social facilities were put forward as to the reasons why labourers were rushing to the towns. On the following day 'The Banbury Guardian' published much of what Mr W. Anker of Cropredy had to say on this matter:

> Mr W. Anker (Cropredy) when discussing the depopulation of the villages said it was nothing to do with the labourers houses but that it was caused by the agricultural depression.
> ... The country had become the dumping ground of the whole world. The surplus of the world's produce found its way here, and the consequence was that prices were lower than they could produce the stuff for. He himself had had a very considerable hand in laying arable land down to grass. He had laid down some of the best land for growing corn one could wish to occupy, simply because it did not pay for cultivation. Now it was laid down to grass it produced a small return. They might as well try to dam the Niagara as to stop the depopulation of the villages. The enormous water power in America had been able to manufacture flour at such prices that the small water mills of this country could not possibly compete against – (hear, hear). They must see that the work in the villages must be a paying work. Small holdings would not remedy the matter ... A great factor in the cause was due to the improved machinery which had thrown so many out of employment – (applause).

Population figures for Over Norton Parish

1801	388	1861	373
1811	356	1871	397
1831	375	1881	444 (440)
1841	400 (402)	1891	342
1851	435 (436)	1901	350
		1998	369 adults

NB: different sources give slightly different figures

Farm workers employed in Over Norton Parish
Details taken from the census returns

Year	1841	1851	1861	1871	1881	1891
Farm Labourers	57	50	57	53	61	51
Plough Boys	-	14	-	*7	-	-
Shepherds	10	6	10	5	6	3
Sheep Dipper	-	-	-	2	1	1
Waggoner	1	1	-	-	-	-
Carter	1	1	2	2	-	3
Total	69	72	69	69	68	58

* The youngest boy [1871] was ten years old

In 1881 there were six boys aged between eleven and thirteen years old working as farm labourers but they were not listed as plough boys. The 1891 census return is difficult to read but no boys under fourteen years of age appear to be listed as farm workers.

In 1851 there were seventy children listed as scholars with five of them having a governess at home. By 1871 there were seventy-nine scholars and two employed children: one eleven-year-old as a 'nurse girl' and an eleven-year-old boy as an 'errand boy'. The number of scholars rose to one hundred and nine in 1881. (There may be slight discrepancies in these figures.)

The number of farm workers employed in Over Norton dropped by fourteen between 1851 and 1891 – this reduction reflects what was happening nationally. By the end of the 19th century sheep farming had decreased and the fall in the number of shepherds employed shows a decline of 30 per cent in fifty years.

List of Farmers in Over Norton Parish 1841 to 1891

Hull Farm [was called New Farm in 1770]
1841 Carpenter Thomas	age 40	
1851 Radford Samuel	age 37	465 acres employing 8 men
1861 Radford Samuel	age 47	464 acres employing 11 men 8 boys
1871 Craddock Robert	age 24	587 acres employing 10 men 6 boys
1881 Craddock Robert	age 34	557 acres
1891 Watkins Henry	age 39	[no other details given]

Hull Farm Cottage
1891 Webb Edward	age 55	[no other details given]
1891 Webb William	age 49	[no other details given]

[1891 Three farmers at Hull Farm in different households]

Priory Farm (on the road leading to Heythrop)
1841 Busby John	age 65)	
Busby John	age 30)	
1851 Busby John	age 43	280 acres employing 6 men 4 boys
1861 Busby John	age 52	" " "
1871 Busby John	age 61	" " "
1881 [Warner John	age 45	Farm Bailiff]
1891 [East Frederick		Farm Labourer living at Priory Farm]

Choicehill Farm
1841 Huckvale James	age 50	
1851 Huckvale Thomas	age 49	213 acres employing 9 men
1861 Unknown		
1871 Fawdry William	age 22	214 acres employing 5 men 3 boys
1881 Fawdry William	age 31	256 acres

Other farmers listed [no details available of number of employees or names of farms]
1841 Huckvale Thomas	age 35	[was at Choice Hill in 1851]
Arkell William	age 30	
Huckvale William	age 50	
Harwood Jonathan	age 25	
Edwards William	age 40	

Colbornes Farm
1851 Phillips William	age 37	160 acres employing 8 men

Manor Farm
[most probably the 1770 West Farm top of Over Norton hill]
1851 Coldicott William	age 44	350 acres employing 8 men

1851 Huckvale William age 64 220 acres employing 8 men)no farm
1851 Edwards William age 56 110 acres employing 4 men)name given

Farm House
1861 Phillips William age 47 356 acres employing 11 men 5 boys

Part of Chapel House
1861 Huckvale Thomas age 59 16 acres Land Agent
            (was at Choice Hill in 1851)

Farm House
1861 Huckvale Rebecca age 75 217 acres employing 7 men 5 boys
(widow of William Huckvale see 1851)
1861 Payne George age 42 8 acres and Jobbing Master

Farm House
1861 Edwards William age 32 122 acres employing 5 men 1 boy

Priory Mill
1871 Claridge Mary Ann age 50 30 acres Farmer/miller employing 2 men
[No farm name given for next two entries]
Edwards William age 43 290 acres employing 8 men 3 boys
Huckvale Harry age 28 220 acres employing 8 men 4 boys

Farm House
1881 Guy Caroline age 42 310 acres
 (Widow)

Centre Village
1881 Edwards William J. age 25 57 acres
1881 Huckvale Harry age 38 200 acres

Main Road
1881 Edwards William W. age 53 260 acres

Priory Mill
1881 Salmon George age 70 Farmer and Miller
Salmon Henry son age 30 " " "

[Ages given on the 1841 census were to the nearest five e.g. John Busby aged 30 on 1841 returns appears as 43 years in 1851.]

Farming from 1900 onwards continues in Chapter 14.

Glossary

teg	–	a sheep in its second year
tod	–	measurement of weight of wool = 28 lbs.
tup	–	a ram
tup - teg	–	a second year male sheep

CHAPTER 9

"What's the use of a book', thought Alice,
"without pictures or conversations?'

The Daly Family and Conversations with: Mr Fred Sole, Mrs Cook, Mr Harry Barnes, Mrs Nolan, Mrs Thomson, Miss Knight, Mrs Pashley and Mr & Mrs Douglas Sheffield.
Also included: Extracts from Mrs K.V. Cambray's book, 'Memories of Over Norton Women's Institute 1933-1964' ; Mrs W. Jasmund's (née Sheffield) 'Letter from America'.

When Col. William Gregory Dawkins left Over Norton House just before 1900 it was leased to the Daly family. Mrs Rose Zara Daly was the second daughter of Mr Albert Brassey and Mrs Brassey of Heythrop. Rose Brassey married Captain Dennis St. George Daly from Ireland, later retiring as a major from the 18th Hussars. They made their home in Over Norton from c.1899. Major Daly bred horses and he was joint master of the Heythrop Hunt with Col. Edwin Brassey (nephew of Albert Brassey) from 1925 to 1934. (Mr Albert Brassey had been master for forty-five seasons from 1873 to 1918.) During the period 1905 to 1910 Frances Witts, youngest of three daughters of Margaret and Frederick Witts (second son of the Rector and Lord of the Manor at Upper Slaughter), kept a hunting diary. Lavinia Jenkinson and Susan Boone jointly edited this diary and published it in 1981. The design and illustrations were by Susan Boone and a preface by Captain Ronnie Wallace was included. Frances who died in 1949 was Susan Boone's mother.

Rosie Daly was Susan Boone's godmother. The diary has been handed down to Mrs de Trafford of Upper Slaughter and her family who own the copyright. They have kindly allowed me to quote the following extracts from *A Diary of a Foxhunting Lady*. These paint a vivid picture of the Daly's involvement with the Heythrop Hunt.

Frid 1st Dec 1905

... Mr Evered very nearly jumped on Rosie Daly but did no more than kick her hat. It looked as if she would be killed ...

Frid 12th Jan 1906

... Capt. Daly let a little of his temper go at Mr Crowder and told him either to go home or hold his tongue! which was the only excitement in a hopelessly bad day.

Mon Jan 15th 1906

... then hounds divided and did not run really well again though we dragged on for some time ... But was consoled by a mince-pie brought me hot by Mrs Daly!!

Sat 27th Oct 1906

... The Nun gave Capt. Daly a fall trying to double a hedge. She lamed herself but did him no harm ...

Wed 7th Nov 1906 Adderbury

Stayed at Over Norton.

Drove with Capt. Daly to the meet 13 miles in 5 minutes under the hour (the diary editor's note i.e. 13 mph presumably in a gig) ... Sturman (kennel huntsman) had his hand rather badly bitten by the fox, so the hounds went home early ...

Frid 9th Nov 1906 New Barn

Felt very grand coming with Mr Brassey and Capt. Daly on the Special [train] from Chipping Norton ... Sturman not out owing to fox bite on Wednesday ...

Frid 23rd November 1906

... Capt. Daly now offered Mabel and me our mounts for Monday which filled me with joy ...

Wed 5th Dec 1906 North Aston

Rode the Nun and stayed at Over Norton ... Had a long ride of about 15 miles back to Over Norton against an icy wind ...

Mon 17th Dec 1906

... Rosie Daly made her first appearance on horseback this season ...

Sat 5th Oct 1907

... Stayed at Over Norton and rode Rex. Rosie [Daly] rode Pioneer, Capt. Daly, Parnell and Ravenbury ...

Mon 28th Oct 1907
... Eileen, Denise and Lilah Daly (aged 9, 5 and 1) were all riding after the hounds, so were Tony Moon aged 8 (from Heythrop Rectory) and a little Hall boy.

Mon 23rd Dec 1907
... Bowes Daly (aged 7) was out looking very smart in new riding kit on the new grey pony ...

Mon 20th Jan 1908
... I fell off Kruger in Over Norton Park. I was talking to Bijou, who was driving, when Kruger suddenly shied away and I toppled off! Capt. Daly lost White Socks, who broke his back jumping a small fence soon after the hounds left Salford.

Mon 23rd Nov 1908 Chapel House
Horses came on by early train (from Notgrove station presumably) and we motored. Found in Walk Gorse, ran round Badger's Gorse, nearly back to Walk Gorse, then left-handed into Heythrop Park through the Ovens ... Trotted back to Salford Osiers where they found and ran back in the direction of Heythrop. We left them as our horses had to catch the 4.45 train. A wonderfully good scent considering that there was a very high wind.

Wed 9th Dec 1908 Adlestrop
... K. Freer had a shaft of a cart run into the shoulder of her horse. Fortunately no permanent injury ...

Wed 17th Feb 1909
Stayed at Over Norton, (Sturman hunting again) and rode Rex, Mabel Lancer, Mother Bogy.
... The day ended tragically as Mr Oakley (of Chadlington) had a fall over a wall and broke his back. They could not get him home for ages ... [He] only lived about a fortnight.
[The accident happened near Heythrop Banbury Lodge.]

During my conversations with local inhabitants and on reading my two written sources, I began to understand what an important role the Daly family played in Over Norton for fifty years. I was aware of deep feelings of nostalgia but memories of any hardship were pushed aside. There seemed to be a strong sense of belonging to Over Norton as definitely a separate unit from Chipping Norton. Strong family ties were also very evident.

Extract from Mrs Cambray's 'Memories of Over Norton Women's Institute 1933-1964'

Mrs Daly brought her spaniel Rascal to committee meetings so we had to be careful where we put our feet under the table as he was a bit touchy. We remember her first born's first tooth set in gold and pearls in the inevitable match box competition [At that time W.I. members seemed to enjoy seeing how many things they could cram into a matchbox.]

Miss Stallard took the first class we had, it was for glove making up in the Playroom [The Orangery in Over Norton Park] and she embroidered the W.I. banner.

'Those Were The Days'. Some of our happiest early memories must surely be of the Garden Parties at Over Norton Park. They used to start at 4.30 (the children all came) with tea provided by Mrs Daly in the Playroom. It was so pleasant for the committee to have a rest and just act as a sort of liaison between us and 'The Kitchen'.

The weather always seemed to be good but there was one evening when we had to stay in the dry and Mrs Sheffield and Mrs Hudson received bouquets made from the flowers on the tea tables as their prizes for skittles and bagatelle.

There was a conducted tour of the garden, and although she kept two gardeners our hostess knew and loved each flower and shrub personally. Then to races and games on the lawn, sometimes country dancing or watching a display of acrobatics by the granddaughter of the house, Miss Claire Shennan.

One evening, the pace grew so hot that Mrs Daly fell when scrambling up a bank and broke her thumb.

For several years we had a competition for the best weight of potatoes grown from one seed and this was always the time for weighing them. The tradition was that each member stood on the scales after her potatoes were done and looking back now one wonders why this operation was so excruciatingly funny but we found it so.

Prizes were presented and we sang our way back to the village in the cool of the evening, nowadays no doubt we should get the cars out to go up there! The Secretary minuted our last visit rather nicely! "We were all sorry", she put "not to have Mrs Daly with us owing to her health, but all members wished her Goodnight at her window".

Little did we know then that we were really saying Goodbye.

Mrs Rose Zara Daly, born October 29th 1872, died January 21st 1949. Her husband Denis St. George Daly, born September 5th 1862, died April 16th 1942. Their daughter, Brigid Mary, born December 11th 1913, was killed in a car accident on August 20th 1932. Major

and Mrs Daly and their daughter Brigid, were buried in Heythrop churchyard.

Senior residents of Over Norton remember three other children, Lilah, Denise who went to Ireland after marriage, and Dermot who had been a prisoner of war and moved to Little Compton when the family gave up the tenancy of Over Norton House.

A Letter from America

Mrs Win Jasmund (née Sheffield) was born in Over Norton. She went to the USA to visit her sister Gladys who was a G.I. bride and Win subsequently married an American and settled in New Jersey. Mrs Jasmund came home to collect her belongings in 1948. She posted the following information recalling her memories of the Daly family.

> The Dalys did a lot for the village by employing mostly the village people. They had a staff of nine in the house: Butler, Footman, two Housemaids, Cook, Kitchen maid, Scullery maid, Lady's maid and Nanny. Outside were Gardeners, Stablemen and Milkman. They kept cows and horses.
>
> The Barnes family did all the Daly's laundry in a house below the Mission Room.
>
> At Christmas they gave a party in the school and each child received a gift. The girls got a flannel petticoat and the boys a scarf made by the lady's maid and nanny who worked on them all year. Before Christmas Mrs Daly would also go around the village and visit the old people, taking a knitted shawl for the women and the men got a pair of socks. As a term of respect, whenever the family went through the village either in pony and trap or car, the boys tipped their caps and the girls nodded their heads.
>
> There was a time when you could go up to the main house and get a can (2 to 3 pints) of milk for $1/2$ penny. We had lots of milk puddings in those days.

In conversation with Mr Fred Sole

A wonderful hour and a half was spent in conversation with Mr Fred Sole of Over Norton, about his connection with the Daly family. At ninety years of age he is very fit and healthy.

He had just driven from Holy Trinity Church after attending Mass, when I joined him to hear about his first job as a fourteen-year-old. He worked as a groom in the Daly's stables at Over Norton

House. His enthusiasm was great, face animated and eyes sparkling as he crouched forward in his chair, re-living the thrill of riding a race horse named Welfare across the top of Over Norton Park whilst accompanying 'Miss Biddie' (Brigid Daly) on her pony, Prince. 'I got on well with Miss Biddie.'

As a boy Fred lived in the Worcester Road, Chipping Norton and his introduction to riding had been on a pony borrowed from Southerndown Farm. Riding, with just a halter on the pony, across the Primsdown was great fun for him.

For a period of just over a year, 1923/24, Fred cycled from Chipping Norton to Over Norton to make a 7am start in the stables. He finished at 6.30pm on cubbing days, but when the horses were out he finished earlier. He also worked Sunday afternoons. Fred's services were retained part-time throughout summer whereas some men were stood off for the summer season. Mr Frank Tanner and Mr Wilmot, the stud groom, and 'Boss' were also retained for the summer period. During winter Mr Frank Worvill, Mr Ernest Moulder, Mr Harry Goodman, Mr George Harris and Mr Jack Worvill were employed as stable staff.

Other staff remembered by Fred Sole were Mr Clarke, the butler, who lived in cottage No. 7, situated to the right of Witts House; Mr Sydney Fox, the cowman and Mr Harry Higgs, from Chapel House, who looked after the traps and motor cars; Mr Blencoe was head gardener and Mr Cyril Moulder under gardener. (Cyril later became head gardener). Mr Blencoe lived in one of two cottages (Keepers Cottage) situated at the entrance to Over Norton House; Mr Cyril Moulder lived down in the village at this time but later moved to Keepers Cottage when he was promoted. The Moulders then were very proud of having their own water tap! Mr George Harris (wife was a Miss Fox) lived at Rose Cottage, School Yard. The stud groom, Wilmot, lived in the stone house now called 'Glovers Close' (1999).

Mr Sam Moulder and his son George did the maintenance of the park's stone walls and trees.

On some occasions Fred Sole was needed to help out during the evening until 8pm to help with the 'medicine chest' and rub ointment on any sore patches found on the horses. He remembers being very hungry and Mr Wilmot provided him with toast and cold black tea.

At that time something unbelievable (in present times) was happening in the wash-house at one of the cottages at the main gate. Mr Alf Messenger was frying battered fish in an old copper! What a treat that was for Fred when he was able to purchase a piece! Alf Messenger used to sell a basketful of fish round the village and any left, was then sold, (cold) in the public houses in Chipping Norton during the evening.

Fred Sole:

> Frank Tanner used to scythe the grass and carry it in a sheet for the horses.
>
> As regards uniforms, the following employees wore grey livery made at Hannis' in Chipping Norton: Frank Tanner, Ernest Moulder and Harry Goodman. Mr Wilmot, the boss, wore a bowler hat. I, as the youngest of the stable staff, wore knickerbockers buttoned up the side.
>
> Mrs Barnes, a wonderful woman, washed the hunting stocks and shirts but the heavier items, including breeches, were taken in large baskets by pony and trap to somewhere in Chipping Norton.
>
> When the snow was on the ground in the Cherry Orchard I put on a little riding show bucking (laughter) an exhibition and the stable men stood around laughing.
>
> Sydney Fox sold two black cows at auction at the Langston Arms, Kingham market. The cows went to Deddington but they found their way back to Over Norton by the following Monday.

Gas lighting was used in the stables and it was Fred Sole's job to wind up the system of circular weights which controlled it.

> I wound it clockwise. There was a big T handle and I had to use both hands to move it. It needed to be done every 4th or 5th day. There was a cylinder of gas.
>
> At Christmas each of the stable staff received a present of a red pullover.

In response to a question about outings or leisure time Fred said that he never went on a visit to the sea or to other venues but he did meet with a lot of success in competitive running sports. He was extremely successful at Great Tew where on one occasion he won race after race and when the presentations were made the presenter said, 'Not you again!' There were also evening sessions of running races held on the Mill Common including the hundred yards and the long distance. On one occasion his father promised to give him his bike if he won; he did win so he received his father's bike and his father bought himself a new Raleigh (bike) from Putmans, High Street, Chipping Norton!

An advertisement (1924) appeared asking for an assistant to Mr Weston at his butcher's shop in New Street, Chipping Norton, 'applicants to be knowledgeable with horses'. Fred applied and was successful and so began a career of fifty-one years in the butcher's trade.

At first he cycled round the villages delivering meat mid-week to Salford, Southcombe and Lidstone and at weekends he did the deliveries using a horse and trap. In later years he had his own butcher's shop in Spring Street; he retained his great interest in horses as a race horse owner.

I Remember, I Remember, the House Where I was Born (Thomas Hood)

In conversation with Mrs Gladys Cook, née Fox, born 2nd June 1907.

Mrs Cook's family lived in a cottage which was part of the existing (1999) cottage named Three Chimneys. They lived at the end which was nearest to the village green.

Mrs Cook:

> I attended Over Norton school until I was fourteen. We went for nature walks to see the autumn berries. We took flowers to school for our painting lessons first I did the stalk, then the leaves.
>
> I remember the globe and learning about the River Severn.
>
> When we went to school we wore a white embroidered pinafore over the top of everything. We wore black woollen stockings held up with elastic garters, a liberty bodice and a flannel petticoat under a woolly jumper and skirt. The Daly's sent us left-off clothes. Their nurse sent dresses and shoes. We bought new shoes at the Co-op with the 'divi' [dividend].
>
> At school we did arithmetic, composition, dictation, geography, history and something on Empire Day [May 24th]. We did a needlework sampler showing how to do different things, buttonholes etc.
>
> I remember going in a horse-drawn waggon it may have been Hospital Saturday or May Day but I was wearing a white dress and flowers and I was about ten years of age.

It was the May Day custom in some villages to ride round the hamlets in a horse-drawn waggon. At Kiddington this was so up to the 1930s when the waggon was pulled round the village and also driven to Gagingwell where on one occasion a 'Stop Me and Buy One' ice cream man on a bicycle was seen by the children for the first time. The children had no money but the May Queen was treated to an ice cream and the rest of the children looked on with envy. The musical accompaniment to the May songs was provided by a harmonium a ludicrous sight the accompanist perched on a stool playing the harmonium in a waggon.

Mrs Cook:

For May Day we picked cowslips, cuckoo pints and marsh marigolds. Mother found a piece of linen we fixed them on it. [This was tied round the head.] I did maypole dancing, just once, when the music was played on a mouth organ.

At Whitsun we wore white clothes to church. I think I was baptised at Over Norton. Mrs Clarke played the harmonium in the Mission Room. The vicar [or Chapel Minister] came on Sunday nights.

At Christmas we had a party at school. The Dalys provided a lovely tea with ham sandwiches, all sorts ginger cake and an orange and sixpence. They also gave the girls pale green flannel petticoats.

Mrs Daly gave the older ladies a crochet shawl/cape at Christmas. Mother's was a mixture of colours and was shaped at the shoulders and it crossed over at the front.

I had a doll's cradle — woven basketwork — and dolls with china heads and shoulders – I never broke them. We had spinning tops and whips on the road and both boys and girls had hoops. We bought sweets — liquorice allsorts and humbugs. They were kept in glass jars and the shopkeeper weighed them out.

I played with Sylvia Miles, my cousin from the Slad Cottage — rounders and tennis — at least our version of it — and hopscotch. I had a Beano comic but I can't recall any books.

I remember sheltering under the big elm tree on the village green [felled 1914].

We had a bath on Saturdays by the fire in a zinc bath like the one we did the washing in. The copper [to heat the water] was in a shed where the wood store was. The water was carried from the fountain tap on the village green.

Sometimes the tap was frozen.

I had diphtheria and I was put in a special room on my own for about a month. Dr King came. A curtain was hung over the door and sprayed with disinfectant and the room was fumigated. During my illness my brother and sister went to stay with Aunt Kate. My brother Reginald was three years older than me — too young to go in the army 1914-1918 — and my sister named Violet Victoria May, after Queen Victoria, was six years older than me. When I was ill the Daly's cook sent nice bits and pieces along.

We cooked on top of a coal fire – an iron was put across to hold a large pan of bacon and onion pudding and vegetables it was lovely. Mother made sweet puddings with a suet crust – spotted dog [currants] and apple pudding.

There was an oven at the side of the fire.

The suet puddings were made with half suet to flour and mixed with water. A family of five would probably use one pound of flour with a little baking powder and eight ounces of grated suet. After mixing it into a dough with cold water it was rolled out. Small pieces of bacon and chopped onion were spread over it. It was rolled up, then put onto a floured pudding cloth, tied at both ends like a Christmas cracker and boiled for one and a half to two hours.

Sweet puddings were made in the same way but dried fruit or jam were used. Washing the pudding cloth – perhaps a piece of old bed linen – was a ghastly job. More knowledgeable cooks added herbs to the savoury puddings. Old country people said that these puddings would 'stick by yu' or 'it sticks to your ribs'. In other words one would not feel hungry for some time.

Mrs Cook:

Coal was brought home from the Co-op in Chippy. We bought many of our grocery things at Over Norton Post Office but we also had things delivered by the Co-op wrapped in a brown paper parcel.

There was a time, before I left school, when Alf Messenger sold fried fish — he brought it round in a covered basket – we found a plate – the fish was warm – we had it for tea.

We bought our bread from the Co-op. It was delivered in a horse drawn cart. We enjoyed the soft bit between the top and bottom of the cottage loaf — we had it with jam which mother had made. We had two cottage loaves from the Bread Charity at Christmas.

I helped my mother by polishing the knives, forks and spoons once a week on Saturdays. We made rag rugs with strips of fabric pulled through sacking [using a rag rug needle]. We had to shake them outside. My mother got me to help her shake the coconut matting from the kitchen floor. I didn't like doing that – the dust got in your eyes and also covered your hair.

We used to see Mrs Daly going by looking wonderful on a horse, riding side-saddle.

In the early evening we went to the Servants' Hall at Over Norton House and paid money to Mrs Daly. I can't remember what it was for. I remember that Mrs Daly looked marvellous. She was wearing a lovely gown – it was jade green and lovely jewellery – her hair was nice and she had a lovely comb in it. I don't remember what the money was for.

Miss Doris Knight:

Mrs Daly collected the hospital club money, twopence a week. We could go to Over Norton House when the Dalys were there and we bought skimmed milk for a half-penny a quart and we were given a basin of dripping.

Mrs Cook:

My father Sydney Fox was a cowman for the Dalys but he did gardening and other odd jobs as well – he enjoyed it. He would go to see to the calves at night. Before he went to work in the mornings at about seven o'clock he had to light the fire to boil the kettle. He churned the milk in the cellar to get the cream. Dad brought milk home. Although the wages were low there were extra benefits, including permission to collect firewood. Once Mr Moulder told us to stop but we said, 'We are not breaking trees'.

We children collected milk – it was cheap for a can full – for Aunt Kate (Mrs Power). We went round to the back of Over Norton House for it.

We used to take meals to the men in the harvest fields – bread and cheese, fruit cake and a can of tea. We took it to Uncle Joseph Power – his wife was Dad's sister – Aunt Kate. Uncle Joseph was a general farm worker.

Dad grew a lot of vegetables in his gardens. He had the piece of ground just up Radbones Hill where two cottages used to be, behind No. 7 [now, in 1999, used as a car park].

Sometimes we went on a bus to Oxford to see Aunt Phoebe (Mum's sister).

As a family we used to walk to the Rollright Stones.

I worked at the tweed mill in Chipping Norton – first as a spinner and then it took me about a month to learn to be a weaver – working from about 7.30am to 6.00 or 5.30pm. We took our mid-day meal to work. I would complete one or two pieces a week – 70 yards in a piece – of a small check or striped pattern. One week I got three pieces off and I received over £3. The speed was according to how well the threads were set up. I used to pay for my keep and then save up for a pretty blouse or a nice pair of stockings.

I left the village for marriage at about 22 years – about 1929 – and moved to Chipping Norton.

In response to a question about wireless Mrs Cook replied:

We didn't have a gramophone or a crystal wireless set at home but after I married, my husband sent away for a wind-up gramophone in a walnut case.

That must be over 50 years ago. We had some records of nice bands.

People now in their seventies, living in Over Norton, recall seeing a 'very smartly dressed' Mrs Cook, walking from Chipping Norton to Over Norton to visit her sister who was living in Rose Cottage, near the chapel.

In conversation with Harry Barnes

Harry Barnes was born August 1913 at the Old School House in the bedroom next to the Chapel. He still (1999) lives in Over Norton. Harry's mother, Mary Barnes, ran a laundry from her home, the Old School House, from the early 1900s. She continued doing this for forty years. She did the laundry for the Dalys, Dr. McKnight of Chipping Norton and for other well-to-do families. She was known to have laundered eighty shirts in two days. She had a copper which held ten to twelve gallons of water which was heated by coal. Harry carried the water from a tap fixed at the side of Rose Cottage just opposite the laundry. At one time there was a severe shortage of water when Witts Farm changed hands and a new farmer Mr Lamb, used more water for his dairy herd. So Harry had to carry buckets of water from the spring in the field just below the bungalow named Pony Close. The laundry work was started early in the morning and went on to between six and eight o'clock in the evening. Mrs Barnes, two daughters and a sister all worked at the laundry full time. The articles were dried in the garden whenever possible. The laundry was never allowed to spread into the Barnes' home and was always done in the end part of the building. On Saturday afternoons, after work was finished, Mrs Barnes still found enough energy to make a cake.

A commercial iron-stand was used for heating up four irons on top and three each side. Polishing irons with a curved bottom used against a board was the method for ironing the fronts of shirts. The mangle for squeezing out the water had wooden rollers and weights each side. Tins of starch came by post from London. It was used for stiffening the shirt collars.

Blue bags were used in the rinsing water for white clothes to prevent them from yellowing and sunshine was used as a bleaching agent.

The Old School House had been a pub or ale-house at one time. Harry said the cellar was good and had an outside access.

The Barnes family made wine twice yearly – eight to ten gallons of parsnip wine. Harry Barnes served for six years in the RAF, during World War Two, and five gallons of wine made prior to the war was drunk to celebrate his homecoming in June 1946. On one occasion his mother sent him a bottle of wine whilst he was in the service, by an airman, who had been home on leave in this area.

Harry spent fifty-one years as a maintenance fitter at the Tweed Mill, Chipping Norton.

Will anyone growing up in Over Norton now have a chance to spend that length of time in a good job which they enjoy doing? As a child Harry remembers playing with 'murrel stones' or 'morrel stones' underneath the old shed which used to be attached to the house on the corner of Choicehill Road. (Could these be morrel cherry stones?) There was a very large stone there with a game scratched on it – also remembered by Mrs Doris Pashley – in the shape of a square with the diagonals marked and with an indentation at each corner and in the centre. Harry has forgotten how to play the game.

Mrs Pashley:

> George Arliss, a well known film star, who used to stay at The Mount, Chipping Norton, frequently walked through Over Norton when taking exercise. He used to stop and play 'murrel stones' with us.

Mr Fred Moulder remembers being given six pence when he opened a farm gate for George Arliss.

Harry has a very early memory of seeing Mr Knight in his soldier's uniform returning to duty during the Great War. Mr Knight said, 'Goodbye' to Mrs Barnes, kissed her and added, 'I shan't be coming back'. This is a particularly poignant memory as Mr Knight was one of the fifteen men from the village who did not return. Two little girls were left fatherless – Doris and Edna. The Knight family lived at Rose Cottage.

Harry was taught by his father how to plant their vegetable allotment which was situated at the top of Choicehill. Harry emphasised the fact that he was never expected to do too much work for his age and that he was sent off to play.

Mrs Barnes was renowned for the wonderful flowers which she grew in her cottage garden and which provided her with the relaxation she needed after finishing the laundry work. Mrs Barnes died in 1969.

As the Barnes' home was just on the edge of Over Norton Park Harry saw something of the Daly's activities. Major Daly would be seen each morning checking his weather vane which was attached to one of the trees which lined the Chapel end drive. Maybe this information was necessary to do with his hunting activities. On Sundays hockey matches were held by the Dalys on the front lawns at Over Norton House.

In conversation with sisters Mrs Thomson and Mrs Nolan, née Shepard.

In conversation with Mrs Nancy Nolan, née Shepard, and her elder sister Mrs Joyce Thomson, I learned that they had, before having homes of their own, always lived at No. 34 Main Street, Over Norton. At that time the house was divided to accommodate two families. No. 34 stands opposite to the end of Choicehill Road and is on the east side of Main Street. It is a Grade II listed building of the mid 17th century, extended in the 20th century.

The Shepard family lived in the part facing the garden. Joyce and Nancy Shepard's father was John Shepard, who worked at the Chipping Norton tweed mill. Their grandmother, Susan Moulder (1860-1951) was married to Henry Moulder, brother of Samuel

Moulder. Henry made leather straps and was also able to do all the repairs to his sons' shoes.

Mrs Thomson recalled, 'When I was in bed I remember hearing Harry Barnes and his friends singing the old songs under the old shed.' On discussing this with Harry Barnes he replied, 'It was the beer!'

School
Both of the Shepard sisters went to Over Norton Council School in Choicehill Road. Joyce started at three years of age and she enjoyed Mrs Padbury giving her rides on the 'swinging' blackboard. As the youngest pupil when the school photographer came, she was honoured by being allowed to hold the small board on which the name of the school and the date were written.

The Shepards' religious education was provided for at chapel at Chipping Norton and at Over Norton Sunday School.

Christmas time at Over Norton School was brightened by gifts from the Daly family. The Daly's cook sent cakes 'and sweets were sent for us wrapped in muslin – all stuck together'. All the girls were given a full length cream flannel petticoat by Mrs Daly. Joyce was pleased with hers, but Nancy was not as she found it 'itchy' to wear and also I suspect that she felt that it was becoming out of fashion to wear such a garment.

The Rollright Stones
Nancy recalled wearing fashionable black, patent leather, ankle strap shoes which became very dusty when the family walked to the Rollright Stones for a picnic in the early 1930s.

> We took a kettle with us and got water from the Toll house, walked along to the stones and then lit a fire to boil the water to make the tea.

In earlier times it had been traditional for all the children of the village to go on a picnic to the stones during Easter time. (Source: George Harris from his grandmother.)

At one time the Thornets lived at the Toll House near the stones and they sold lemonade at one penny a bottle. (From Harry Barnes but not remembered by septuagenarians living in the village.)

No doubt the parents and older brothers and sisters would have enjoyed passing on the legends and rhymes of the Rollright Stones. It is certain that they would have talked about the king and his army who were believed to have been turned to stone by Mother Shipton and of her words:

> Seven strides thou shalt take
> If then Long Compton thou canst see
> King of England shalt thou be.

... but before he could reach the top of the mound she said,

> Stand still, stone;
> King of England thou shalt be none.

Legend has it that the king was turned into stone as was his army forming the circle ...

> while the five knights still hold aloof and whisper treachery together against the king. [Ravenhill 1926]

Generations have passed on to each other the suggestion that it is impossible to count the stones correctly and have told the story of the baker who tried to do it by placing a loaf on each stone.

As the children returned home down Little Rollright Hill and over the Choicehill Bridge they would have discussed the story, feeling slightly apprehensive, of the large stone which was moved by the Lord of the Manor to bridge Rollright Brook. Supposedly it was moved there with great difficulty but when the Lord became frightened, due to noises during the night, it was returned to its rightful place quite easily. Did some of Over Norton's stones mentioned in an earlier chapter come from this site? A Chipping Norton historian thinks that it is a possibility.

Recent studies and excavations have shown that there could be a time difference of as much as one thousand years between the construction of the Whispering Knights, probably a Neolithic free standing tomb c3000 BC, and the King's Men. Picnicking families would have been unaware of this. Other sites surrounding the area include Bronze Age burial mounds and Iron Age and Roman farming settlements and an early Saxon cemetery. (George Lambrick – from a talk given to Over Norton History Group March 1998.)

When talking to siblings, a fascinating picture of social history gradually emerges. In listening to Mrs Nolan and her sister, Mrs Thomson – with only three years age difference between them – it is amazing how the development of social change emerges as when they were talking about their dolls...

Mrs Thomson:
> I had a china doll.

Mrs Nolan:
> My doll was a celluloid one from Woolworths.

... and as mentioned earlier, their attitudes concerning flannel petticoats.

Celluloid dolls were not very attractive. They did not break as a china doll would but quickly became full of dents. They did not have hair as such but the head was moulded to represent hair. Legs and arms were moveable as they were attached to the body with elastic. These dolls could be produced cheaply and formed a large part of the doll market in the 1930s. Dolls were not available during the 1939 war and parents looked out for 'Doll For sale' advertisements in the local papers. The skills learned at the Women's Institute became very important and toy patterns were eagerly sought.

In the early times of the Woolworths stores articles were priced at threepence or sixpence each. One could even buy fabric for dressmaking at sixpence a yard.

Mrs Thomson:
> The girls had wooden hoops and the boys had metal ones.

Mrs Nolan remembers buying a plain wooden spinning top from Putman's, High Street, Chipping Norton, and then decorating it with coloured chalks.

At this time the children were safe from traffic although at Great Rollright some children were whipped by a man in a horse drawn vehicle. They could play with whips and tops on the road. Young children would wind the whip cord – (you were lucky if you could get hold of a leather shoe lace) – round the top and then balance it in the mud on the roadside before flicking the whip away to set the top spinning. If luck held, the top would be kept spinning by continually hitting it with the whip. Older boys were able to make their tops 'jump' and loved to pronounce that their tops were 'window smashers'.

Mrs Thomson:

> My granny – who was a Stickley from Kitebrook – told me that on Sunday she used to take a batter pudding, when she was a child, to Laburnum Cottage, just across the road, to be baked.

Mrs Thomson's granny died in 1951.

Mrs Thomson:

> I remember seeing the old ladies carrying their Christmas charity loaves, holding them up in their long black aprons. They were also given half-a-crown [two shillings and sixpence]. My grandmother lived with us and she used the money to buy the ingredients for the Christmas pudding.

Leisure

As late as the 1930s most village people did not venture very far afield, partly due to cost, but also because working hours were very long. Later, during the second world war years, transport was a problem. Villagers had perhaps one excursion a year.

Mrs Thomson recalls going to Barry Island but Miss Doris Knight says that she did not see the sea until after she was eleven. Leisure time spent locally included a visit to Dunthrop to see The Prince of Wales – (Duke of Windsor) – racing in 1927, when Mrs Thomson was five years old. Magic lantern shows given by the Revd. Arkell were enjoyed.

Miss Doris Knight also mentioned the Prince's racing event:

> A visit to Dunthrop to see horse racing was arranged by the Daly's. Children went up in a horse-drawn waggon. The Prince of Wales (later Duke of Windsor) was taking part. The horses were flying over and we didn't know who was who. Mrs Daly also organised buses to take us to Conservative fêtes.

Just before, and during the war, young people of this area spent some time socialising at Reg's Cafe and Swimming Pool which was situated between Southcombe and the turn to Chalford on the A3400. On an 1860 map, public baths – an extension of the Over Norton stream – were shown along the Cleeves just on the Over Norton Parish boundary. There was also a café at Chapel House run by Micky Wood's family.

Leaving School
Dr. Brigg, from Chipping Norton, had cause to treat Mrs Thomson following an accident when she was fourteen years old. He asked her if she would like to become a nursemaid to his children, assisting their nanny. She was very pleased to be able to take up this position with such a prestigious family but later, when war came along, she had to register for war work so she served in the W.A.A.F. as a cook from 1942 to 1946. Mrs Nolan worked at the tweed mill, as had her father, through the war years. This was counted as war work as they were making cloth for the forces' uniforms.

Mrs Thomson admits at this time to having a photograph of David Niven, a popular film star, on her bedroom wall. 'Pin-ups' were just becoming fashionable but prior to that it was quite usual for bedroom walls to be adorned with nothing more than a biblical text.

Beauty Preparations
The two sisters were discouraged from wearing make-up by their grandmother. Many girls at this time were buying 'vanishing cream' foundation and face powder from Pearce's chemist shop on Chipping Norton High Street. Mrs Pearce sat, whilst serving at the counter, and she set an example of perfect grooming, wearing make-up and an immaculate 'ruffled and frilled' blouse.

According to Mrs Doris Pashley she and other girls stained their legs during the war with permanganate of potash crystals in order to economise on stockings – she having obtained her crystals from her brother's greenhouse!

By around 1946 servicemen returning home from the Far East were bringing their girl friends the 'new stockings' made from nylon.

It was common at that time, if you were fortunate to have been given nylons, to hear remarks such as 'Mind your nylons' as you got on a bus. Where groups of girls were living together in hostels or colleges nylons were frequently stolen. A little difficulty arose with the first nylons. Suspenders, two to each stocking, were always slipping off them!

Mrs Thomson: 'Mother made our clothes'

Families whose mothers were 'good with a needle' were indeed fortunate. Adult clothes were cut down to children's sizes. The Women's Institute arranged classes to improve all handwork and needlework skills and many women of this village would have learnt a lot at these. Money was very short for many families and no scraps of fabric were wasted; the smallest pieces being used to make pot holders and kettle holders – a necessity – as the iron pot handles and kettle handles became extremely hot as they were heated on an open fire, oil stove or primus stove before electricity came to the village. Pieces of old felt hats were often recycled for use in this way. In Spelsbury's W.I. late 1920s record there was a mention of a competition to make a pair of baby's knickers out of the thick welt at the top of a stocking.

Sewing skills took on another important dimension during the 1939-45 war when 'Make Do and Mend' became the vogue. At this time, and even right up to the early 1950s, many people would expect to make their children's play coats from adult coats bought at jumble sales and teenage skirts were made from men's old grey flannel trousers. Blouses were made from discarded summer dresses. During the war some Chipping Norton County School pupils had their school blazers turned. To do this the blazers were completely unpicked and re-made with the inside of the fabric on the outside so the worn parts did not show. One pupil had her school blazer made into a shaped jacket by her mother in readiness for starting work.

Mrs Doris Pashley (née Harrison)

The Harrison family lived at the corner of Choicehill Road. Information from Mrs Doris Pashley, born in Over Norton, is dispersed throughout this book. As regards her childhood she was well protected and looked after by her father especially as she was the youngest member of the family – a daughter after six sons. She was devoted to her father who died when she was only ten years old.

Her father obtained an old horse-drawn carriage for her to have in the garden to be used as a play house and after this she had a Co-op baker's cart for the same purpose. She also had a very deep metal doll's pram which was based on the design of baby prams of the late 1920s. (See photo)

Mrs Pashley went to Over Norton School and when it closed, transferred to the British School in New Street. Here she remembers going to cookery lessons in the newly built centre in the grounds of the Green School. Little did she know that one day she would hold a very responsible position as cook supervisor at the St. Mary's Primary School which was built on 'The Green' site. Previously she had done war work.

When it had been time for her to take 'the scholarship' at eleven years of age she had been told by her mother that should she gain a free place to go to the Chipping Norton County School she would be unable to take it up as they would be unable to afford it. Mrs Pashley made no effort to pass the exam which she could have done quite easily. At that time – until the Education Act 1944 – a document had to be signed promising that the pupil would stay at the County school until sixteen years of age, whereas at the non-selective school they could leave at fourteen and start earning something towards their keep. Parents had to provide a school uniform for pupils at the County School (some help could be obtained for this) and pencils, pencil crayons, pens, inks, blotting paper, ruler, set square, protractor and a pair of compasses. (Ball type pens did not come on to the market until the Biro (1947) when they were still very scarce and cost today's equivalent of £6.)

County School Christmas parties ceased in 1939 but that year one first-year girl did not tell her parents that a party had been arranged as she knew that they could not afford to buy her a party dress. However, her parents did get to hear about it from a friend and finding that the lack of a party dress was the reason the little girl pretended she did not want to go to the party, took her to the Co-op in Chipping Norton and bought a pretty yellow one. The girl's pleasure at having the dress was still heavily marred by the fact that she knew her mother was having a problem to make ends meet as her father had been unable to work regularly through the 1930s due to war wounds (1914-18).

In conversation with Mr Douglas Sheffield and Mrs Eileen Sheffield.

Douglas was born and brought up in Over Norton and Eileen also has an interest in the village having lived in Blue Row for a few years after their marriage. She helped with the Women's Institutes coach teas in recent years. Doug recounted some of the events in the life of his father – William (Bill) Sheffield. His mother was Amelia Ellen Sheffield, née Eley, from Enstone. Mr and Mrs William Sheffield were very helpful members of this village's community.

William Sheffield, born 1889, came from Enstone to Over Norton and lived in Blue Row. In his younger years (14 to 16) he worked in Knightsbridge, London, for Harvey Nicholls, a large departmental store, where he wore formal clothes including a bowler hat.

Whilst at Enstone he took part in sports which included carrying a two and a quarter hundred weight sack of barley twenty yards. Today this seems to be an impossible task but farm workers then were used to carrying heavy loads as was Walter Symonds, head carter, on the Kiddington estate. As part of a normal day's work he carried newly threshed sacks of corn up a flight of steps to the corn storage. Walter could cope with this all day long from seven in the morning until evening.

When Mr Sheffield came to live in Over Norton he worked as a farm worker for Mr Walford and was called up for war service in the 1914-18 war.

Mrs Jasmund (Née Sheffield, sister to Douglas)

He was in the last batch of agricultural workers to be taken. He reached the rank of Sergeant in the Oxford & Bucks and he was stationed in Cologne in the army of occupation. He returned in 1920 when he went back to farming.

Later he found employment as a furnace man at the Hub Ironworks, Rowell's, Chipping Norton, where about twenty men were employed in making such things as road signs and man-hole covers. Douglas, his son, used to cycle down to meet him at about 5.30pm at the end of the day shift. Throughout the daytime the moulds for the castings were made. At the end of the daytime shift, between five and six o'clock, the clay bung was taken out of the furnace and the ladles were filled with molten iron which was poured into the moulds. There was a man holding each end of the ladle but one huge ladle was operated by a crane. A 7ft long steel rod with a pointed end was also in use in connection with the furnace. When scrap iron was being used a small quantity of pig-iron was added to it.

Due to ill health Mr Sheffield left the Hub Ironworks to work for the council but returned there during the war (1939), when he, and one other man, were employed to work over night to empty the mouldings ready for the day shift. Previously the day shift had done this but with the new arrangement more work could be completed within twenty-four hours.

Some items for use in the war effort were made. Mr Sheffield retired in 1954 aged sixty- five. Mr and Mrs Sheffield became the first caretakers of the new wooden village hall (1934).

Apparently Mr Sheffield often walked across the park to Mr Goodheart's at Chapel House to get the bookings list for the hall.

In the days when the present chapel was a Mission Room, run by the Church Army, it was used as a venue for concerts. Local inhabitants did 'turns' and Bill Sheffield made a contribution by singing 'Little Brown Jug'. On a 1953 Coronation Tea photograph both of the Sheffields can be clearly seen in charge of the tea urn! Mrs Sheffield was caretaker at one time of the school which was in Choicehill Road.

CHAPTER 10

Schools in Over Norton and Chipping Norton

Dame School and Public Elementary School (Mrs Joines' taped memories)—Fees National School Chipping Norton 1880-1891—Board School, Over Norton and Church letters of opposition 1896—Log Book July 1900 to April 1933—Chipping Norton Schools' Log Books: fairs, holidays, treats and entertainment 1880 to 1913—Over Norton Monitress (Mrs Padbury's Memories)—St. Cecilia's School (Dorothy Rudge)—Banbury County School (Roy Worvill)—Chipping Norton County School—Today, January 2000.

The first official factual reference to an Over Norton school seems to be the one contained in the Parliamentary Gazetteer of England published in 1840 based on facts collected at the close of the year 1839. It states that Over Norton had a daily school at that time and Chipping Norton had '12 daily, 4 day and boarding, and 3 Sunday Schools'.

It is likely that some Over Norton children attended school in Chipping Norton as it would have been within easy walking distance for them. (See later references) Events in Chipping Norton have been of great influence on the lives of people living in Over Norton.

The majority of children had no formal education in the early 19th Century for there was no state provision. Two main church societies, the Church of England National Society of the Poor and the Nonconformist British and Foreign Schools Society had been established in 1811 and 1814 respectively and had set up schools. The education provided in them was poor and consisted mainly of pupils being drilled in answering set questions. Monitors, older pupils who were taught by the Head Master to pass on information, took charge of groups of pupils.

Dame Schools, usually run by women who were themselves often of low educational standard were in operation at this time and continued for many years. The 1840 government report stated:

> Dame or common Day-schools ... cannot be said to amount to education; it can have little effect in expanding the minds of the scholars ... or in giving them a desire for further knowledge ...

A later report from the the Newcastle Commission 1861 stated that

> Dame Schools are very common in the country and in the towns [and that they were] generally very inefficient.

The number of schools in Oxfordshire in 1839 was recorded as 66 Infant Schools; 510 daily schools including 39 boarding schools; and 284 Sunday Schools. There was a mixture of funding sources which included fees, subscriptions and endowments with the Sunday Schools having a large endowment input. The Sunday Schools had been started at the end of the 18th Century for children who were working six days a week in industry. They were to provide moral education and to see that the children did not 'rise above their station'. Pupils were expected to learn to read, mainly from reading the bible.

In the early 19th Century the government appeared to do very little to support education for the masses although in 1816 they appointed a committee to 'institute inquiries respecting the education of the poor ...' but it was not until 1833 that £20,000 was granted to the two main church societies for school building.

When the Revised Code 1862 became law the government started a system of payments to schools based on results, the elements considered being; the children's yearly examination in reading, writing and arithmetic and the pupils' attendance. Teachers' salaries were paid from this grant too.

Attendance was poor as children were ill-clad and so had to stay at home in bad weather. Illness was common with serious epidemics of measles, mumps, chicken pox, scarlet fever, consumption and diphtheria, all made worse by poor home conditions and an inadequate diet. There were many deaths. Poor parents could not see the

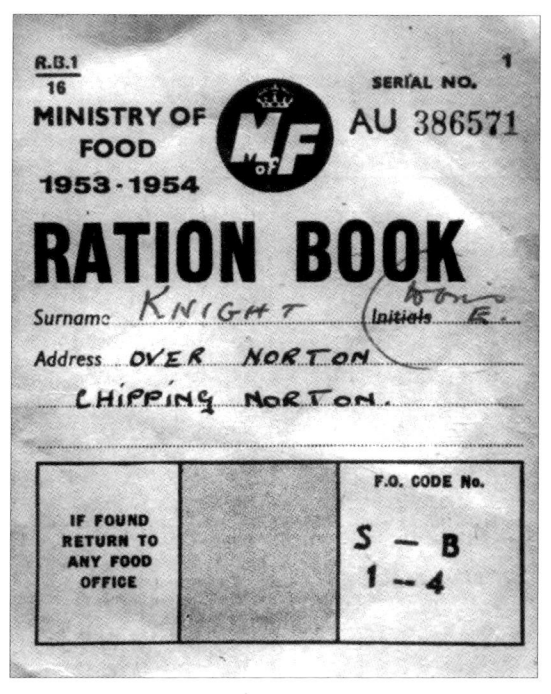

Above: Doris Knight's Ration Book.

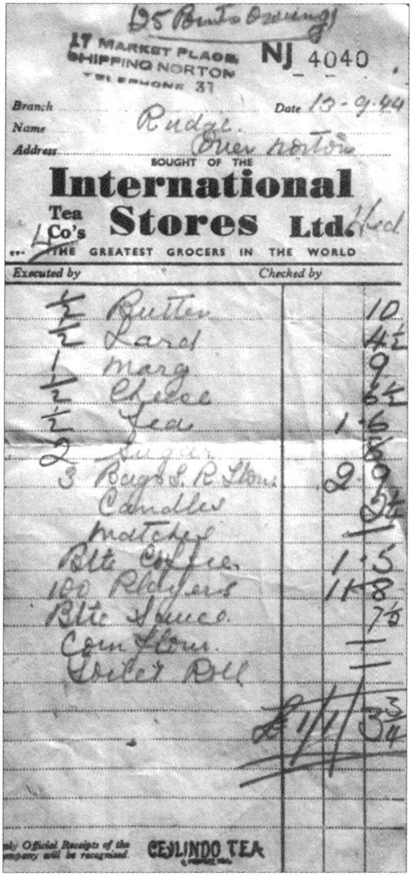

Right: A war-time bill see Chapter 12.

Below: Identity Cards had to be carried during the 1939-45 war years and shown on demand of officials.

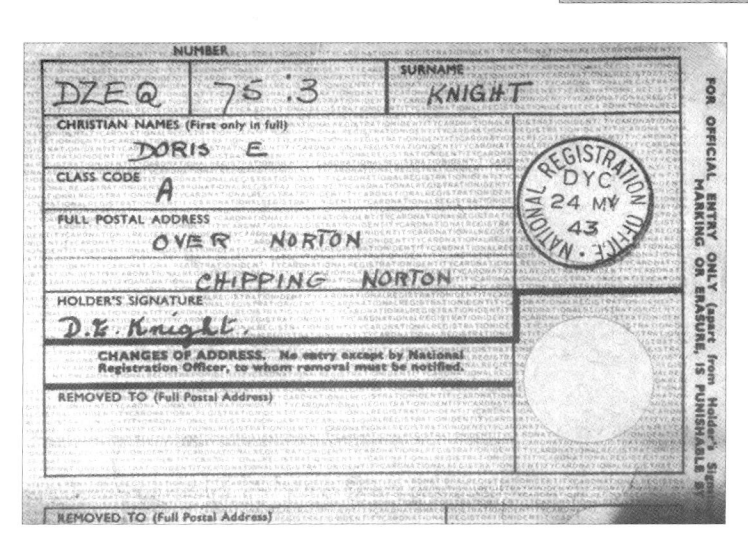

Public seat given to Over Norton to commemorate the Golden Jubilee of the W.I. movement. Joe Roughton chairman O.N.P.C. with members of Over Norton W.I.

Xmas 1968 Entertainment provided for the residents of Castle View by members of O.N.W.I.

Honey from Australia in 1947 and groceries in 1946 were given to O.N.W.I. members.

George Webb, with his horse Punch, collected skins from Banbury Station. They were tanned at Distons Lane, Chipping Norton for the gloving industry.

Receipt.
CHIPPING NORTON UNION.
PARISH OF OVER NORTON.

The 12th day of Feb 1909

Received of Mr W. A. Fawdry's Exors the

Sum of Sixteen Pounds, Eleven Shillings,

and Seven Pence, in respect of the POOR RATE of the above Parish, viz.:—

Assessment Number		£	s.	d.
1	RATE made the 4th day of Nov., 1908, At 3s 0d in the £ on £ 37 – 0 – 0 Rateable Value of Buildings and other Hereditaments not being Agricultural Land	5	11	–
	At 1s 6d in the £ on £ 14 – 1 – 0 Rateable Value of Agricultural Land	11	–	7
	Arrears of former Rate			
	Total £	16	11	7

...ance to Owner at .... per cent.

Received from Owner £

.... Assistant Overseer.

Above: Poor Rate receipt W.A. Fawdrey's Executors 1909 (Choicehill Farm).

Right: From Samuel Moulder's ledger of estate work 1911.

Aug
26 Casing of Powells bedroom floor
27 Rep door spouting at Worells
28 Rep of Powells pig stye
29 Rep of Dunfords pig stye
30 Tree felling
31 drawing timber

Sep
2 Sawing
3 drawing material to yard
4 make gate
5 Hanging gates posts at rick yard
6 Repairing Smiths gates
7 making gates

9 Make gate for Park
10 Painting of Betteridges doors
11 Rep Willmotts Spouting
12 Limewashing Powells bedroom
13 Ditto
14 Rep Smiths gates 6 days

War work for Women September 1916. Man in charge Doris Knight's grandfather from Chapel House. (Firs Farm)

Below Left: Firs Farm 1909-1912 – William John Weale – farmer and wheelwright with daughter Primrose.

Below Right: Mrs Weale with daughter Violet Rose and Grandmother.

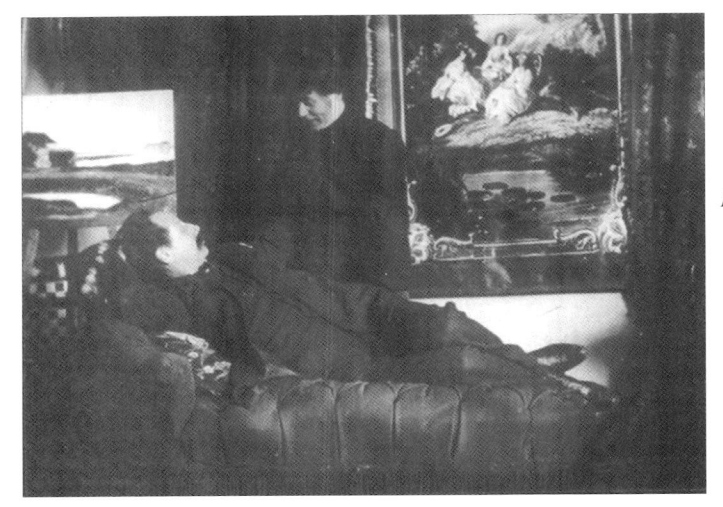

The Firs – Hippolyte Langlois – the famous theatre giant – with wife Dora. (Early 1900s)

1911 Hippolyte Langlois in Jack the Giant Killer with Little Tina, his daughter. (This photo was sent from Australia)

*The Saunders family.
Back row L/R
Agnes, Esther, John,
William, Annie, Kate
Front row L/R
George, John,
Martha, Amelia.
Probably taken to
celebrate a golden
wedding.
Annie Saunders
married George
Dunford and was
John Grantham's
grandmother.
(John Grantham
living at Salford
2000)*

*Chipping Norton Peace
Celebrations – A car load
from Over Norton.*

*Caroline Colyear
Cottages about
1950.*

Top Right: An appointment card received by Albert Saunders, Grocer, Over Norton 1922.

Left: Showing that Hughes supplied Princess Mary's wedding cake. (But still found it worthwhile to do business with Albert Saunders at his small shop in Over Norton.)

Bottom Right: Hull Farm House about 1950.

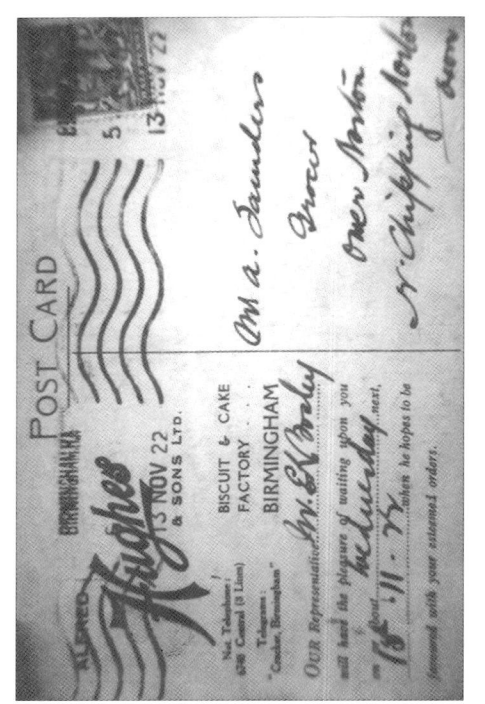

relevance of school for their children and needed them to go to work as soon as possible to bring home a few pence to supplement their meagre earnings. Boys had time out for seasonal farm work and girls were kept at home to do domestic duties.

The upper classes thought that it was unnecessary, and at most harmful, to educate the masses – once they could read they would be in a position to read seditious material!

> ... the poor should not read, and of writing I never heard for them, the use.
> (John Byng)

The sentiment expressed in, 'God bless the Squire and his relations and keep us in our proper stations' was not eradicated until World War Two. There were some good, kind and understanding 'Landed Gentry'.

Forster's Education Act of 1870 introduced School Boards, but more about this later and the furore it created between Over Norton and the Chipping Norton Vicar. It was not until 1880 that school attendance became compulsory for children up to ten years and was raised to twelve in 1899 and fourteen in 1918. Attendance at school became free in 1891 but previously pupils had paid a few pence weekly. The School Boards were abolished in 1902 and then the schools became County Council schools.

That many people were without the most rudimentary knowledge of reading and writing as late as 1900 was shown recently when a family will was studied showing that several of the beneficiaries were unable to sign their names but made their mark.

Over Norton's school situation was very reflective of what was happening countrywide. Much oral evidence exists about Over Norton's schools but it must be remembered that at each telling of the story slight changes are made. This is well illustrated in the telling of the first Christmas story in the gospels. There is always a great deal of truth in oral history much of which can be verified from documents but frequently a 'telescopic happening' is reported – this being a well-known feature of oral history when two elements of a different time become intertwined.

Dame School 'Three Chimneys'

Oral evidence that a Dame School operated in the north end of the cottage named 'Three Chimneys', comes from the previous mentioned tape recoding. (See Chapter 3)

Mrs Joines' memories:

> In the cottage where my grandmother went to school there was a small window that faced the house where the lady of the manor lived. The husband of the school teacher was a painter and he used to watch from this window so that he could tell his wife when the lady of the manor was coming through the park gate. She financed it in some way. She was over it. What he painted I don't know, but after I was married I lived in it, and one of the bedroom window sills was plastered with paint of all colours.

Mrs Joines is also reported by Mrs Garrod, as saying that the Dame teacher was referred to as 'Old Mother Gulliver', and that the children weeded the pleasure walks at Over Norton House for 'the lady of the manor' to cover their school fees.

Further on in Mrs Joines's tape-recorded memories she talks about another school.

> ... That was the school which is now turned into a chapel. My mother went there to school where she paid fourpence [presumably weekly]. When her mother was at work, my mother and her sister used to play truant and spend the fourpence. [See details later of school fees at the National School Chipping Norton.]

To add written recorded facts to oral accounts the Over Norton Census Returns from 1841 onwards have been scoured. There is no mention of a teacher in the village in 1841 but in 1851 Sarah Joynes widow aged 62 was listed as a school mistress. Sarah was included on the 1841 census as being of Independent Means as was her twenty-year-old daughter Ann. Was Sarah Joynes a Dame teacher? In 1851 the Martin family came on the scene: Charles Martin, aged 56, a decorative painter from Middlesex, and Ann, his wife, aged 53, school mistress from Oxford St. Mary V [as written] and three daughters, the youngest aged 11, born in Over Norton. It would appear that they just missed the 1841 census return. They were also listed in 1861, Ann being described as a School Mistress Day, and Charles a

House Painter. By 1871 he had become a Painter Glazier and Ann was not working.

Was it Charles that kept an eye out for the arrival of the school children's benefactor, Mrs Dawkins? Was it at the present St. James' Chapel and Old School House site where blocked windows can be seen on the walls facing Over Norton House. Did the Martins leave the school house and move to No. 9 (part of Three Chimneys)? In 1871 a record reads:

> one [house] uninhabited Chapel and School House for Boys and Girls. [No teacher is recorded in 1871.]

By 1881 Mrs Louisa Thornly, aged 22, school mistress, with Alice, her daughter, aged 2, and Sarah Turner, a servant, aged 16 were living at No. 3 School Square. No. 2 School Square was listed again as being uninhabited.

1891 saw Emily Hyatt, aged 36, school mistress, living at No. 5 the village (as written), with her widowed mother and unmarried brother and sister.

In 1898 William S. Foote was the Principal Teacher and in July 1900 John Lane was Head Teacher with Miss C. Smith as Assistant Teacher. These last two teachers moved on from the school in the chapel to the new school built in Choicehill Road 1901.

Searching for 'old Mother Gulliver' I discovered that she did live at No. 9 (Three Chimneys) in 1899, by then a widow, aged 64, and was employed as a caretaker. Living with her were Minnie (or Marinie) Wheeler aged 16 whom Mr and Mrs Gulliver had adopted – referred to as a Border [sic] – and Florence Miles aged 6, a scholar, born in Worcester. Prior to this date Ann Gulliver born at Charlbury and James aged 43 her husband, born at Hook Norton, were living in Over Norton in 1871. James was a baker. They both appear again on the 1881 list, living in Choicehill Road, when Ann was described as a 'baker's wife'.

As the census returns only occur every ten years it would be pure conjecture to try to establish what happened in the intervening years. (See Chapter 8 for census returns giving numbers of scholars 1851, 1871 and 1891.)

The school room, (now St. James' Chapel) probably converted from a cottage, measured thirty feet six inches by thirteen feet. At some stage an extension of fifteen feet by fourteen feet was added forming an L shape. At one time there was another floor with a communicating door to the School House. Dancing was supposed to have taken place at this 'bedroom' level. (Source: Mrs Garrod) The steps from the 'Old School House' bedroom which linked to the school are still in existence and the recess so formed used as a wardrobe.

Children from three years upwards to twelve year olds [by 1899] were taught in one room. Conditions were very cramped.

Advice for teachers as to how to make a happy start in school for their new pupils was published in 1846 and included the following advice:

> 1. On a child's first morning, as children are registered, they are handed over from parent to teacher who comforts them with plums, cakes etc. Thus obstruction of parents is removed.
> 2. To gain new children's attention teacher should stamp and generally gad about the room throwing balls at them and patting them until all are induced to a chair and have stopped crying. 'Simplicity and patience; Christian grace and comfort must be resorted to'.
> 3. First week to be devoted to order and precision of acting and speaking, i.e. simultaneous actions as in a company of soldiers – viz. hands on knees, heads up, mouths shut, etc. Simple number verse action commences.
> 4. Monitor selected to teach each class of seven or eight. He received lesson board from teacher and instructs his little charges.

(Source: 'The Infant Teacher's Assistant for use by Schools and Private Families' by T.Bilby and R.B. Ridgway)

It is difficult to imagine the above advice being put into action in Over Norton's little school.

School Attendance Certificate:

Mrs Doris Pashley (née Harrison) who has lived in Over Norton all her life has her father's, (James Harrison), Certificate of School Attendance at 'Over Norton Public Elementary School'. He is recorded as having made the following attendances after 5 years of age

1890   301
1891   306
1892   301
1894   306
Signed 1st day of February 1898
William S ? Foote

School Fees National School Chipping Norton

1880 5th November
Sent Theresa — home for her school fee

1882 7th February
Emily Stickley was sent home for her school pence this morning.

1884 4th April
Annie Watts sent home for her school pence [she did not return that week].

1884 7th November
Punished Leonard Widdows on Wednesday for spending his school money.

1891 28th September
I forgot to mention that school is 'free' since the holidays.

Board Schools

Forsters 1870 Education Act said that if there were not enough school places provided by the voluntary societies such as the British & Foreign Schools (as in New Street Chipping Norton), the National Society (the Church School) near St. Mary's, Chipping Norton, or other religious groups then School Boards had to be elected by ratepayers. Women could vote if they were householders although not allowed to in parliamentary elections. The Board were allowed to levy a school rate and use it to build and maintain Board Schools.

The Board Schools were independent of religious bodies. Voluntary organisations tried to increase their number of school places and to keep the 'godless' Board Schools out. Only 12 per cent of Oxfordshire villages had Board Schools by the mid 1890s (Malcolm Graham).

'Echoes of the Week' J.O.J. Sat Sept 16th 1899

... An elementary education crisis is familiar enough to most towns in Oxfordshire, a crisis prolonged for the most part, during which the voluntary school system, with more or less of hope and of heroic effort, struggles to hold the field and to keep out the Board School and its accompanying rate ... Banbury is going through such a crisis ...

There was a bitter battle going on between some inhabitants of Over Norton and the Vicar of Chipping Norton regarding the setting up in Over Norton of a Board School which is clearly shown in the following four letters. [Chipping Norton never had a Board School]

> The Vicarage
> Chipping Norton
> 19 Feb 96 [1896]

Dear Mr Brownrigg,

Another question viz: of a School Board for the Hamlet of Over Norton in this Parish is to be decided by vote in this village on Wednesday next; the squire is practically without funds – all his property is over mortgaged, but he is a Radical of the bitterest type and is dead against Voluntary Schools; tho' the expense will be serious to his estate (or rather to the mortgagees) he has applied to Ed. Dept. for a School board because the little School is not a Church school, but an undenominational school – (practically a British) is £20 in debt & the Farmers won't help him. So he [?funds it] himself. Of course I, though I cannot enter the school and am kept off the com^c have nothing to lose by it becoming a board school, but at the same time I do not like a Board School in my parish at all; it comes uncomfortably close to Chipping Norton Town. I am inclined therefore to take some steps to stop it. What can I do besides putting out leaflets giving "comparative costs" in other places & trying to get the farmers to pay up. I feel sure they won't & I can't.

If you have any up-to-date leaflets on the money question please send me ? of each...

P.S. The Hamlet is 1 mile off our schools. I suppose the Hamlet children can come to them if their school is closed.

[Signed Rev. Littledale]

Extract from a letter from Mr Brownrigg to The Lord Bishop of Reading dated Feb 20th 1896

My Dear Bishop

I hear that there is a grave danger of a Board [school] at Over Norton... it will be well to try and keep a Board out of Over Norton ...

The Vicarage
Chipping Norton
23 Feb 96 [1896]

My dear Bishop of Reading

Yes, there is danger of a School Board being formed for Over Norton in this ecc^l parish, it is a separate <u>civil</u> parish so will not involve us directly; but indirectly it affects us.

It will make people who now resist the intrusion of a B^d feel that there is little use keeping up their opposition, & that a Board is sure to come to C. Norton. Personally, I also object because I dont want a board in any part of my parish nor do I want any "surrender" to emanate f^r this part of the diocese! Besides our subscribers at a distance may easily think, as it is in my parish, that we have <u>failed</u> over our school question w^h we have not. Far from it; we have scored several great victories for the Church – though we are not at a haven of rest just yet.

By way of action I propose to attend the meeting w^h is to be at O.N. on Wed. evg: Col. Dawkins has been going round his villagers with a paper w^h they sign – most of them without reading it! asking Ed. Dep. for a school B^d because he can't get enough money to go on: they are some £30 in debt: but the reason the farmers or some of them wont subscribe is that the school a/cs have been so badly managed. The farmers dont want a B^d nor do the villagers really care to any great extent. If I can get some of the farmers to agree to make another effort <u>under new management</u> it w^d be the best thing; or if a B^D is <u>vetoed</u> at the meeting as it may be & if Dawkins wont go on as a voluntary sch; then I shall say "<u>close it</u> and let the children come to C.N.: w^h is only 1 mile away".

This I presume the Ed. Dept. Wd allow if the school was closed & w^d not compel a Board to be formed. If you can tell me by Wed. whether this is the case or not it w^d guide me in what I may say. But I suppose you know that the school in question is not a Church School at all; nor even a British tho' it is worked on "British" lines for the sake of excluding the clergy! The Building is Dawkins' private property and he has always kept me and any other churchman off the management; the school too has always been ?starved & once "warned" I never may use it, not even for a Good Friday service or mothers' meeting. Dawkins lets the Wesleyan hold a Sunday Evg. Service there. Consequently though I have £120 allowed ... for a Curate "on condition that he is employed at Over Norton" through Col. Dawkins' continued boycott we can only work there by visiting; no services, no mothers' meetings no teaching by clergy in day school.

A B^d School therefore in some ways w^d be an advantage to me for I c^d sometimes (I sh^d suppose) secure the use of it for services, & the children w^d probably have a better paid Master than the present man. But on the whole I feel that the possible advantages of a <u>Board</u> are so small that we ought to do what we can to keep it out.

It is very disagreeable for all of us having to cross swords with Dawkins, but he has been upsetting all his tenants lately & the mortgagees of his property are so pressing that many think that he cannot stay on at Over Norton much longer; in fact he is little more than nominal owner as it is.

Under these circumstances I am quite for holding out against a Board. Excuse such a long effusion.

>Believe me
>my Lord Bishop
>Y[ts] obediently
>Godfrey A. Littledale

re Over Norton (Undenominational) Sch

>The Vicarage
>Chipping Norton
>19 June 1896

Dear Mr Brownrigg

The enclosed is the sequel r[e] the Over Norton School in our parish (one mile from Chipping Norton; pop. 342).

We had a public meeting in the village some months ago, and all the farmers and practically every rate payer except the Radical-Church-Association Col. Dawkins and a few of his cottagers, were in favour of the Voluntary School being maintained and some £40 was forthwith collected by a Mr Scholfield who is a sound churchman and the secretary of our School Building Fund and who is intending to go up to the Educ[n] Dept. on Monday next about this Over Norton Question, and also to see the mortgagees of the Over Norton Property and ascertain if they wish for a Sch. B[d].

I am writing this partly to let you know of what is taking place and part to ask you to render Mr Scholfield any assistance you can. Our difficulty is that Col. Dawkins owns every inch of available land on w[h] we might erect an iron school.

>Yrs very truly
>G. A. Littledale

Over Norton Board School was started, the exact date unknown; but then in 1902 an Education Act stated that Board Schools were to become County Schools.

Records, from the Over Norton Board School log book, are available from 9th July 1900.

1900 July 9th
Today, I, John Lane, trained, certificated master (Period of Training) (1896-7-8) take charge of the above school
        Staff   John Lane Master
                   Miss C Smith Art 68

These premises are temporary, the new buildings being expected to be ready in six months time. [Not ready until November 1901] This school is at present poorly furnished with apparatus. Am making list of requisites this week.

One of the early tasks of the new headmaster was to prepare a list of 'Object Lessons'. These had become compulsory for Infants and Juniors in 1895. The following list is taken from the school log book.

Object Lessons

Standards	Infants
1. Roots of Plants	A Slate
2. A few curious roots	An Umbrella
3. Stems of Plants	A Brick
4. Climbing Stems	A Table
5. A First Lesson on Leaves	A Basket
6. A First Lesson on Forms of Leaves	A Tallow Candle
7. The Margins of Leaves	A Bell
8. The Veins of Leaves	An orange [as written]
9. Some leaves compared	An Apple
10. Parts of a Flower	A Sponge
11. The Primrose	Different Kinds Paper [as written]
12. The Daisy	A Grocer's Shop
13. Insects and Flowers	Tea
14. Vegetation in Autumn and Winter	The Cat
15. Vegetation in Spring and Summer	The Dog
16. Wheat Plant	The Cow
17. Some Common Grains	Winter
18. Butter and Cheese	Ice
19. The Potato	Rain
20. Bread	Money

This Arithmetic Exam paper was taken from the Over Norton Board School Log Book 1900 and is copied as it was written.

Arithmetic Third Exam (Quarterly)
(1) Cost of 2850 art @ £2.17.9 each (Practice)
(2) 19lbs @ 8½d per lb, 17½ lbs 8d per lb
14¼ lbs @ 11d per lb, 20 lbs ½ per lb (Bill)
(3) 3/7 of a field were sown with wheat 2/9 with barley and the remainder with oats. What part was sown with oats.
(4) If 2 tons, 15 cwt are carried 70 miles for £1.17.6 how far would 3 tons 10 cwts be carried for the same money.

IV. (1) Multiplication (2) Division
(3) If a boy takes 2 steps each 2½ ft long in a second how far would he walk in 2 hours
(4) If I bought 3 chests each containing 2 cwts of tea at £3.18.0 per cwt, and sold it at 1/1 per lb what would be my profit

III. (1) Addition, (2) Division 11,001 divided by 110 (Dictated)
(3) From a purse holding £5.11.6 a man pays the Butcher 17/9, the grocer 9/9½d. and buys a hundred ½d stamps. how much has he left?

Std II From Cards 3rd Quarter's Examination

Extracts from the Over Norton School Log Book follow:

1900 July 13th
There were present 31 children this week there being a preponderance of infants. Only one boy attended in the standards. As the school has been closed for 3 months, and the school year begins Apr 1st, I have marked the registers in the Second Quarter and will select only twenty object lessons for stds. I, II & III.

1900 July 16th
... Admitted Charlotte Powell, a trifle over three years of age.

1900 July 18th
Today have written to Mr Holmes (HMI) with reference to the granting of the usual Midsummer Vacation.

1900 July 27th
Have received word from the Board that there will be no Midsummer Vacation this year [for Over Norton Board School].

During the three months closure of Over Norton Board School some children attended schools in Chipping Norton therefore the Head Teacher, at Over Norton, must have been very surprised to find that they did not qualify for a break from school during August 1900.

(See extracts further on from Chipping Norton Schools' Log Books ref Over Norton pupils.)

1900 July 23rd
This morning Edith Brain returned to school. This is her first appearance since the re-opening. In the afternoon her sister Fanny returned, as a half-timer. Edith takes her place in Std II and Fanny in Std V.

1900 July 25th
John Moulder returned to this school from Chipping Norton British School. He attended this afternoon. He has been placed in Std II.

1900 July 31st
This afternoon Ada Moulder returned to this school. I have placed her in Standard IV. This makes 38 on the books all of whom are present this afternoon.

1900 Aug 3
... There will be a holiday on Monday next (Bank Holiday).

1900 Oct 10th This afternoon there is a very poor attendance in consequence of a Fair being held at Chipping Norton. It has been usual to give a half-holiday on this day in past years. The whole of the Betteridges and Hopkins' are away. I sent specially to both people but without avail, the only answer from them being that they were going to take the children down to The Fair. I am praising those children who have come this afternoon and shall have a hard word for the absentees when they return. It is self-evident though that the fault is the parents.

[See later explanation of Chipping Norton's Fairs]

1.2.01 Poor attendance 10 children absent due to Chicken Pox

8.2.01 We have been grappling with the metric system this week in the upper standards.

1901 22nd February 47 children on the books 1901 28th February Her Majesty's Inspector [H.M.I.] said 'Maps and pictures urgently needed'.

1901 15th March Visited by teachers from the National Schools (Chipping Norton). [One would have thought that this would have been discouraged by the church!] Lesson on the census. [This census return should be released in 2001.]

1901 29th March
... Infant work and discipline leaves much to be desired... also the opinion of H.M.I.. the standards satisfactory... praised girls of the First Class for their paper work and made a pleasant little speech of encouragement to the

standards concerning their removal, shortly, to their new school [being built in Choicehill Rd.]

1901 17th April
This has been a miserable week. No satisfactory work has been done. [The Head Teacher had a bad throat and the Infant Teacher was absent.]

1901 30th April
... holiday on account of the May Day Festivities held in the village.

1901 14th June
Fanny Brain helping with the Infants.
Mr Allen checked the registers.

1.7.01
To satisfy the new rule concerning Drill I shall give the last 5 minutes, now devoted to Mental Arithmetic each morning, to the practice of Exercises learnt. [What pleasure for the children to be allowed to stretch themselves!]

The following extracts taken from the Chipping Norton National School Log Books give a broader view of Physical Education as taught around the turn of the 19th century.

Military Drill

In 1888, in the school near the Church, the teachers were trying to get the children to 'drill and sing' at the same time and this proved impossible. Later they were allowed to use the church choir's harmonium.

Now at the new school Burford Road:

1897 12th March
'Musical Drill' – elder girls in the class-room, juniors in the school-room – harmonium placed between the rooms.
[Not surprisingly]
We find it impossible to drill all the girls at the same time.

1901 26th July
... commenced military drill in the playground.

1901 1st August
Playground examined – needs smoothing for drilling purposes.

1901 13th September
Revd. W.C. Page Lieutenant of the Boys' Brigade gave a dozen girls a lesson in drill.

1902 31st October
Sergeant Burford of the Volunteer Corp has been appointed to give the staff of the Girls and Infant Department a few lessons in Military Drill according to the latest requirements. Mrs Burbidge appointed by the Managers as a lady visitor... witnessed drill and checked the registers.

Further extracts from Over Norton Board School Log Book:

1901 5th July
Received 8s.2d for sale of garments made by the children.

1901 12th July
First class have this week mastered metric money.

1901 19th July Lesson taken outside – suitable place for learning a poem "My Shadow". A chrysalis brought in by a child.

1901 24th July
Very wet day. None of the children who live at long distances are present this morning. Present 34 [adequate clothing was not available].

1901 26th July
Standard I and II Reading is wretched and I shall have to devote the whole of their reading lesson time to them alone for some time.

1901 2nd August
Tomorrow I meet with the Board to make arrangements for providing the children with a treat.
A broken dish fell on Rose Batt's foot – bandaged it – Edith Brain lent a slipper.

1901 9th September
Today is to be performed the opening ceremony of the New School. We do not commence work today in consequence of this. The Village will be en fête today.
Miss Spearmint will be unlocking the door.

1901 20th September
History books arrived. I hope we shall move to the new school, in a few days.
We are now waiting for slates to arrive. [The main part of writing was still done on slates using a slate pencil.]

1901 1st October
The Clerk instructed close [school] at once [due to measles outbreak].

1901 2nd October
We are to re-open in the new school on 21st October.

1901 21st October
Re-opened [still in the old school] Apparatus (sewing materials, slates) not yet ordered as far as I am aware [by the Clerk]. We are in great need of pictures slates and pens.
Measles – almost free now.
Playground of the new school nowhere near completion.

1901 1st November
We have no sewing materials. I shall see the Clerk of Board with reference to ordering it. I sent in some over three weeks since. I wish the Drawing Bks and C? were arrived.

1901 6th November
Received sewing materials from Smiths Chipping Norton.

1901 8th November We have now got nicely into the swing of work again. I hope we start in the new premises on Monday.
I hear that the list of requisites which I sent in has been ordered.

New School
Over Norton Council School, Choicehill Road, was ready for opening on 11th November 1901. According to a 1924 Kelly's Directory it cost £1000 to build and was planned to cater for sixty children.

1901 11th November
Enter the New School today. No cupboard on the premises so books are stored on window ledges and chairs.
We are without pens, ruler and slates but expect them any moment.
Although the fires have been kept going for a week the walls are too damp to display pictures. [No positive comments were recorded whatsoever on entering the new school. There were two classrooms; each measured 18 feet by 17 feet.]

1901 12th November
I have bought a box of pens so that we may continue our paperwork uninterruptedly. Coal scuttles, brush, tongs etc arrived.
Fenders and fireguards to follow. [Surprisingly allowed to function as a school without the provision of fire guards.]

1901 15th November
Clock fixed in the school today.
Fanny Brain [believed to have lived at Honeystones, Over Norton] again to assist Miss Smith. I am looking for material improvement from now onwards.

1901 22nd November
Still without a cupboard.
The north wind is drawing smoke down the chimneys making work anything but pleasant.

1901 29th November
The playgrounds are now almost finished.
The gates leading to them about to put in place.
Cupboard and table not yet come.
The Infants have taken nicely to colour work.

1901 4th December
The cupboard arrived today table also.

Mr Holmes H.M.I. called on 5th December and remarked that the classroom is very badly lighted. He suggested that if the upper panels of the wooden partition were glazed the classroom would be able to 'borrow' light from the main room. He also said that proper apex ventilation seems to be needed in both rooms. [What grave problems to surface so soon after newly opening!]

1901 5th November
Mr Mace, Clerk to the Board, announced the holidays – 20th December to 6th January. I showed him the H.M.I.'s entry – he said he would report to the Board. Mr Lucas called – the children read to him.

1901 20th December
On Xmas Eve Mrs Daly of Over Norton Park gives children tea and prizes as ast year.

1902 10th January
Received keys for out offices [outside bucket toilets].

1902 30th January
Inquest on death of an Infant in school at 7pm.

1902 31st January
Smoke trouble – children taken out to play 'till hometime.
Several [pre-school] children died of whooping cough.

1902 28th February
Received a Map of England.

1902 7th March
Inquest [in school] at 2pm on the body of an elderly woman.

1902 30th April
Tomorrow will be a holiday on account of the May Day festivities held in the village.

1902 1st May
Today is an annual holiday. The children will have a Tea in the schoolroom this afternoon after the May Garland.

1902 2nd May
Received a gift of a picture of Queen Victoria. Have taken it to the Clerk of the Board to have it framed.

1902 22nd May
Have hung the picture of Queen Victoria in the Schoolroom today.

Annual Report 1902
No grant is payable under Art. 105 of the Code since H.M.I. (Her Majesty's Inspector) is unable to report that the staff is efficient or the school well taught within the meaning of that article.

1902 6th June
Average attendance 56.3 – highest yet reached.

1902 13th June
We are busy now in preparation for the Coronation. The girls utilize their sewing lesson in making sashes and frocks to be worn on Coronation Day.

1902 25th June
On Monday next mugs and flags given by Mr Brassey to be distributed.

1902 11th July
We want ... and a map of the Empire ... [There was a great emphasis placed on learning about the Empire and of learning patriotic songs and poems].

1902 18th July
Miss Insall (new teacher) working very hard with Infants.

1902 25th July
Half-holiday for Lord George Sanger's circus in town.
[Followed by five weeks Summer holiday.]

1902 8th September
Partition glazed during holidays.

1902 19th September
Two boys absent for harvesting.
Annie Moulder has applied for a half-time certificate.

1902 24th September
Being a fine day visiting Choicehill stream for an Object lesson on the river.

1902 3rd October
The Infants have made very little headway with the 'Phonic Method' of Reading and I think it will be best to return to the 'Look and Say Method'. [The arguments for and against these methods have raged for years and are still going on in 1999. 'Phonic': using letter sounds; 'Look and Say': learning words without sounding out the letters and instead learning the 'shape' of the word.]

1902 8th October
Today is Fair day at Chipping Norton... children asked to return at one o'clock and we shall close at 3.00pm. There are 48 present. This afternoon we have six less than this morning all of whom had neglected to bring their dinners and had evidently been anticipating a half-holiday.

1902 9th October
The fires smoked abominably and something must be done.

1902 15th October
Today is Chipping Norton Great Fair Day only twenty-four present this afternoon.
Heavy storm... lowest attendance in new school.

1902 7th November
This morning locked out several children who were late. Result – no late arrivals this afternoon.

1902 28th November
Have had several rambles with the scholars this last fortnight. [Natural History was beginning to take on a new importance and being studied from real life and not only from pictures.]

Mrs Beck still has her poetry book which she used at Over Norton School – 'Oxford Elementary School Books' 'Fourth Book of Verse' O.U.P. and it is from this that these extracts are taken.

   ... Come forth into the light of things,
   Let nature be your teacher ...

   Come forth and bring with you a heart
   That watches and receives

                                         Wordsworth

Summer

Why, one day in the country
Is worth a month in town,
Is worth a day and a year
Of the dusty, musty, lag-lost fashion
That days drone elsewhere.

Christina Rossetti

1902 28th February
Recorded by the Head Teacher [Brave man!]
As will be seen by reference to date 26th we received visit from the Lady Inspector who undoubtedly violated Art. 18 (Circular to Inspectors) by her harsh manner. The children were quite cowed, and unable to do themselves justice. A method of working a problem not giving satisfaction she remarked, "Heaven alone knows how long that will take". A Std V girl was so 'badgered', (which is the only word appropriate to the irritable manner in which the girl was treated) that she burst into tears. In many other ways which I shall not detail here, was a most miserable morning caused. I must add, however, that the Lady Inspector admitted upon leaving that perhaps she had been a "trifle impatient".

It is because I have felt so strongly upon the matter that I have made the foregoing entry. I must also add that I was dictated to, by her, in the presence of the scholars, and I think I am quite justified in my asking the Clerk of the Board to make suitable complaint to the Head Inspector or the Board of Education.
[Mr Lane, Head Master, left the school on 19th March 1903.] From Over Norton Council School Logbook

Chipping Norton Fairs: extract from 1852 Directory

... there are fourteen fairs held in the year; viz. on the Wednesday after January 1st, and the last Wednesday in every month excepting December when it is held on Wednesday after the 11th. Cattle and sheep in large numbers are brought hither for sale and the fairs are usually frequented by a goodly number of farmers and dealers. There are also statutes for the hiring of servants on the Wednesday before and after October 10th.

The Statute Fairs were a remnant of the 'Statutes of Labourers' from Edward III's reign (1327-1377) which were enforced due to a shortage of agricultural labourers and usually took place at Michaelmas when the magistrates' decisions as to wages were declared at the Statute Sessions. Queen Elizabeth I (1558-1603) abolished the 'Statutes of Labourers' but kept the Sessions – employers and men met to listen to the rates of pay and conditions of work and hiring agreements were made. (*A Dictionary of British Folk Customs*, Christine Hole. pub. Hutchinson & Co. Ltd. 1976) Fairs developed around this and people seeking employment provided a symbol of their trade – e.g. a shepherd his crook; the dairy-maid a pail. When an agreement of work had been made the farmer paid the worker a 'fastenpenny'. In Chipping Norton if the employer and worker did not get on they returned to the 'Runaway Mop' on the Wednesday after 10th October and negotiated again with someone else.

Chipping Norton National School Log Books

There are many entries concerning half-day holidays for the Chipping Norton Fairs from October 1880 up to the beginning of the First World War.

> 1880 14th October
> Half Holiday – 2nd Mop Fair
>
> 1886 22nd October
> A holiday on Wednesday ... being the last of the mops
>
> 1895 Half-day holidays given on:
> 11th October – 1st Mop
> 18th October – 2nd Mop
> 25th October – 3rd Mop
>
> [These dates do not quite fit the Statute Rules]

An interesting item recorded on 19th October 1885 was:

> Several children left the town it being the time for labourers to change their situations.

In May 1890, it was noted that

> The 4th [standard] children lingered at the fair.

A fun-fair – ' The Chippy Mop' – is still held in the centre of Chipping Norton each September (1999).

Other holidays, treats and entertainments during the years 1880 to 1913 included: The Band of Hope Festival July 1880; the Wombell's

Menagerie February 1882 and September 1887; The Blue Ribbon Movement at the Town Hall 1882; Sports on the Common ... Club Day July 1889; two days holiday ... Royal Wedding July 1893 [Duke of York]; half-day for ... Relief of Ladysmith 1st March 1900 and for Peace at end of Boer War 2nd June 1902; a week's holiday to celebrate the Coronation of Edward VII; Day Schools treat at Glyme Farm July 1912; aeroplane exhibition February 1913; Choir Boys taken to the Isle of Wight July 1902 and to Chepstow and Ilfracombe; half-day holiday Empire Day – children drilled with flags 24th May 1910; school closed ... a new organ dedicated at Church 26th July 1910.

An unofficial treat in September 1903 took place: Several boys accompanied their parents to Birmingham Onion Fair.

Extract from the Log Book of Chipping Norton National Girls' School Burford Road

> 1900 July 13th
> Nine girls from Over Norton school who were admitted here, during the temporary closing of their school have returned as the school is re-opened. [Names listed included Susan Keen, Margaret Ebborn and Esther Honour]

and from the Church Infants' School, same date,

> Several children from Over Norton left this week as the school in that village has been re- opened.

There is no information available on this subject from the Chipping Norton Boys' National School Log Book as the first entry was dated 14th October 1901.

The new Chipping Norton National Girls' School and Church of England Infants' School were opened 14th January 1897 when:

> Re-opened school today in new buildings, Burford Road. 111 present. Visited the new schools – closets temporary. Signed G. Littledale.

A calamity occurred on the first day when,

> a trestle table tipped and blotted the register. [Registers were sacrosanct]

By April the Head Teacher recorded

... Much healthier here.

The Chipping Norton Boys' National School Log Book:

1902 6th November
Opening of the Parish Church Room [former school] by Hon. Albert Brassey – [a tea provided].

1903 6th March
Monetary rewards of 3d per quarter given to regular scholars. 24 boys received the gift ... children turned the age of 14 have left school.

1904
Admitted Percy who has been attached to a travelling roundabout.

1906
Received a portrait of the King and Queen in Coronation robes.

Some children were sent away from the Chipping Norton National Schools and between 1901 and 1914 three boys were sent by Magistrates to an Industrial School – one for repeated truancy; a boy was removed by the Poor Law Authorities to 'Stanley Park Colony'; and four Union (workhouse) children were transferred to the Cowley Poor Law Schools.

Monitress Over Norton School

Mrs Minnie May Padbury (née Burtonshaw) of Hook Norton, began her teaching career at Over Norton Council School. She came to work as a monitress when fourteen years old having been educated at Chipping Norton Church School (situated in the Burford Road at the junction with Albion Street). Beginning her duties in 1920 she stayed for one year and she still has the testimonial dated Nov 20th 1921 which Mrs Meredith, Head Teacher, wrote for her. Mrs Padbury received a salary of £1.6s.8d a month.

She recalls walking to Over Norton School from Chipping Norton, in the company of Freda Padbury (family were Newsagents) a teacher, at the school.

Extract from Log Book Girls' School, Burford Road, Chipping Norton:

Freda Padbury began her teaching career, as a monitress, on 8th October 1909 [and she] resigned as monitress 12th December 1913'.

Although Miss Burtonshaw married and became Mrs Padbury, there was no family connection with Freda Padbury, the teacher of 1920.

Mrs Padbury was the daughter of Thomas Burtonshaw (1833-1917), the manager of the gas works at Chipping Norton (near the Tweed Mill). He was also an inventor and designed a tar burner – the "Excelsior" Tar Burning Arrangement. Better results were claimed to be (i) far better and more regular heats, (ii) more gas per ton of coal for less labour and a gain of 2/6 to 3/- per day per furnace. Many people travelled to buy these tar burners at £1.1s.0d each. Mrs Padbury recalls:

> The components were bought from Hartwells, Ironmongers, in Chipping Norton and they were assembled in our cellar often by my mother. There was apparatus in the cellar for printing the advertising leaflets. Once a Mr Evanson came from Ireland and gave me a doll. [The gas works were moved from Distons Lane to the Bliss Mill in 1856/57.]

Miss Burtonshaw was an extremely talented young woman having inherited her parents' abilities. Unfortunately she was unable to take advantage of many opportunities due to lack of finance. Her father died when she was 12 years old. Although she won a place at Banbury School she was not allowed to go there. In her late teens she won a scholarship to the British Dominican School of Drawing in London, but was unable to take it up.

As a monitress, her education was continued at the Guildhall in Chipping Norton where a Technical School had been set up.

> The old Guildhall, which had been converted into an up-to-date Technical Institute was the scene of an interesting ceremony on the occasion of the formal opening (1901). Mrs Brassey unlocked the door. Others present included The Mayor and Mayoress, Deputy Mayor, Vicar Revd. C.A. Littledale, Captain Scholfield and Dr O'Kelly. At the Town Hall, during the evening Mr P.E. Good gave a short address, in which he set forth the benefits accruing from technical education. (From The Oxfordshire Weekly News)

In 1921 a Mr Liddell, came from Oxford, on Saturdays, to teach the 3Rs in the morning and art in the afternoon. Lessons were conducted upstairs and Mrs Padbury recalls

> ... the boards were wonky.

> Miss Winifred Bennett (born 1893) a monitress at Church Enstone School when she was twelve years of age (1905) was paid half-a-crown a week. She stayed at that school for ten years (1915) and during that time she had to walk to Chipping Norton on Saturdays to prepare for the Senior Oxford Examination. The tutor for this was Mr H. Liddell M.A. and the sessions lasted from 9.45am till 3pm, with three-quarters of an hour dinner break.
> (From: *A Review of Enstone* pub. Enstone Parish Council 1971)

Mrs Padbury later travelled, by train, to Oxford, on Saturdays, to study at the school in Gloucester Green, Oxford. (At one time called 'The Central'.) At Oxford the number of subjects was increased to cover chemistry, physics, geography and history. She attended this centre for two to three years and she sat for her examinations in the Examination Schools in Oxford High Street. She passed her preliminary exam at 17 years.

Mrs Padbury recalls that there were pupil teachers attending the centre from Stonesfield, Charlbury and Witney.

After completing a year as a monitress at Over Norton School Miss Burtonshaw moved to Heythrop School, as a pupil teacher, and subsequently had a very successful teaching career and was still teaching children to read, at her home, when she was 90 years of age.

Whilst a monitress at Over Norton her duties were to help in many ways under the teachers' directions. She recalls taking the children for nature walks towards the allotments and picking wood anemones.

She helped in the Infant Class with:
(i) plasticene modelling
(ii) paper folding
(iii) coloured paper work (children favoured red and green)
(iv) drawing

Singing games included:
(i) The Farmer's in His Den
(ii) Ring-a-Roses
(iii) Oranges and Lemons
(iv) I Sent a Letter to my Love

Other games she remembers are:
(i) Marbles
(ii) Whips and Tops
(iii) Hoops
(iv) Hopscotch
(iv) What's the Time Mr Wolf?
(vi) Hide and Seek

Skipping games included
(i) 'Salt, Mustard, Vinegar, Pepper'
(ii) My mother said, I never should
Play with the gypsies in the wood
If I did, then she would say
Naughty girl to disobey!

(iii) Nebuchadnezzar king of the Jews
Bought his wife a pair of shoes
When the shoes began to wear
Nebuchadnezzar bought a bear.
When the bear began to kick
Nebuchadnezzar bought a stick
When the stick began to break
Nebuchadnezzar bought a snake.
When the snake began to sting
Nebuchadnezzar bought a ring.
When the ring began to rust
Nebuchadnezzar was turned to dust.

Another singing game played was:
Round and round the village (rep 3x)
As you have done before
In and out the windows (rep 3x)

>   As you have done before
>   Stand and face your play-mate (rep 3x)
>   As you have done before
>   Take him/her off to London (rep 3x)
>   As you have done before
>   Bring him/her back rejoicing (rep 3x)
>   As you have done before.

The children made a circle and held hands high to form arches. The child chosen, ran between the children, under their arches during the singing of 'In and out the windows'. The rest of the rhyme is self-explanatory.

Mrs Padbury, monitress, has a good memory for the names of the pupils in 1920/21 and quickly recalled the following:

> Winnie and Gladys Sheffield, from Blue Row,
> The Moulders, Harry Barnes, Bertie Harrison, the Tomlins,
> Halls from Firs Farm, Marie Powell and Gladys Fox.

She said that the children wrote on chalk-boards. The Physical Education consisted of 'Drill' which would have been quite formal exercises. The children went home to mid-day dinner.

When the Over Norton School closed on 12th April 1933 having been in operation for just under thirty-two years, the village children had to attend schools in Chipping Norton. The free schools available for them were the St. Mary's Church Schools and the British School in New Street.

Teacher Training at the National School, Chipping Norton included:

> 1894 9th March
> Pupil teachers to have instruction at the Head Teacher's house from 5pm to 6pm as this will be more convenient than the dinner hour.
>
> 1895 28th March
> Pupil teachers taught by the Vicar at weekly classes 9.05am to 9.45am.

1897 14th June
Miss Pratt, Assistant Teacher, and two pupil teachers attended the Service and Art Examination at the Town Hall.

St. Cecilia's School (1935-37)

Some families, mainly farmers, elected to send their children to St. Cecilia's School, a private school, which was located at the back of Dunstan House, New Street, Chipping Norton. It was run by Miss Shrimpton and Mrs Taylor. Miss Shrimpton was very keen on music so that is a possible explanation as to why she named her school after the patron saint of music.

Miss Dorothy Rudge, with her brother Tom, attended St. Cecilia's and recalls that there was a lot of glass along one side of the building. This conservatory effect can be seen in an old photograph. Dorothy Rudge recounts:

> The school consisted of one room heated by a tortoise stove. All ages were taught in this room with Mrs Taylor teaching the younger children. I remember looking out of the school room window and seeing a waterwheel – not working – but to my young mind the water seemed really deep. Part of Dunstan House was used by the Church Army. There was a billiard room in their part; we used to pop in and buy 1d bars of chocolate from their shop.
>
> The Over Norton Mission Room was run by the Church Army.
>
> The school choir was about twenty-three members strong and we took part in music festivals where we were very successful. We were presented with a shield at Banbury for winning at singing. On this occasion, one Over Norton boy, was asked to mouth the words instead of joining in. Our uniform was blue and white.
>
> We played tennis at school. We also did pantomimes and performed in the Town Hall and at the Workhouse.
>
> Miss Lawrence, daughter of the huntsman at Heythrop Kennels, taught dancing at the school. These dances were performed in the pantos. I have photographs showing my brother Tom and me dressed in our panto costumes.
>
> There is also one of us in Woolliams's garden [Home Farm]. My panto ball gown was of yellow taffeta and was made at Webb's shop in Chippy [now Somerfield Supermarket 1999].
>
> Miss Simpson and Mr & Mrs Taylor lived together in Horsefair, Chipping Norton, in a house which is now 'The Cottage Restaurant'. They gave music lessons after school. I took piano lessons with Miss Shrimpton.

Dorothy Rudge's memories of the names of her school mates include Richard and Audrey Woolliams and Pat Cambray of Over Norton. She remembers Diana and Pauline Flick (the latter, the owner of The Rollright Stones until recently) and the two Major boys, Noel and Murray (Young/Major garage family).

Before coming to live in Over Norton in 1935 the Rudge children had been taught by a governess at their farm bordering Great Tew. That arrangement came to an end when the farm workers began quarrelling over the governess.

Dorothy Rudge, summing up her two years at St. Cecilia's says:

'We didn't learn a lot!'.

This must be a gross understatement as Dorothy and her brother Tom, went on to farm, with their parents, at Witts Farm, Over Norton, and subsequently took over the running of the farm, which they did very successfully, when their parents were too old to continue.

Tom and Dorothy Rudge both live in Over Norton, in their respective homes, converted from farm buildings, Endall's and Well House.

After leaving St. Cecilia's, Dorothy Rudge and Audrey Woolliams moved on to Chipping Norton County School as fee paying students, at £4.4s.0d. a term.

By 1939 eleven-year-olds went either to The County School, Burford Road – Headmaster Mr Steward – if awarded a Special Place or as fee payers. If neither of these they went to the Secondary Modern School in The Green. (1999, this is 'St. Mary's Primary School' and the old 'County School' is now 'Chipping Norton School', providing comprehensive education for all 11 to 18-year-olds.) When the older children were split between the two schools it was very divisive. Children starting at the County School through selection, seemed to lose all their friends. One lone boy was terrified of being ambushed by the Secondary Modern boys on the way home to Over Norton.

This form of selective education had begun after 'The Education Act of 1907' stated that a quarter of all places, at rate-aided grammar schools, had to be kept as free places for children who were attending elementary schools. It was hoped that this would provide a good opportunity for some working class children. It was the beginning of the eleven-plus selection system.

Banbury County School

Banbury County School, called Banbury Grammar locally, served this village prior to 1928 when Chipping Norton County School was built. At one time the school in Banbury was named Banbury Municipal School and was later re-named Banbury County School.

As far as is known, there is no Over Norton resident living in Over Norton (1998) who won a scholarship to Banbury County School.

Information about pupils from this area, who attended the Banbury School, has been gathered from Mr Roy Worvill of Chipping Norton. Roy was born of Over Norton stock and has happy/sad memories of attending Banbury School. A certificate was awarded to him on his gaining a Junior County Scholarship July 1925.

> First I passed an examination in English and Arithmetic which was held at the British School, New Street, Chipping Norton where I was a pupil. This was followed by an oral exam in Oxford, held at the County Education Offices in New Road.
>
> I started at Banbury School at eleven years of age in 1925.
>
> We travelled by train, on free tickets, to Banbury, a journey of fifty minutes passing through Bloxham, Adderbury and Kings Sutton. We were always late and missed part of assembly.
>
> We did have a lot of fun on the train journeys. I remember the windows on the carriages had the following notice:
>
> 'To Lower Window Pull the Strap Towards You'. With a bit of scraping off of some letters it could be made to read: 'To Love Widow Pull Her Towards You'.
>
> There were no school meals so we took sandwiches and we made cocoa in the Physics Laboratory. [No Health & Safety Regulations!]. The school building was red brick. Girls and staff used the main entrance and the boys had a dingy entrance through the basement cloakroom. There were A and B streams about 200 pupils.
>
> The uniform for girls was navy blue, and for boys, red and black. The boys' caps were red and black with a real silver badge bearing the school motto,

'Dominus Nobis Sol et Scutum'
(Our Lord is our Sun and Shield)

One day we were reported to the Head Teacher by a passenger on a train, for singing 'The Red Flag'. Our school caps were confiscated as a consequence of this behaviour. My mother wrote and complained and reminded the Head Teacher that she had bought the cap and so it was her property! Of course, I knew Wilf Harrison well. We were old friends at Banbury School and then at Chippy when the school opened in 1928. Wilf went to Banbury a year before I did. We were second cousins, as I am to all the Harrison family including Mrs Doll Pashley.

Roy Worvill was unhappy at the Banbury School, and one male teacher was particularly unpleasant (too mild a description!) to him, comparing him, unfavourably, with an older brother, Norman. (Norman Worvill passed External London Intermediate BA, usually taken at university, in the 6th Form and the whole school was given a half-day holiday to celebrate this.)

Roy Worvill went on to have an extremely successful life, having transferred to Chipping Norton County School, when it was built in 1928. He gained a BSc and MSc external London degrees and a teacher's certificate at Bangor. He wrote many books, including some Ladybird Science Books. He was frequently asked to review science books including some written by Patrick Moore, the astronomer.

Roy Worvill's grandparents lived in Choicehill Road in Over Norton. His grandfather, Henry Worvill, was a farm worker who lost a hand below the wrist, in a threshing machine accident caused by momentary inattention when he drew out his watch from his pocket and his sleeve caught in the machine. He was taken to the Radcliffe Infirmary Hospital, Oxford, by horse and cart. After this accident a metal cap and hook were fitted to his arm.

Henry's wife was Eliza who was previously married to a Mr Webb. There were two children of her second marriage, Bernard (1883-1965) and Albert.

Colonel William Gregory Dawkins did many oil paintings of young people living in the village. He painted Bernard as a young boy, in 1894, holding a half-eaten apple. Bernard told his son, Roy

Worvill, that he got very tired of posing for the picture and that he was given a golf ball to hold in the early stages.

Eliza Worvill was a Liberal. It is believed that Col. W.G. Dawkins was also. The two had a disagreement at one time and Col. Dawkins is reported as saying that Eliza ordered him out of her house – although he owned it!

A baptismal card shows that Eliza Worvill was baptised as an adult at Chipping Norton by the Revd. Ths Bently on June 30th 1881.

Bernard Charles Worvill went to school in Over Norton. At that time the school was held in the present (1999) St. James' Chapel building. He left school at eleven years of age and went to work for the Co-operative Society in the packing room and also in provisions. (The Co-op had an excellent delivery service to outlying villages – at first by horse-drawn vehicles.) Wilf Harrison (deceased) of Over Norton, brother of Mrs Doris Pashley, 'passed the scholarship' and went to Banbury School in 1924. He went on to train to be a teacher at St. Luke's College, Exeter, and taught at London and Reading.

Chipping Norton County School

Most girls going to the County School were proud to wear the school uniform. Mrs Alma Millard (née Joines) of Over Norton started there in 1939 and was proud to have hers. She had 'won a scholarship' to enable her to go. Full school uniform was worn at that time but it relaxed, just a little, as the war years ground on. By about the fourth year, girls began to rebel a little, and one student, having earned some money pea-picking, bought pink knickers instead of the regulation dark green. She was mortified when running round the sports field to find that the elastic in one leg had broken and a trail of pink began to show beneath the regulation tunic. This same student also bought brown suede, squared-toed shoes with orange stitching to emphasise the square look. They should have been 'sensible' black leather lace-ups. Another 'fashion enhancer' was to wear stockings inside out so that the seam up the back of the leg showed up strongly. Miss Jones, Senior Mistress, called frequent spot-check meetings to ensure uniform regulations were being obeyed. Hats – dark green felt in winter and panama with hat band in summer had to be worn in town and were quickly replaced or removed at the 30mph signs.

Boys wore grey trousers and a green blazer. School caps were worn by the younger boys.

War-time conditions presented many difficulties and the upshot was that very few students stayed on after taking the School Certificate Examination. There were perhaps two or three students in the sixth-form. Alma Joines, a very able girl from Over Norton, was one student who was asked to stay on – the only one as far as I know in 1944 – but her family were unable to allow this. Girls did not get the same chances as boys. Families often thought that girls would marry and their education would be wasted but that boys would need to be the bread earners. (What is more important than the mother's role? Why should it need less education?)

CHIPPING NORTON COUNTY SCHOOL
LIST OF CLOTHING FOR GIRLS IN 1936

A. COMPULSORY.   PRICES.
1. Two regulation school blouses. Summer or winter qualities.   S. Pale green tobralco blouses, 6s. each.
   W. Pale green winter blouses, 9/9d. each.
2. Dark green serge tunic of standard pattern.   24" 27" 30" 31" & above.
   16/6d. 17/6d. 18/6d. 19/6d.
3. School mohair girdle.   School colours, 1/6d. each.
4. Two pairs of green knickers to match tunic.   Green woven, 1/10d. per pair.
5. Black stockings, extra long.   3/6d. per pair.
6. Dark green felt hat.   6/6d. each.
7. Panama hat for summer.   White panama, round brim bound with green, 6/3d. each.
8. School hatband and badge.   2/9d. each.
9. School tie.   1/6d. each.
10. Black gymnasium shoes (Plimsolls).   )
11. Black low heeled slippers for wear during school hours.   ) These articles are not obtainable
) through the school.

B. DESIRABLE, BUT NOT COMPULSORY.
1. White knitted sweater for sports and gymnasium.   6s. to 7/6d. according to size.
2. Overcoat in good quality green velour cloth.   From 30s. according to size.
3. School Sports Blazer.   21s. each.
4. Scarves in school colours.   2/6d. each.
5. Regulation summer tunic.   27" - 32" 32" - 36"
   17/6d.   18/6d.

6.	Regulation Summer Dress in Green Tobralco.	11/6d. to 13/6d. according to size, knickers to match, extra 3/6d. to 4s. per pair.
7.	Overalls for certain lessons.	Not obtainable through the school.

C. PRICE OF MATERIALS AND PATTERNS.

1.	Blouse material.	Tobralco (Dyed specially) 1/9d. per yard Winter blouse material, 3s. per yard.
2.	Tunic material, 54" wide.	8/6d. per yard.
3.	Patterns, tunic and blouse.	Price 6d. each.
	Gymnastic tunic material (Sparva).	1/3d. per yard. Pattern for tunic obtainable at the school.

100/6/36/ [June 1936] [See Boarding School, Chapel House, chapter 4]

Now in January 2000 the primary stage of education (5 years to 11 years) for Over Norton's children is provided for by two schools in Chipping Norton. The Holy Trinity Roman Catholic Primary School in London Road, Head Teacher Jane Fetherstone, has five Over Norton children on roll. Janet Thornton is Head Teacher at St. Mary's Church of England School in The Green and there are nine Over Norton children there. Chipping Norton School, a comprehensive school, catering for eleven to eighteen-year-olds have eighteen children from this village – Head Teacher Richard Graydon. A few children are educated privately.

Bernard Aries has a happy memory of walking to school in Chipping Norton after the Over Norton School closed in 1933 when on St. Valentine's Day the children scrambled for sweets thrown to them by shopkeepers. When they heard the school bell ring they rushed off to school. Prior to this custom I am told that the shopkeepers used to throw hot pennies for the children.

An excellent range of adult courses is available (year 2000) through Chipping Norton Community Education Council – Mike Bardsley being head of this. Courses are held at Chipping Norton School and at the ACE Centre which includes the Computer Training Centre (junction Albion Street and Burford Road). In 1999 there were twenty-nine applications for courses from Over Norton inhabitants – a good response from a small village.

Over twenty clubs and societies are affiliated to the Community Education Council ensuring a good social life for the years to come for local inhabitants.

CHAPTER 11

Lest Ye Forget Those Of This Parish Who Fell During
The Great War 1914-1918 and During World War Two 1939- 1945

29552
Pte Lionel Benfield
2nd Batt. Royal Berkshire Regiment
Died of wounds 7th August 1917 Age 23
Buried in St Sever Cemetery Extension Rouen, France. Block P Plot 2 Row A Grave 1B

32762
Pte Philip Charles Benfield
6th Oxford & Bucks Light Infantry was killed in action 7th october 1916 Age 27
No known grave but is commemorated by name on the Thiepval Memorial, France. Pier 10 Faces A & D

[Number not available]
Bernard Cyril Benfield
Formerly of the Hampshire Regiment
Died of wounds at home May 1921 Age 21
Buried in Chipping Norton Cemetery 31st May 1921 Lionel, Philip and Bernard were the sons of Charles and Mary Benfield.

225421
Pte Frederick Thomas Clarke
'D' Coy 2nd/1st Batt. London Regiment Royal Fusiliers
Killed in action 29th December 1917 Age 20
Buried in Mendinghem Military Cemetery, Belgium. Plot 6 Row B.B. Grave 51

Pte Clarke was the son of Herbert and Mary Clarke of Over Norton.

277996
Pte Henry Harrison
5th Batt. Oxford & Bucks Light Infantry
Killed in action 3rd May 1917 Age 36
No known grave but is commemorated by name on the Arras Memorial, Fanbourg d'Amiens Cemetery, France. Panels 23 and 34

Pte Harrison was the husband of Laura Harrison and the son of George and Rhoda Harrison of Over Norton.

220270
Pte Frank Keen
8 Batt. Royal Berkshire Regiment Killed in action 23rd October 1918 Age 23
Buried in the Highland Cemetery, Le Cateau France. Plot 11 Row A Grave 13

9085
L/Cpl Joseph Henry Keen
1st Batt Oxford & Bucks Light Infantry
Died as a prisoner of war of the Turks on 6th August 1916 age 28 after being wounded at the siege of Kut.
Buried in the Baghdad (Northgate) War Cemetery, Iraq. Plot 21 Row D Grave 40

Pte Frank Keen and L/Cpl Joseph Keen were the sons of Joseph and Patience Keen of Over Norton.

14532
L/Cpl William Knight
2nd Batt. Oxford & Bucks Light Infantry
Killed at Arras May 1st 1918 Age 30
Buried in the Cabaret Rouge British Cemetery, Souchey, Belgium. Plot 8 Row Q Grave 4

L/Cpl William Knight was the husband of Annie Knight, the father of two daughters and the son of William and Rose Knight of Over Norton. [Grandfather of Richard Benfield]

8625
L/Cpl Ernest Margetts
2nd Batt. Glos Regiment
Died of wounds 11th July 1915 Age 25
Buried in Erquinghem-Lys Churchyard Extension, France. Plot 1 Row D Grave 4

L/Cpl Margetts was the son of Thomas and Eliza Margetts of Over Norton.

7169
Pte Frederick J Moulder
2nd Batt. Oxford & Bucks Light Infantry
Killed in action 31st October 1914 Age 33
No known grave but is commemorated by name on the Ypres (Menin Gate) Memorial, Belgium. Panels 37-39

Pte Moulder was the son of Henry and Sue Moulder of Over Norton, one of eight brothers who formed a brass band.

G/39081
Pte Ernest Sandles
7th Batt. Queens Royal West Surrey Regiment
Killed in action 10th August 1917 Age 20
No known grave but is commemorated by name on the Menin Gate Memorial, Belgium.
Panels 11, 13 and 14.

Pte Sandles was the son of George and Sarah Ann Sandles of Over Norton.

19189
Pte George Albert Saunders
3rd Batt. Coldstream Guards
Killed in action 15th September 1917 Age 19
Buried in the British Military Cemetery Mendinghem, Belgium. Plot 7 Row C Grave 3

Pte Saunders was the son of Albert and Lizzie Saunders of the Shop and Post Office, Over Norton.

19509
Pte Tom Trace
2nd Batt. Oxford & Bucks Light Infantry
Killed in Action 30th July 1916 Age 19
No known grave but is commemorated by name on the Thiepval Memorial, France. Pier 10 Faces A & D

Pte Trace was the son of the late Thomas Trace and Mrs Ruth Trace of Over Norton.

G/39394
Sgt Samuel James Webb
25th (Garrison/Service) Batt. The Middlesex Regiment
Died in Siberia 13th September 1918 Age 42
No known grave but is commemorated by name on the Vladivostock Memorial, Chukin Russian Naval Cemetery, Soviet Union and now on the Brookwood (Russia) Memorial.

Sgt Webb was the husband of Rose Hannah Webb of Bledington, the father of three children and the son of Thomas and Eliza Webb of Over Norton.

14266301
Gnr Philip Lionel Bernard Hiatt
8th Medium Regiment Royal Artillery Killed in action 8th May 1944 Age 20
Buried in The Imphal War Cemetery, India. Plot 6 Row F Grave 5

Gnr Hiatt was the son of Ernest and Linda Hiatt of Over Norton.
Gnr Philip Hiatt was the nephew of Privates Philip, Lionel and Bernard Benfield who were killed in the 1914-1918 War.

L/Cpl Ernest Margetts and Pte Tom Trace are not recorded on the Over Norton War Memorial.

[Information by courtesy of Chipping Norton Museum.]

CHAPTER 12

Village Memories of the Second World War and The Women's Institute from 1933

W.I. formed 1933—War-time—A.R.P.—Evacuees—L.D.V.
Home Guard—Food Rationing—War Work for Women—War memories from the Children (Tom and Dorothy Rudge, Don Cambray and Pat Randall, née Cambray)—American Forces—Gas Masks—W.I. Drama Productions—Electricity arrived.

Mrs V. Cambray and Mrs Bickford arranged a meeting to discuss the formation of a Women's Institute

> ... and so on 26th January 1933 there were twenty-four of us in the lovely garden-room at Cleevestones full of talk and enthusiasm and on the 16th February 1933 the inauguration meeting was held. We were very happy in the school for twelve months but then it was closed and sold. [K.V.C.]

The members were soon dealing with some very serious subjects; writing by July 1933, to Major Edmondson M.P. (Sandford St. Martin) urging him to do all in his power in connection with the passing of the bill against 'Trapping of Wild Birds'. In April 1939 they supported the O.F.W.I. resolution, that

> Education Authorities be asked to reduce the limit for providing transport of children to school from three miles to one mile.

It is one mile from Over Norton chapel to the old 'British Schools' in New Street, Chipping Norton, where Infant Children (age five years to seven years) were taught at one time. Transport for young children continued to be a problem and resulted in the O.N.P.C. writing to the Director of Education October 1957 asking if the school bus could be re-routed through the village especially in view of the fact that the hutments in 'The Park' would be closed within the next three months.

A reply in February 1958 promised that this should be so

to convey Infants to school in Chipping Norton.

In 1950,

the fifteen or so huts in the ex-Prisoner of War camp (Over Norton Park) were let by the West Oxfordshire District Council to various displaced persons for a few years. [C.J.D.]

In December 1937 when war was approaching, O.N.P.C. sent the names of men who would be prepared to act as wardens in the event of an air raid to the 'Air Raid Precautions Committee' Messrs W.J. Cambray (Firs Farm), H. Goodhart (Chapel House), E.J. Joines, W. Sheffield and W.L. Woolliams (Home Farm) volunteered.

Children in the school playgrounds were singing:

Underneath the spreading chestnut tree
Mr Chamberlain said to me
If you want to get your gas mask free
Join the blinking A.R.P
[This rhyme may have originated from an Arthur Askey programme]

N.B.: No other references to either of the two world wars 1914-1918 or 1939-1945 have been found in the O.N.P.C. records.

On 29th September 1938 at 2pm the Over Norton Women's Institute called an emergency meeting. The members were informed what their duties were considered to be by the Oxfordshire Federation,

in view of the fact that England was on the verge of war. [W.I. minutes]

A promise had been made to the Clerk of the Rural District Council that

... we would arrange for the billeting of as many London school children [evacuees] as possible. Mrs Marshall, Mrs Shepard, Mrs Pearman, Mrs Bennett, Mrs Smith and Mrs Sheffield each undertook an area [in the village] and Mrs Goodhart, Chapel House.

Their reports were handed in to Mr W. Cambray, the Billeting Officer. From other reports it seems that Mrs Cambray acted as Billeting Officer. These plans for evacuating children from the danger areas did not take place until September 1939. O.N.W.I. had made further plans in June 1939 when they

> decided to assist the Billeting Officer in the reception of evacuees by providing cocoa and biscuits in the Village Hall.

Mrs Goodhart promised to provide these commodities and Mrs Haigh, Mrs Pearman, Mrs Bennett, Mrs Harrison and Mrs Goodman were to undertake the work.

Evacuees arrived in the village the day before war broke out and

> By 3pm on that Saturday (2nd September 1939) all was ready at the Village Hall, but at 9pm we were still alone ... our centre had received the wrong train, and our contingent, instead of being twenty-five school children as scheduled, turned out to be sixteen mothers and twenty-one very small tots. Everybody rose to the occasion magnificently but it was no joke to find that where you were expecting a little boy or girl about the same age as your own Tom or Mary, to share his or her bedroom, you had a mother and two or three children to squeeze in goodness only knows where. Many candle-lit excursions were made to attics that night to unearth cots; somehow or another everybody was bedded down and the Billeting Officer, Mrs Cambray, returned to her well earned repose. But what a rude awakening she had in the morning. Early on, housewives fetched up on her doorstep with one and all the same story, 'That's a nice little woman we've got but she is going to have another baby soon and we cannot possibly keep her'. However, after a time they were sorted out and where necessary moved on to billets near their Nursing Homes and all was well. The next party, ten school children, fitted in quite happily. Also as time went on and the blitz really started in earnest, large family parties arrived unofficially and were absorbed.
>
> Of course, evacuation to a village like ours, in common with many more, was terribly difficult. All water has to be fetched from communal taps yards away from the cottages – there is only one room down and two or three up in most of them and worst snag of all, no sanitation. We have been brought up to accept as part of our normal scheme of things, a bucket, the contents of which have periodically to be given decent burial in the garden, but the Londoner had never imagined a land in which flush lavatories do not grow as it were on every tree, and they could never bring themselves to do anything in the way of officiating at these interments. However, after many –

and some bitter vicissitudes – we parted good friends and this summer [1965] several vaccies have reappeared in their old billets to spend a holiday – one lad of sixteen started work as a farm labourer which apparently was what he was always meant for but didn't know it until he got here. Lots of our local boys and girls have had lovely visits to London since the end of hostilities and have seen all the sights. [K.V.C.]

Cambrays accommodated twenty-five evacuees.

The Prime Minister, Mr Chamberlain, made a broadcast to the nation at 11.15am on September 3rd 1939:

> I am speaking to you from the Cabinet Room in 10 Downing Street. This morning the British Ambassador in Berlin handed the German Government a final Note stating that unless we heard from them by 11 o'clock that they were prepared at once to withdraw their troops from Poland, a state of war would exist between us. I have to tell you that no such undertaking has been received and that consequently this country is at war with Germany ...

The L.D.V. (Local Defence Volunteers) – or 'Look Duck and Vanish' as they were jokingly called – was set up in May 1940 following the fall of France and the evacuation of the forces from Dunkirk. The volunteers were unpaid, had no uniform but wore an arm band. By July this force was re-named the Home Guard and were provided with uniforms.

The first three men to join The Home Guard from Over Norton or it may have been the L.D.V., were Mr Rudge (Witts Farm), Mr Cambray (Firs Farm), and Mr Woolliams (Home Farm). Dorothy Rudge told me that her father, having heard the announcement on the radio collected the other two men on his way to report to the Chipping Norton Police Station – but they were premature as the duty constable knew nothing about it. When the Home Guard closed down uniforms were returned but it is said that very little was left to return of Mr Cambray's boots he having made good use of them on the farm.

> The Wardens had a very thin time of it to start with having no headquarters at all. The poor chaps congregated under what is locally known as 'The Shed', our village Houses of Parliament, which is actually nothing else but a roof supported by wooden pillars on to a cottage wall. ... they acquired a

sort of superior shed as official post where they enjoyed the comparative luxury of stove, lamp and chairs ... [K.V.C.]

I am not going to perpetuate the many humorous but sometimes derogatory stories which circulated about the Home Guard. It is understood that in difficult times humour helps to keep the spirits up but these men who gave great service to their country deserve respect and gratitude. They gave up an enormous amount of their lives often being on duty right through the night. The Over Norton men carried out a very difficult task described by Mrs K.V. Cambray in her book, 'War Records of Over Norton' when she wrote;

> Nobody will ever forget that ghastly morning when a bomber and a trainer plane collided in mid-air and hurtled to earth a mile away from our sleeping homes. Pieces of planes and engines rained down in our gardens, the Home Guard spent the morning searching the fields, some of them so very young, in a few years to see death in many parts of the world saw it for the first time in their lives that morning.

A plaque has recently been placed in Church Street, Chipping Norton in memory of the eight airmen who died.

Over Norton's Home Guard was called to cover duties in Chipping Norton. One night they guarded a crashed Spitfire which was on display to prevent 'souvenir pieces' being removed. This exhibition was probably part of the launch of the 'Spitfire Fund' in October 1940. Many war fund-raising weeks were held in Chipping Norton.

During food rationing families had to register with a particular shop. The shop assistants cut coupons from the customers' ration books. Food rationing began in January 1940 first with bacon 4oz, butter 4oz and sugar 12 oz. By March meat was rationed not by weight but by price. At one time each person was allowed 1s.2d. worth per week. July saw tea (2 oz) and later cooking fats (6 oz), jam (2 oz - 4 oz) and cheese (10 oz to 8 oz) curtailed. At one time eggs were rationed to one per fortnight but if living in the countryside this caused no hardship. Dried egg powder was on sale. A points system operated giving a little flexibility to the shopper. These could be used for example if tins of fruit or spam etc. became available.

The Rudges war-time food bill (1944) from the International Stores Ltd, 17 Market Place, Chipping Norton, tells quite a story (see illustration). Notice that four people were registered – i.e. Mr & Mrs Rudge, Dorothy and Tom. At the top of the bill: 25 points owing. Several items were unavailable: matches, bottle sauce, cornflour and toilet roll. Candles were listed at 2¼d – a reminder that there was no electricity available and that farthings (four to a penny) were still a useful coin in our currency.

The three Cambray children quarrelled over their food allowances so their mother provided each one with their own rations. Arguments ceased but bartering went on! (Source: Don Cambray and Pat Randall (née Cambray)). Some food rationing continued after the war into the 1950s. A student in a London Teachers' Training College 1946-48 recalls having to provide a tin in which to store her individual rationed goods and this was taken to the dining hall at meal times. For a newly married couple in 1951 their meat ration for a week consisted of two lamb chops!

The Women's Institute movement did a great deal to ensure that all members were aware of how to feed their families a healthy diet even during war time. It is believed that the war-time diet produced healthier people and improved the diet of the formerly disadvantaged groups.

Mr Fred Burbidge, in October 1939, gave a talk to the O.N.W.I. on 'War-time Gardening'. (W.I. Minutes) This subject was taken up by many subsequent speakers throughout the war years. The growing and preservation of food was high on the agenda at all times with bottling and canning (led by Mrs Joines) and jam making. At least five W.I. members promised to attend a canning class in July 1947. At the beginning of the war in September 1939,

> It was decided to try and obtain 1 cwt of sugar (112 lbs) from the N.F.W.I. for preserving.

The members were encouraged to pass on surplus crops

> ... surplus fruit should be taken to Chipping Norton jam centre... [W.I. Minutes April '42]

Honey was in demand as a sweetening agent and a 'Bee Club' was formed – the bees were installed at Cleevestones. Members were to buy one shilling shares. (May 1940) This club did not flourish as the bees disappeared. [K.V.C.]

Gifts of food arrived from Australia and in May 1947 'Queensland Country Women's Association' sent a tin of honey. Earlier in June 1946 a box of groceries was received from them.

Continuing on the food theme Mrs Goodhart described South African sheep and ostrich farming, Mrs Joines took charge of the 'Government Pie Scheme' and in November 1940 Mr J.E. Sims gave a talk on 'How to Feed and Care for Rabbits' including the uses to which their pelts could be put. Many people 'farmed' rabbits in barns and chicken houses partly to support their diet but mainly for extra income. Country people had always made use of the wild rabbits which could be poached or purchased from local men – at half-a-crown each in 1949. Many women made rabbit-fur-backed mittens in the war years. February 1942;

> ...demonstration in Glove Making ... everyone keen to save [clothing] coupons.

Clothes were rationed in 1941 and sixty-six coupons a year were allocated. This was not entirely due to a shortage of fabrics but because the government wanted to divert the textile workers, many of whom were women, to war work. (Quotes are from W.I. Minutes)

Many women were employed in local factories. Mrs Pashley, along with Mrs Edna Benfield and Miss Jean Worvill from Over Norton, worked at Rowells factory, which was situated in Albion Street, Chipping Norton, opposite the new Co-operative Super Market. This factory was separate from the Rowell's Foundry. At the factory the girls put threads on shell cases. The components were delivered in a rough state and had to be finished. Some workers were making sockets and weights for sea mines. At times the workers were not told exactly what it was that they were working on. There were three working shifts covering all night and day: 6am to 2pm, 2pm to 10pm and 10pm to 6am. On asking Mrs Pashley what it was like getting up so early in the winter months she replied,

> I used to go and give my friend Jean Worvill a call. She lived up Choicehill Road. I got the primus stove going and then she came down and had a cup of tea with me before setting out at twenty-five to six (am). We collected Edna Benfield on the way. There was a canteen at work. We were provided with overalls.

In replying to my comment that they must have been exhausted working until 10pm she replied,

> Not too tired to go to the R.A.F. dances along the Chadlington road.

During this period of her life Mrs Pashley was keeping house for her brother Oliver. I have heard of one girl who travelled to Oxford to work in a factory.

Three girls of the village joined the Land Army. Mrs Kathleen Allen (née Bennett) told me that some girls had to leave working at the Tweed Mill and join the forces so she with one other Over Norton girl joined the Land Army and were posted to Curbridge. After serving for approximately two years she was allowed to leave on marrying. Mrs Allen, when young, lived in Paynes Yard just off Choicehill Road.

There was no electricity in Over Norton until 1946 so...

> ... a demonstration (Nov 1942) of Hay-box cookery proving what a saver of fuel this method of cooking can be ...

...would have been popular.

> Hay-box cookery is a form of 'fuel less' cookery. For example, a casserole dish would be partially cooked in an oven and then transferred to a nest in the hay-box to finish cooking. The box was well insulated with hay, cork shavings, newspapers and flannel fabric. During the Second World War people were encouraged to revive this old method of cooking to save fuel. It was estimated that it would reduce fuel consumption by at least a half. (Source, oral, from Jane Runacres)

The W.I. tackled many worthwhile undertakings:

> 14 March 1940
> ... It was decided unanimously to form a National Savings Group. Members agreed to let non-members join ...

These groups were actively encouraged by the government when collectors went round house to house to sell National Savings stamps. Schools took part too.

The members viewed a

> ... very interesting film entitled "Salvage."

All paper, tins and bones were collected for the war effort. A child collecting salvage in a nearby village was given a badge to wear. It was red in colour and formed in the shape of a cog to show that the collectors were part of a greater war effort machine.

Mrs Pat Randall (née Cambray):

> I went round the village collecting salvage – probably once a month. I was in charge of the pony and the four-wheeled trolley which it pulled. My father had made this out of the chassis of an Austin Seven. My helpers went collecting house to house. [See illustration]

Knitted articles were provided for European People in July 1944. O.N.W.I. had a sale in October 1944 to provide Christmas gifts for 'Men and Women of the Forces'. It was recorded in August 1945 that the

> Members unanimous in their wish that any women of the village discharged from their war work should be invited to our Christmas Party.

Tom Rudge, a very young boy at the beginning of the war and his sister Dorothy have vivid memories of the main part of their home, Witts Farm, being commandeered by a party of guardsmen. One night Mrs Rudge, on answering the door, was confronted with,

> 'We wish to take over your house for forces accommodation'.
>
> She replied, 'I'll have to ask my husband'.
>
> 'No need, Madam, we have the authority to do it',

and so the Rudge family were squashed into the back of the house and the army took over all other rooms, including the kitchen. Tom believes the 'party' included Lord Denbigh, plus six or eight officers and their batmen. The Rudge family were provided with meals.

The Guards at this time also requisitioned the old wooden village hall and were described by Mrs K.V. Cambray as follows:

> When our W.I. Banner was made and embroidered with care, little did we dream that one day it would have military honours. One memorable weekend a detachment of Coldstream Guards descended upon the village and demanded billets, among others, the Village Hall, and it was arranged that all our precious effects should be moved during this hectic tenancy. The men attacked the job in the right spirit, and great was our delight to see our banner waving gaily along the street borne by a hefty Guardsman and accompanied by Colour Party with perfectly serious faces and marching as only the Guards know how. [Depicted on the W.I. wall-hanging made in 1997]
>
> Our little wooden Hall had several [interesting] lots of tenants during these few years, [including] the Church Lads' Brigade from Hendon who had their living and being there for a fortnight, working on the local farms and generally enlivening the neighbourhood. [See photograph]
>
> Then for several days there was a most intriguing party in occupation – military, very hush hush and important. Nobody knew anything about their doings except the caretaker, Mrs Joines, and that was only that they were a radio unit of some species. Mrs J., who can never resist doing a bit of mothering on the side, did some cooking for them and was very touched when clearing up afterwards to find a hoard of their egg shells neatly autographed 'Mother J. bless her cotton socks' and so on for each member of the family.

Tom Rudge recalls that there was a searchlight battery on high ground beyond Sandfields Farm, with 'dug-outs the Rollright side of Pearman's'. (Sandfields Farm) The Captain in charge, and his wife, lodged with Rudge's for about a year. His batman, named Bunker, lived at the searchlight site. Dances were held in the hut there – just to the right of the Great Rollright road. Wives of pilots stationed at Chipping Norton aerodrome also stayed at Witts Farm and the wife and children of a man called Ottewell– 'a high-up' were there too. Some interesting people stayed at the beginning of the war, including Leonard Busfield believed to be lead violinist of the BBC orchestra, whose wife had a permanent room there; the leader of the orchestra also stayed. At times as many as twenty guests were in the Witts Farm dining room. Mrs Aries helped Mrs Rudge with domestic duties. There was only one toilet in the house but chamber pots were provided under the beds!

I'm told that in early summer 1940 hundreds of soldiers back from Dunkirk – the Durham Light Infantry – were discharged from the trains at Chipping Norton to spend time in this area to recuperate. Mrs Pat Randall (née Cambray) has a very clear memory of seeing the soldiers resting in Chipping Norton and was very touched by the incident when a soldier gave her a penny as she was going to school. Just pre-war one could buy four chocolate toffees for a penny or a packet of broken crisps; she thought it was very generous as these men had lost all of their personal belongings in France. Don Cambray as a small child remembers sixteen soldiers sleeping in their barn at Firs Farm and also many being accommodated in the Coach House at Over Norton House and Kings House. Tom Rudge talks about the hay-making that year and how the soldiers were around chatting to the farm workers. A soldier made Don a wooden rifle and one gave him a 'bugle' badge from a forage cap.

November 1946 saw what now seems a peculiar request

> ... a letter from the Alexandria Musical Society [to W.I.] asking for gifts of cigarettes and other comforts for hospital patients at Christmas. Resolved that each member bring a small donation of cigarettes to the meeting...

More understandable is

> ... all members promised to bring at least 1 oz margarine to next meeting, with other commodities if possible ...towards a cake for the Christmas party.

Soap had been rationed but in January 1948...

> ... Mrs Buckingham a lucky winner of a cake of soap . [W.I. Minutes]

> ... The hours we spent knitting, biking to Chipping Norton to stand heated hours behind the counter of the British Restaurant, lacerating our fingers on camouflage netting, and the hours we spent preparing for the things that mercifully did not happen – fitting gas masks, attending First Aid and Anti-Gas courses, making beaters ready for fires in the corn, the dawn to dusk patrol of the L.D.V., the chilly watches the Wardens kept – all for the things that did not happen ... [K.V.C.]

Dorothy Rudge and Pat Randall (née Cambray), when school girls, spent time rolling bandages and sprinkling white power on them.

They think that the bandages, three to four inches wide were cut from old sheets. It is thought that the powder was plaster of Paris which when wetted was used to support broken bones. The Red Cross organised this work through the leadership of Miss Griffin, Head Teacher of the Girls C.E. School; the work was carried out at Chipping Norton Hospital.

The American Forces billeted in Over Norton Park caused a few difficulties but

> ... the youth and beauty of the village had plenty of cinema and dance dates ... [K.V.C.]

One very major problem occurred when they polluted the Over Norton Village water supply. Important looking notices were put up to say that 'all water must be boiled before drinking'...

> The old inhabitants however knew of a spring on the opposite and therefore untainted bank, whence we would wend our weary way with buckets, day after day, until the position was satisfactory. This was all very nice for the folks living near, but for those at the farthest end of the village it wasn't so funny. The water ran from a pipe in a stream not as big as one's little finger, so there we would queue, smoking, knitting, gossiping, young and old, rich and poor, reduced to a common level by our urgent need, the whole thing taking the flavour of the old village pump at its best ... [K.V.C.]
> [See illustration]

Gas Masks

Everyone was fitted with a gas mask. You were supposed to have them with you at all times and they were carried in brown cardboard boxes held across the chest with a strap. Ones for babies were made so that the child was put inside and so was completely covered; when in use an adult had to keep foot pumping to guarantee an air supply. In schools gas mask drills were held when the form teacher would check the fit of the gas masks by placing a piece of card over the bottom of the gas mask. The result desired was that the whole 'snout' should be sucked up towards the chin showing that no air was getting in except through the filter. Now it has been discovered that asbestos was used in the filter!

Those residents who were children during the war seem to think that their gas masks were issued to them at school, although their

Chapel House Hotel (now Chapel Farm House with top storey removed).

The timber yard – an early photograph taken by Sam Moulder.

1930 Four Over Norton boys in Over Norton village. L/R Bill Hemmings, Frank Sheffield (Douglas' brother), Fred Moulder, Fred Harrison (Mrs D. Pashley's brother). The three-wheeler was constructed by Fred Moulder. (Courtesy of Mr E. Jones.)

Gentlemen of the village. (Date and names unknown)

Photograph by Sam Moulder before Nos.1-4 The Green were built. Taken from the garden of Firs Farm.

Mothers and Sons 2nd May 1921 in the centre of Over Norton village.

The Fete at Over Norton Park probably 1928.

The Old Shed Meeting Place bottom of Choicehill Road.

Over Norton Park about 1935 L/R Mrs Shepherd, Mrs Joines, Alma Joines, Mrs Goodman and daughter-in-law Beryl Goodman.

The Boys' Brigade with centre L/R Mr Woolliams, Mrs Joines, Mr Cambray, Mr Rudge.

1st Over Norton Cubs showing their shield and certificates. Back Row left to right: Philip O'Neil, Andrew Thompson, Tom Dunn, Patrick Nolan, Leslie Harris, Richard Benfield, Ian Mackenzie, Robert Moulder.
Front Row Martin Moulder, David Moulder, James Thompson, Christopher Nolan, David Mackenzie. Scoutmaster Mr Jackson.

At No.7 Main Street about 1951. L to R: Margaret Evans, Pat Orme with brother David.

The Old Shed meeting place or Over Norton Town Hall L/R Francis Worvill, Tom Rudge, Arthur Worvill.

The Timber Yard. L/R Cyril Clifton, Jack Harrison, David Pearman. (Courtesy of Mr F. Moulder.)

Rick building at Witts Farm Left George Harrison, Mr Harrison on rick, Mr Rudge standing.

Witts Farm Tom Rudge on Fordson tractor, Dorothy Rudge operating Albion binder.

Witts Farm Dorothy Rudge tractoring. (A Fordson tractor was bought from Fitts in 1942 and replaced in 1944. A Fordson Major tractor was purchased in 1946.)

Cleeves Corner. (Photo by courtesy of Ron Stares) L to R: Janice Worvill Terry Warner Steven Moulder Stephen Warner Mark Roughton (Warner's Dog, Judy)

Phyllis & David Pearman on their wedding day 1947. The Larches, Salford.

Chapel House Crossroads   The Steps entrance to Over Norton Park.

The Castle Banks, Chipping Norton.

The Fountain – a woman going to fill her kettle.

Over Norton Road, Chipping Norton.

memories are very hazy. Richard Woolliams is sure that he was fitted for his gas mask at Cleevestones by Major Haig. Mrs K.V. Cambray writes about the fitting of gas masks by the Head Warden when,

> ... after one or two frenzied tussles with luxurious buns and complexities of pins ... he left the female members of his entourage to cope ...

Memories of the few times spent in concrete air raid shelters at the County School have not faded. These shelters were built at the edge of the playing field running parallel with the lane leading to Glyme Farm. Some recesses had hessian curtains, perhaps covering toilet facilities. All school windows were given protection by either having small mesh wire battened with wooden bars over them or by gummed brown paper strips stuck on them. Some of this work was carried out by senior boy pupils. Charlbury school sent a small group to cover the windows with wire at Enstone, Spelsbury and Kiddington schools. They were driven out to them by Mr Osborn, the Headmaster, and left to get on with the job. At Kiddington during their dinner break they were tempted to go fishing in the little river Glyme. Having caught a six pound pike they thought the wisest thing to do with it would be to hide it in a tree. At the share out it was cut into three pieces of equal length but the head section was not a very good bargain!

The end of the war came in 1945, Winston Churchill announced victory in Europe on the 8th May and V.E. (Victory Europe) Day was celebrated on 9th May and V.J. Day (Victory in Japan) announced 14th August and celebrated 15th August.

From the O.N.W.I. Minutes:
May 16th 1946 Outing suggestions were received for the Victory Parade:

> Whipsnade [Zoo] and the sea-side

but the celebratory outing was in fact a River Trip (Oxford) in August. The outing to Whipsnade Zoo took place in July 1947 and

... was very much enjoyed by all, the weather being glorious.

Don Cambray remembers going on this trip.

Over Norton W.I. always had lots of fun times and were very good at drama putting on many plays after the war, which they performed in local villages.

MRS JARLEY'S WAXWORKS – This started in a small way written and produced by Mrs K Cambray as entertainment for a group meeting but it gathered momentum and showed in fourteen villages and the Norton Hall, Chipping Norton. Some of the players and all of the props packed into a Vauxhall van and Mrs Pashley nearly lost an ear when the driver had to brake hard at the Hospital corner and a pole went through the window. An out-of-doors performance at Little Compton was found unwise as midges nearly upset the immobility of the waxworks, as did a cat at Swerford who rubbed round their ankles. Nell Gwyn created a diversion once by fainting just before the curtain went up. We'd had a long wait in a cold dressing-room and she had laced her pregnant self too tightly into her costume. [K.V.C.]

REDHOT CINDERS – A private effort for our Christmas Party when Mrs Joines ran herself up a little thing in muslin and tinsel as the Fairy Godmother, not letting anybody forget that she had left off her long sleeved winter vest for the occasion. Mrs Tait was much too attractive as an Ugly Sister but the Producer made a last minute grab and she went on with a red nose whether she liked it or not. [K.V.C.]

MY HORNBOOK AND MY TOP – Oxfordshire Rural C.C. Festival. We thought we had chosen a good play and quite a poetical one but were a bit deflated at hearing the dialogue referred to by the adjudicator as "pseudo Elizabethan". Although the author was to blame for this we were in the wrong for choosing it but the production and acting were praised. Much amusement and interest was had from making costumes, entailing drawings from Mrs Goshawk, books from the Library and a visit to a tomb in Chipping Norton church. At the beginning of rehearsals for this production Mrs Adams retired owing to an impending happy event and the next play we started Mrs Bignall was unable to perform for the same reason. As this one was to have featured flowing Greek draperies we did wonder whether she could get away with it, but it was decided not. "Even unto the next generation", Producer Cambray started being busy with grandchildren and apparently owing to this startling rise in the birth rate, the Drama Group folded up and has not been seen alive since. [K.V.C.]

Mr Richard and Mrs Peggy Adams with daughter Rosalynd and son Nigel came to Over Norton in 1957. Peggy was immediately pressed to join the W.I. drama group by Kathleen Cambray as one member had withdrawn from the current production. This was the beginning of a long association with O.N.W.I. for Peggy. For many years she made a tremendous lively contribution to all aspects of the W.I., both at village and county level. She still does so (1999) at another local village and she is part of the county team who organise W.I. holidays both in England and on the continent. She was president of O.N.W.I. for many years. Her daughter Rosalynd Garrod is mentioned in the schools' chapter. Richard Adams and Nigel's association with the village is covered under farming. The Adams family moved in December 1958 from their temporary home in the village – No. 37 attached to Cleevestones – to Hit or Miss Farm, Chipping Norton. Aldwyn, the Adams' second son was born there.

Richard Benfield, writing from the U.S.A. after the death of his mother in 1995, expressed very clearly the great value of the opportunities provided by Over Norton's Women's Institute:

> ... As we all know she was the last surviving founder member of the Over Norton W.I.; a fact in which she took great pride. She commented many times just how much the organization had provided for her during the times when, as a family, we had little money, no car and hence a very small geographical area in which to function. The W.I. ... gave her both warm intimate friendships but also a worldly view ... She was eternally grateful and so am I ...

Electricity

Mrs Cambray:

> We were practically blacked out before the war with every cottage window only showing a faint glow from an oil lamp behind cozy winter curtains.

Oil lamps had been used since 1860 and it was almost a hundred years before all Over Norton people owned an electric reading lamp. (Paraffin oil was discovered about 1820.)

The O.N.W.I. had been trying since 1933 to get electricity to Over Norton, first by sending a delegate, Mrs Goodhart, to a meeting on the subject of 'Electricity for the Villages' as early as October 1933.

This was followed by a resolution sent to government by O.N.W.I. in April 1936 which urged

> the extending of the Electric Grid to all villages ... where a local electricity company holds out against the grid it should be obliged to render the same service at the same prices as the grid charges ...

Records of O.N.P.C. include in November 1945:

> A letter was read from the Village Hall Committee asking the Parish Council ... to induce the Wessex Electricity Company to arrange for a supply of current in the village and suggesting the Council might take a census of those who would make use of the current when available.

A reply from the Wessex Company stated that

> a scheme had been prepared ...

but they were unable to say when it would be in operation.

Over Norton residents eventually had the opportunity to be connected to a supply. Four local farmers, Mr Rudge, Mr Woolliams, Mr Cambray and Major Campbell, had to guarantee to use £50s worth a year. Witts Farm had one central light and one socket installed in each room. It is believed that electricity had been carried across to the American Forces when they occupied Over Norton Park.

By March 1949 O.N.P.C. was authorized to

> spend up to £30 in the ensuing twelve months for the purpose of providing public lighting

and in July 1949 'The Board' (S.E.B.) agreed to install three lamps for £40. By September 1964 an estimate of £168 4s.1d. was given for providing four street lights at Over Norton Hill when 'full agreement' to this was given.

From the first discussions in 1945 up to March 1967 there are at least twenty-eight recorded minutes (O.N.P.C.) to do with street lighting.

CHAPTER 13

Occupations 1841 to 1891

Gloving Industry—Bliss's Mill, Chipping Norton. Other occupations 1841 to 1891 from Census Returns.

Glove making has been an important part of the economy in West Oxfordshire throughout many centuries. Woodstock, the surrounding villages and Charlbury, have played an important part in its development. Many women found working in the gloving industry in their own homes provided a very useful income.

Benjamin Bowen from Worcester introduced the gloving industry to Chipping Norton in 1825. Members of the Bowen family are listed in the 1841 Over Norton census return as follows:

John Bowen	40	Glove Manufacturer		Not born in Oxon
Selina (wife)	30			" " "
Constance Bowen	19			" " "
John	"	15		" " "
Charles	"	7		Born in Oxon
Louisa	"	5		" " "
Alfred	"	4		" " "
James	"	2		" " "
Walter	"	7 months		" " "

As the relation to the Head of the family was not given in the Census 1841 we can surmise that Constance Bowen and John age 15 were John Bowen's brother and sister or cousins and that the children, from Charles downwards, all born in Oxfordshire, are John and Selina Bowen's children.

John Bowen compiled the 1851 census and he began it by explaining the areas which made up Over Norton Parish:

> The whole of the Hamlet of Over Norton including Chapel House, Priory Farm, Priory Mill, Hull Farm, Choicehill Farm and the village of Over

Norton. Also Taylors Cottage in the cleering [as written] and the Cottages at the New Barns in Mr Coldicott's Grounds.

There were ninety-one houses listed and John Bowen placed his family at the end of the census. They were living at Colbornes Cottage. (Colbornes Farm was 160 acres and farmed by Mr William Phillips). He described himself as a Glove Manufacturer from Worcester St. Swithins, employing 6 men 140 women 40 girls and 2 boys.

Living in his household in 1851 were:

				Where Born
John Bowen		49		Worcester St. Swithins
Selina Bowen	Wife	39		Hadson
Louisa Bowen	Daughter	15	Milliners Asst.	Over Norton
Alfred "	Son	14	Scholar	" "
James Henry "	Son	11	"	" "
Walter "	Son	10	"	" "
Selina "	Daughter	7	"	" "
Louis "	Son	5	"	" "
Elizabeth "	Daughter	4	"	" "
Agnes "	"	1	"	" "
Taylor Emma	SV	16	General Servant	GLS Oddington
Gibbs Elizabeth	SV	13	Nurse Maid	Over Norton

Constance, John (15 in 1841) and Charles were no longer with the family.

An 1852 directory clearly states that at Over or Upper Norton

> .. in the village is the glove factory of Mr John Bowen, in which about 200 hands are employed ...

and under Chipping Norton

> ... A considerable quantity of gloves are still made here by the Messrs. Bowen ...

Under Glove Manufacturers are listed just two names: Bowen Benjamin and John Bowen (marked to indicate he lived at Over Norton).

John Bowen and his family were not listed as living in Over Norton in subsequent years, except for his son Walter, who in 1861, was living in 'Chapel Villa' at Chapel House.

The entry is as follows:

				Where Born
Walter Bowen		20	Commercial Traveller Glove Department	Over Norton
Anne Marie Bowen	Wife	25	Milliner	War. Leamington
Theresa Bowen	Dghter	1		Chipping Norton
Cornelius Hey	Boarder	25	Officer from Ireland Revenue (Excise)	Ireland

1851 - Living at a separate address from John Bowen there was:

				Where Born
George Bowen		32	Glover	Worcester St. Johns
Sarah "	Wife	34		Oxf Long Coomb
George	Son	8	Scholar	" " "
William	Son	5	Scholar	Over Norton

[As the last child was born at Over Norton they must have moved to Over Norton approximately 1843 to 1846.]

1861 - George Bowen's family were still in Over Norton but he had remarried:

Glove Manufactory				Where Born
George Thos Bowen		42	Employing 2 men and one boy	Worcester
Anne	" Wife	49	Glover's Wife	Oxon Gt Rollright
George	" Son	18	Glover's son	Oxon Long Coombe
William	" Son	16	" "	Over Norton
Joseph	" Son	9	Scholar	" "
Mary	" Dghter	5	"	" "
Sarah Mitchell	SV	16	General House Servant	Oxon Spelsbury

1871

				Where Born
George Thos Bowen		52	Glove Manufacturer employing nine men and two boys	Worc. St. Johns
Emily	Wife	45		London Stoke Newington

231

Mary	Dghter	15		Over Norton
Lucilla ?	SV	17		Oxon Swerford

[Emily appears to have been George's third wife. Her birthplace is given as three different locations in 1871, 1881 and 1891.]

1881 [95 households]
Main Road Over Norton
Glovers Hall

				Where Born
George T Bowen		62	Glove Manufacturer	Worcester
Emily L "	Wife	55		Mid. London
Sullivan Bridget	SV	17		Gla. Cardiff

This address is believed to be Glovers Close [1999] opposite Witts House [formerly Witts Farm].

The small cottage No. 8 Main Street set back into the ground belonging to Glovers Close with separate access (see road 1770 map) was, according to oral sources used as a workshop for the glove trade. Mrs Harris, (George Harris' mother) formerly of The Post Office, Over Norton, told the present owner of Glovers Close that she remembered going there to the gloving premises where her mother was working at the turn of the century.

1891

				Where Born
George Thos Bowen			72 Glove Manufacturer	Wor. St. Johns
Emily Lydia "	Wife	64		London Hackney
Eleanor Mary Elizabeth	Visitor	?		Hanley Staffs
Anne Elizabeth ?Keen	SV	22 Domestic Servan		Lydney Glos

George Bowen died 27 December 1895 and at that time had been living at 30 Pembroke Street, Cowley Road, Oxford.

By 1851 a family – name Chetwins – had come from St. Peter's Worcester and seven of them were working in the gloving industry.

Stephen Chetwin		47	Glover Cutter
Mary Ann "	Wife	48	Gloveress
Edward Stephen Chetwin	Son (m)	26	Glove Cutter
Mary Ann "	D/Law	30	Gloveress
John "	Son	18	Glove Cutter
Mary "	Daughter	15	Gloveress
Ephraim "	Son	14	Glover's Apprentice
Anna Matilda "	Daughter	8	Scholar
Mary Ann "	G/daughter	1	

Henry Talbot, Lodger, 41 years, Glove Cutter also from St. Peters Worcester was living at the public house, the Horse and Groom. The victualler at this time was George Payne age 36 years from North Aston. It is believed by Mr C.J. Dawkins that No. 40 The Green was a public house so that seems to rule out the suggestion that Bowens had a warehouse there for glove making. (see Chapter 2) It is possible that present day No. 50 was used as No. 40 and No. 50 are thought to have been one building.

In 1851 four women were working as gloveresses, the youngest being twelve and there was one man listed as a 'glove leather parer'. In 1861 Thomas Simms aged 17 years was described as a 'skin grounder'.

Number of Over Norton's Inhabitants Engaged in the Glove Industry

1841	1851	1861	1871	1881	1891
None	12	8	8	10	8

These figures do not include the Bowen family as they were employers. Of the eight employed in 1861 six were gloveresses.

The most important workers were the cutters. Two other processes were carried out by leather parers and leather grounders. The parers had to reduce all parts of the skin to an equal thickness and this was done by using a circular paring knife the centre of which was cut away and its wooden handle was fixed across this. The leather was held in a 'perch' over a horizontal pole and the parer's left hand kept the leather taut whilst he cut away some of the flesh side. The grounding process was very much like paring except that it was done with an emery covered crescent shaped piece of wood and was used to smooth the surface of the back of the leather. It is not known at what date these tools were first used. (*Glovemaking in West Oxfordshire*, by N.L. Leyland and J.E. Troughton. Oxford City and County Museum Publication No.4) Dennis Lewis, in his booklet *Distons Lane Chipping Norton* (1993) (Pub. Chipping Norton Local History Society and obtainable from Chipping Norton Museum) writes that during his boyhood when he was watching the men working in the tan-yard ...

> One man ... was engaged in stripping the fat from skins. They were spread over a piece of marble and pared with a very sharp knife. Every now and then he would cut off a piece of fat and eat it ...

In St. Mary's Church baptismal records a Joseph Baldwin was baptised on 8th February 1824 son of William and Sarah Baldwin – father a shoe-maker – and earlier on 22nd October 1815 John Baldwin, son of William Baldwin Cordwiner (sic) and Sarah was baptised. In the 1851 census William Baldwin aged 61, born in Little Compton, with a wife named Sarah, born in Over Norton, was listed as a Pauper Cordwainer. There were seven other people listed as paupers. The use of the term 'pauper' was later banned from use.

Bliss Tweed Mill, Chipping Norton

My 1852 Directory informs me that:

> The manufacture of woollen girths and horse cloths, and of press bagging for oil crushers, as well of that of tweeds and ladies cloaking and shawls, are still carried on here by Mr William Bliss, who gives permanent employment to about 150 persons. The ancestor of Mr Bliss was the sole inventor of that most durable of all materials for 'trowsering' [as written]   tweed.

People from Over Norton were being employed at Bliss' Mill by 1861 – there were none recorded in 1851.

The Number of Over Norton's Inhabitants working at William Bliss' Tweed Mill

	Tweed Burler	Weaver	Labourer	Spinner	Dyer	Total
1861	6	3	1	0	0	10
1871	4	6	0	1	1	12
1881	1	5	2	2	2	16

(a feeder to weaver, a piecer, a warper and a tweed knotter)

| 1891 | 0 | 7 | 1 | 2 | 1 | 15 |

(plus a feeder, a winder, a shawl fringer and a shawl huckster (seller))
[Burler: a dresser of cloth]

The labour force at Bliss Mill was increased from eleven in 1839 to over a hundred in 1879 – this is reflected in the 1881 figures for Over Norton.

The Lower mill had been destroyed by fire in 1872 but not one worker lost his job. It was rebuilt within a year.

William Bliss II died in 1884 but his son William III was unable to keep financial control within the family. By 1895 it became a limited company. The mill closed in 1980. (See conversations: Mr Harry Barnes, Mrs Cook and Mrs Nolan — chapter 9 and Mrs Allen — chapter 12.)

Census 1841. Occupations of Over Norton Residents excluding Farming, Gloving or working at the Tweed Mill.

Baker, Blacksmiths (2), Cabinet Maker Apprentice, Carpenters (2), Exciseman (from Ireland), Hostler (living over stables at Chapel House), Millers (2 water mill), Postman, Postboy (living over stables Chapel House), Shoe Makers (3), Slater, Stone Mason, Tailors (5), Turnpike Gatekeeper (John Jacques), Victualler (John Purnell). Total 23 men.

John Kendall is listed as a shoemaker in 1841 but as a cordwainer (one word) in 1851. In 1861 William Worville is listed as a Cord Wainer (written as two words). (Nuttalls (1919) Dictionary: cordwainer (one word) = a worker in cordwain; a shoemaker.

Cordwain: Spanish leather; a goat-skin tanned and dressed.)

Lists follow of other employment featured for the first time.

1851 Dressmakers (4), Sempstress (1), Laundress (1), Roadman (1), Shopkeeper (1), Shoe Binders (3) (All young girls: Emma Betteridge 16 years, Hannah Marshall 17 years and Lucy Betteridge 14 years); sock-weaver (Sarah Marshall 15 years).

1861 Female Toll-gate keeper age 23 years, Straw Bonnet Maker (Esther Sellars) who had moved to Chapel House from Hertfordshire, Milliner (1).

1871 Beerhouse keeper (George Payne age 55), A Bill Sticker, Coachman, Dentist, Pharmaceutical Chemist (Richard Hopgood), Engine Feeder at Factory, Grocer (2) plus one man employed, Portable engine-driver, Shoeing smith, Wheelwright.

1881 General Dealer, 'Minds house' (Esther Jarvis age 12 years), Shop-keeper (Elizabeth Smith, Chapel House)

Domestic Servants
1841 Over Norton Parish
In 1841 there were 32 people employed as domestic servants – 22 female and 10 males. There were seven farmers employing 17 of them and the rest were as follows: (F.S. = Female Servant, M.S. = Male Servant)
   Baker 1 F.S., Blacksmith 1 F.S., Victualler 1 F.S. and 1 M. S., Miller 1 F.S. and 1 M.S.
   Three people of independent means:
   Ann Beck, Chapel House, employed 2 F.S.
   George Wells, Woodbine Cottage, employed 1 F.S.
   Henry Dawkins employed 4 F.S. and 2 M.S.

1891
The list of Domestic Servants for 1891 included:
2 Housekeepers, 1 Housekeeper/Domestic Servant, 1 Cook/Housemaid, 2 Laundresses, 11 Domestic Servants, 1 Mother's Help, 1 Butler – a total of 18 female servants and 2 male servants.

The Oxfordshire Weekly News, December 20th 1899 carried forty-four advertisements for Domestic Servants. There seemed to be two main domestic agencies operating: Long's and 'Mrs Bates' Select Registry'. The latter was offering £24 to £40 for Good Plain Cooks [i.e. plain cooking!]; Cook Generals £16 to £22; Parlour-Maids £22; House Parlour-Maids £16 to £20 – all wages quoted were yearly. Three other categories of domestic servants were required: Stillroom Maids; Between Maids [working between helping the cook and the housemaid in the bedrooms]; and Stop Gaps. Further vacancies were couched in such terms as Wanted: A Respectable Girl about 15; a Clean Active Girl; a Strong Country Girl about 16.
   A Mother and Daughter were wanted for a Cottage Laundry (one other kept): £12 a month.

In the same newspaper a dentist, Eskell of Beaumont Strett, Oxford, offered 'Special reduced fees [on three days a week] for servants and others of limited means'.

As already mentioned details of 'Servants Taxes' paid in Over Norton between the years of 1790 to 1796 have survived. These appear on the same returns as the window taxes. Male servant taxes were levied from 1777 to 1852 and female servant tax from 1785 to 1792. I have found no returns for female tax but there are entries for male servants tax:

> 1790 Executors of the Late Mr Kerby [Chapel House]
> One male servant £1.5s.0d.
>
> 1795 Henry Dawkins Jun. Esq
> Male servants £6.0s.0d. [Does not work out equally at £1.5s.0d. for each servant]
>
> 1796 Henry Dawkins Jun. Esq
> Male servants £6.0s.0d.
>
> 1796 Henry Boniface [at Chapel House, I think]
> Male servants £1.5s.0d.

Information taken from 1891 Census Returns for Over Norton Parish follows:

> 168 males including children living in the Parish
> 176 female   "   "   "   "   "   v
> 112 men and women were employed
> 12 employers
> 4 widows
> 43 wives not following any employment

Employment details taken from the 1891 Census returns for Over Norton Parish
[Excluding Domestic Workers]

Farming
<u>Land owner William Gregory Dawkins The Mansion</u>

> 1   Land agent
> 8   Farmers
>   Edward Webb   Hull Farm Cottages) two separate
>   William Webb   "   "   ") households

237

	Henry Watkins	Hull Farm House
	Henry Harris	Chapel House
	George Jarvis	" "
	Wilmot Walford	The Village
	Ann Baughan	Choicehill Road
	William Albert Fawdry	Choicehill

- 1 Miller/Farmer
- 2 Farm Bailiffs
- 1 Farmer's Son (Albert Busby)
- 1 Farm Servant
- 1 Farmer's Assistant (Nephew to Ann Baughan – lived with her)
- 2 Grooms
- 1 Groom/gardener
- 1 Gamekeeper
- 3 Shepherds
- 3 Carters
- 1 Sheep dipper
- 51 Agricultural labourers
- 1 Gardener

Woollen Industry Presumably Chipping Norton Tweed Mill

- 1 Wool Sorter
- 1 Woollen Dyer
- 7 Wool Weaver (one listed as Tweed Weaver Wool)
- 1 Wool Feeder
- 1 Woollen Winder
- 1 Wool Spinner
- 1 Land Spinner
- 1 Shawl fringer
- 1 Shawl Hucksterer [seller]

Glove Trade – Leather

- 1 Leather grounder
- 1 Glover
- 4 Gloveresses
- 1 Glover's assistant
- 1 Glove machinist
- 2 Factory operatives
- 1 Machinist
- 1 Factory Mill ? man
- 4 Factory hands

Clothing Trade

- 1 Seamstress

2   Journeyman Tailors

Leather Industry
1   Saddler's Assistant

Food
2   Grocers
1   Baker
1   Dealer (shop)

Roads
2   Road Contractors
1   Highway Repairer

Building
1   Mason's Labourer
2   Stone Masons (Father and Son)

Miscellaneous
1   Caretaker (Female)
1   School Mistress
1   French Polisher

CHAPTER 14

Farming in Over Norton from 1900

Conditions 1900 to 1939—Dawkins Estate Sales 1897, 1918, 1925 and 1926—
War-time Agriculture—Post War Reconstruction—Fifteen Farms: Witts, Firs,
Sandfields, Walk, Home, Cleeves, Choicehill, Halt, Hull Farm and Priory Mill,
Chapel House, Merryweather, Wynmere, Shepherd's Dean, Elmsfield—
Dawkins Involvement from 1950

The Smallholdings Act had been passed in the early 1900s to try to help improve agricultural employment opportunities following the farming depression (see Chapter 8) and County Councils had the power to buy and lease land and to let it in holdings of up to fifty acres.

O.N.P.C. 1907 December 16th recorded in their minutes:

> ... to consider the Small Holdings Act ... to inform the County Council that no further allotments were required by the Parish ... being already well supplied with same ...

For many years school summer holidays had been delayed to allow schoolboys to work on the farms and they often worked during term time too. O.N.P.C. (July 1910) wrote to the County Council to say that in their opinion

> the holiday at the County School should have been postponed to the season of harvest as being more useful to employers and employed.

Records in the Chipping Norton Boys' National School Log Book show that in 1902-4 boys were needed to work on the farms:

> working in the hay-fields and doing odd jobs; ... assisting in the harvest work; ... engaged in potato planting and picking; and ... gathering blackberries.

Farmers had a period of agricultural prosperity during the First World War, 1914 to 1918, when a huge increase in the production of cereal crops was demanded. In 1917 the government guaranteed prices to growers and forced them, through the County Councils, to plough up more land. A Wages Board fixed a minimum wage for agricultural labourers at 25s a week rising to 46s.6d. in September 1919. Through the 1920s more arable land was laid to permanent pasture a repeat of the end of the 19th century scenario. Fewer workers were needed for dairy farming. Following the war (1914-18) there was a short boom time when British exports and industry flourished but suddenly in 1920-1 exports slumped causing a rise in unemployment. The Wall Street crash came in 1929 with British exports almost halved between 1929-31. Massive unemployment followed. (From oral sources, but verified in *A Short History of British Agriculture*, John Orr. O.U.P. 1922)

Dawkins Estate Sale 1897 - 1918 - 1925 - 1926

Many country estates were sold after 1918 but the sale of parts of the Dawkins' estate in Salford and Over Norton began in 1897.

> On 5th May 1897 auction of Lot 1 A freehold and tythe-free farm situate on the Choicehill Road, Over Norton. 38 acres 2r 36p in the occupation of Mr William Charles Jefferies ... well watered ... the Arable excellent sheep and turnip land ...
>
> Lot 2. — All that well-built stone and slated Freehold Messuage or Dwelling House situate in the centre of the village late in the occupation of Mr East. [Large house detailed but no name given] The Buildings; Ten-stall Cow Shed, Stabling for Five Horses with Loft over, Three-bay Waggon Shed, Four-bay ditto, Coach house, large Barn with Stack Yard adjoining.
>
> Lot 3. — All that substantially erected Stone-built and Slated Freehold Messuage or Dwelling House known as King's House containing Entrance Hall, Two Sitting Rooms, Four Bedrooms, Kitchen with Storeroom over and Brewhouse, also capital underground Cellar together with Front and Back Gardens also garden on the opposite side of the road, capital stone-built and Slated Two-stall Stable with Loft over Coach-house, and small yard, now in the occupation of Mr Richard Hamblett at a yearly rent of £15. [House 18th century/early 19th century, the front constructed of limestone ashlar with pilasters. See photo of Chapel House Farmhouse similar.]
>
> Lot 4. — Two stone-built and slated Freehold Cottages or Tenements containing Two Rooms up, one down and Pantry ... Washhouse and Outbuildings ... stone-built and slated Hovels and Pigsties on the opposite

side of the road ... in the occupation of Mr G.C. Miner and Mrs Castle at a rental of £5.4s. per annum.

Lot 5. — All that Freehold Stone-built and Slated Messuage or Dwelling House ... three bedrooms with Two Attics over, Two Sitting-rooms, Kitchen, underground cellar ... Garden Ground in front and Outbuildings ... Stone-built and Slated Blacksmith's shop with Shoeing House attached. Stone-built and Slated Stable with Loft over, and Three-bay Stone-built and Slated open Shed with Yard adjoining – Piece of Productive Garden Ground on opposite side of the road, together with the stone-built and slated Hovels and Pigsties thereon.

Let to Mr Charles Gibbs annual rent £10 with the exception of the Blacksmith's Shop and Shoeing House.

Lot 6. — Two stone-built and slated Freehold Cottages – centre of village – occupied by Messrs William Jarvis and Samuel Wheeler [Not Fountain Cottages as they had thatched roofs]

Conditions of sale included:

Lots 1 to 6 inclusive ... no Church Chapel, or Schoolroom, or other School Buildings shall ever be erected thereon. [See chapter on Schools regarding Board/National Schools]

Following William Gregory Dawkins' death in 1914 George Henry Dawkins (1854-1945) of Wilcote, (son of James Annesley Dawkins 1828-1913, who was William Gregory's younger brother), and Sir Charles Tyrrwhit Dawkins K.C.M.G., (second son of James Annesley), were joint beneficiaries of William Gregory's will but Sir Charles died in 1919 and his son Hereward, 1888-1914, became joint owner. Hereward's mother was daughter of Sir Hercules Robinson who had been the first Governor of Hong Kong (1863) then,

went out and governed New South Wales, and then was Governor General of Cape Colony, (as Lord Rosmead) . [C.J.D.]

What was left of the Dawkins' Estate after William Gregory Dawkins death had to be sold within a few years except for the triangle* of Over Norton Park. An auction sale was arranged for 24th July 1918 of twenty lots which included Witts Farm, approximately 193 acres, Chapel House Farm, 86 acres, and forty-six cottages – the whole having brought in an annual rent of £632.

Lot 8 consisted of:

> Two Stone-Built and Slated Cottages and Parish Room The one occupied by Ernest Barnes at a Rental of £3.0.0. (see my Conversations – Harry Barnes) and the adjoining   Capital Parish Room now used as a Mission Room [former school till 1901, Chapel in 1999] The cottage opposite, named Rose Cottage 1999, was let to Mrs Knight, Doris Knight's mother, at £3 and is early/mid 18th century. The Old School House opposite is late 18th/early 19th century.

* Over Norton Park in this context means all the land within the area enclosed by Over Norton village (B4026); Over Norton road to the apex with Banbury Road, Chipping Norton; to Chapel House roundabout and back to Over Norton House. Locally it is referred to as the triangle of Over Norton Park although much of it is in Chipping Norton parish. Kite-shaped rather than triangular would be a more accurate description of this piece of land.

A contract shows that Wilmot Poole Walford of Over Norton, gentleman, bought lots 10 and 16 from George Henry Dawkins of Wilcote and General Sir Charles Tyrwhitt Dawkins of 21 Emperors Gate, SW. Lot 10 included two Stone-built and Slated Cottages let at £5.10.0. to Sydney Fox [see conversations: Gladys Cook née Fox] and William Winnett (Mrs Joines' family). One hundred pounds was paid for the two cottages (now Three Chimneys 1999 with an Estate Agent's price guide of £180,000 Freehold) and Lot 16 included the five cottages known as Blue Row: Rent £15 and occupied by S. Moulder, B. Aries, A. Moulder, W. Sheffield and J. Powell. Four hundred and fifty pounds was paid for the five cottages. A deposit of £55.00 had to be paid. Lot 17 was King's House tenanted by Mr Alfred Wood at a rental of £15. Pencilled in the catalogue is '£300 Thornton'.

Alongside the Witts Farm auction details (1918) is written 'withdrawn' but another document shows that Witts Farm was sold to George Richard Lamb in 1919. He died 21st September 1934.

At the time of the 1918 sale Mr William Tombs was renting the Witts farm and two cottages (now Fountain Cottage) for £184.7.0d.

All rents given on the above properties were annual.

1925 brought the auction of Home Farm (Corn and Stock). The tenant was Walter Webb of the house and buildings plus 72.420 acres at an annual rent of £102 and Richard Hall was tenant of 36.901 acres at £27.10.0d. per annum.

At the same sale 'The Firs Farm' an area of about 83 acres – tenant Richard Hall rent £95.00 per annum was offered, as was Hill View Farm (The Cleeves 1999, see Lamb) of approximately 172 acres, a corn stock and sheep farm tenanted by Tom Jakeman and let at £205.0.0d. plus a fourth farm – Hill Side [previously known as The Folly] with an area of 55 acres and two small cottages also tenanted by Jakeman which produced an annual rent of £55.0.0d. The total acreage offered for sale was approximately 515 acres which had brought in a total of £674.16.0d. rental for land and buildings.

Prior to the sale, Albert Saunders, sitting tenant, bought the Post Office and Lot 17 – Broad Close – an area of approximately 2 acres. (A. Saunders was George Harris' grandfather.)

A 1926 auction sale was described as a

> Sale of the Remaining Portion of the Over Norton Estate including Two Medium-sized Farms [Home Farm and The Firs Farm – both had been advertised in 1925] including Seven Cottages and Gardens and Pasture Land [in all about 208 acres].

Included in the freehold of the cottages was,

> ... wash houses and earth closets used solely by the occupier or where used in common with others the perpetual right of such user in common.

War-Time Organisation of Agriculture

(The following information is based partly on Mary Marshall's work *Part 56 Oxfordshire of The Land of Britain Survey. The Report of the Land Utilisation Survey of Britain* Edited by L. Dudley Stamp, and also compiled from information from local farmers.)

During the 1939 war, committees made up of local farmers liaised with the War Agricultural Executive Committee which represented the Ministry of Agriculture. District officers acted as advisors and covered all aspects of farming. They checked that the ploughing orders to plough up grassland were carried out. (Just before the war, Mr Rudge, when taking over Witts Farm had promised not to plough up grassland! See Witts Farm)

Every farm in the county was surveyed in summer 1940 by the Executive Committee and according to their quality were put into one of three categories: A, B or C. Powers were given to replace 'C' farmers by more efficient ones. In the Chipping Norton area ninety farms were designated A, two hundred and sixty-two were B and forty-three as C. One farm bordering Over Norton Parish Boundary was put in category C and officials placed someone to oversee the running of the farm.

Land Utilisation: reconstruction after the war

A Land Utilisation Report on Oxfordshire was begun in 1931 organised by the Director of Education, Mr T.O. Willson. Most of this work was destroyed at the Survey's London premises when they were bombed in 1941. The survey was eventually published in May 1942.

A very detailed survey was done of 'Forty Squares Miles' in the Hook Norton area and in 1946 a film – still available today on video cassette – of that name was made showing all aspects of country life. The information gathered was to serve as a basis for reconstruction after the war. A book, 'Country Planning': A Study of Rural Problems by the Agricultural Economics Research Institute Oxford O.U.P. published in 1944 gave all the details of the study.

On the shortage of farm labourers it was thought that more attention needed to be given to the workers' interests and social conditions and that with improved communications workers would no longer need to live in isolated cottages.

It was said that workers should have houses in towns or villages with water, electricity and gas on hand. Roads should be metalled and bus services easily available. A farm motor van would pick up the workers each morning and key men would ride to work on motor cycles or in small cars.

Some re-planning of farm boundaries was suggested to improve access for mechanical cultivation. It was thought that farms would need to be of 450 acres upwards to be successful.

Witts Farm

In 1905, a solicitor's communication to William Gregory Dawkins included a cheque value £34.6s.7d. 'in account of the half-year's rent due Lady Day last' from Mr J.W. Badger for Witts Farm.

By April 1906 Mr Percy Smith of Witts Farm was recorded by O.N.P.C. as being appointed to the Parish Council and he was also

> ... elected [as] a manager of the Public Elementary School ...

of Over Norton at the same meeting, in both cases due to Mr W.F. Marshall having removed from the neighbourhood.

To recap, Mr William Tombs was renting Witts Farm in 1918 and Mr George Richard Lamb bought the farm in 1919 from the Dawkins family.

Eva and John Parker rented the Witts Farm from sometime during the 1920s until 1931/32. Their eldest son Maurice and his children also shared the house. Geraldine Parker, Maurice's daughter, was born there in 1926. Both Mrs Edna Benfield and her sister Miss Doris Knight worked for the Parker family helping to look after the children. Unfortunately the depression in farming was being experienced and so the Parkers left.

Maureen Shepherd of Manchester House, Chipping Norton, confirmed that Eva and John Parker were her maternal grandparents and her mother was Chrissie Stanley (née Parker).

Alan Gibbs whom many local people still remember at Chipping Norton County School, particularly for his musical brilliance, was the son of Eva Gibbs (née Parker). His mother who played the organ at the Methodist Church, Chipping Norton, passed on her love of music to him and Alan has had a successful full-time musical career. Alan Gibbs wrote a book of Twenty Poems called *Oxfordshire Memories* published 1983 and poem XVII records the Parker's farming moves:

Farms in the family flourished.
Farmer Parker meant
My grandfather, uncle, cousins,
And each place was an
Animal Farm

Run by the animals, with humans allowed in
On sufferance.

At Towersey you were welcomed by a wet terrier nose
While cats cowered in curious safety,
Threaded your way through the cowpats
Amid flurries of fowl-feathers
And wide-beaked protest.

My aunt appearing at the kitchen door
Flushed with effort and wiping red hands on her apron,
Seemed just another species
In this cosy menagerie.
Life was full as a bran-tub,
Every minute a task –
The feeding of the chickens,
The milking of the cows

(None of your newfangled metal, these were hand-milked
And stood calmly chewing and turning their heads this way and that
To the beat of the spurt in the bucket,
Taking it all for granted).

Everywhere smelt of animal and straw:
Not a cosmetic city-smell this
But a fundamental life-redolence,
Invigorating and vital.

To Thame market my uncle would regularly
Transport his experience,
Wander between wicker-shaped cattlepens
With a purposeful roving eye seeking out healthy beasts
To team with a fresh milk-yield,
While on all sides cries
Of higher against lower bid
Rang out staccato above an accompaniment
Of lowing, bleating
And indignant grunts at the odd
Experimental prod.

Gagingwell
Engaging name!
Was where my mother's fondest memories formed
At the little farmhouse on the hill.
Then came Arncott, Kidlington – and then another,
Crucial,
Move to Over Norton.

How sad it must have been to see
The farm dug like a weed into the ground
By the Depression
When Kidlington would have prospered,
But it brought my parents together.
So changed the course of all our lives,
Including mine not yet begun,

For although the animals rule the farm
It is the humans who have to make the decisions.

Mr and Mrs Barrett and their two sons Alfred and Harold followed on after the Parkers left Witts Farm. Alfred married Mary Moulder – Fred Moulder's sister. Because of this connection, Fred, as a child, spent some time going round their farm and recalls the work being done by shire horses.

Mr William Albert Rudge took over the tenancy of Witts Farm in September 1935 (242 acres). Extracts from his 'farm tenancy conditions' which follow are typical of that period.

Richard Lamb who had bought Witts Farm in 1919, died 21st September 1934. His wife was the beneficiary.

> Landlord agrees to let and the Tenant agrees to take all that Farm, farmhouse, building and land known as Witts Farm, Over Norton 242 acres 2 roods 37 perches. Tenancy to begin 29th September 1935 for one year and so on until the Tenancy be determined by either party giving twelve calendar months notice. Rent £250 annually. The Landlord reserves all timber, trees, saplings, woods and coppices, (except that willows and poles may be lopped for repairs [to] fences), quarries, minerals, stone and gravel and with liberty for (Landlord) herself, her friends, agents, servants and others to enter for cutting and carrying away timber and working quarries.
>
> Tenant to pay all Rates and Taxes except Tithe land Tax and Landlord's Property Tax.

To keep all ditches, mouths of drains well and sufficiently cleared, ... all walls, stiles, rails, fences and gates [in good repair] materials from the Landlord but Tenant to do hauling free of cost ...

... keep the inside of Farm house and cottages and buildings and glass in the windows [in repair]

To Reside upon the Farm

not to underlet any part

not to remove or sell any hay, straw, roots or manure

lawful to sell a portion of the hay or wheat straw in any year except the last year of tenancy, upon returning the equivalent manurial value

Not to plough up any meadow or pasture under penalty of £20 an acre.

To stock, manage, till and cultivate the farm in good husbandlike manner ... [to] throw down and spread anthills and cut all thistles ...

Landlord agrees

To keep the roofs main walls and exterior tenantable. Tenant to find straw for thatching

To supply pipes for drainage.

On the determination of the Tenancy the Landlord or Incoming Tenant to pay for hay and straw of last years growth for young seeds properly planted etc.

Landlord's son to be allowed to shoot occasionally on the farm.

Witness to the signature of Jessie Lamb [was] James Sturrock a farmer of Herefordshire and to William Rudge, D.P.Tustain, Upper Grove Ash, Great Tew, Oxford.

In conversation with Dorothy Rudge she recalled being driven to see Witts Farm prior to moving there by an aunt who drove them in a Packard car – Dorothy, her brother Tom and her father seated in the dicky seat and her mother in the front. Dorothy did not like the situation of the house and farmyard as it was too close to the road.

The farm was run 'half-and-half' as a mixed farm – dairy and arable.

The Rudges employed John Saunders, cowman, and Bernard Aries, carter. They also employed casual labour at times but not female labour except for Land Army girls at threshing time during the 1939 war. Dorothy, who could tackle anything, worked on the farm after leaving school and was subsequently joined by her brother, Tom.

They had a dairy herd of about thirty Friesian Cross and two bulls up until 1947 when it was decided to go in for fattening beef cattle. A selection of calves, but a few days old, was brought to them from which they chose some at something like £10 to £15 each. They were sold at two-and-a-half to three years for about £50 each. They were kept under cover in winter, fed on hay silage which had been made in a pit in the ground from green grasses and molasses. April 17th was the date for releasing them into the fields. They were sold through the Fat Stock Marketing Corporation. This part of the business carried on until Mr Rudge retired about 1968.

Prior to that the dairy cows had been fed on root crops – swedes and mangolds. Kale was cut and taken to the cows and hay too. They were also fed 'bait' which consisted of chaff saved from threshing, ground up barley, minerals and ground swedes and mangolds.

Cattle cake was also given to the cows and rock salt was provided for them to lick. There were no problems concerning a water supply. Electricity was not connected until 1948 so the milk cooling system was operated using running water. The cows had to be hand milked morning and night with the milk put out in ten gallon churns by 7am ready for collection by the United Dairies, Banbury, and later the Milk Marketing Board. The churns were left on a milk trolley at the farm entrance. A few customers bought a jug of milk at the side door to the farmhouse.

The farmland was good ground for growing barley, but did not quite measure up to producing 'malting barley' – it was tested by cutting the grain to see if it was suitable. Wheat crops were good but the ground was not suitable for growing oats or potatoes. The latter was tried out on a small acreage due to war-time pressure.

Hay was sold to Col. Chamberlayne for his hunters.

The Rudges kept a few sheep for fattening, but none for lambing. Some of their ground was boggy where the fluke would thrive and so could cause illness in the sheep. A few hens were kept for their own use and about thirty turkeys were produced for the Christmas market. Pigs were kept for domestic use only.

As electricity was not available paraffin was bought from Hartwells in Chipping Norton and was stored in a tank of approximately one hundred gallons. The mention of Hartwells reminded us that the 'accumulators' which powered the wireless sets were re-charged by them – people who lived out in villages served by a bus route sent theirs in by bus for re-charging. Dorothy said they were only allowed to listen to the news. This was probably just for the duration of the 1939 war when the news was of paramount importance.

Mr Rudge was a champion hedge-cutter. He entered competitions where the competitors drew lots to see which length of the hedge (a chain = 22 yards) they were to cut.

The Rudges farm machinery consisted of a double-furrow plough, an Albion Binder (see photograph) and a series of tractors: the first one being a Fordson in 1942, the second bought in 1944 and the third a Fordson Major in 1946, all bought from Fitts of Little Tew at about £400 each.

Three shire cart-horses were still in use.

Mr Rudge bought Witts Farm from Mr Wells who had bought it from Lambs in 1964. Mr Wells was a draper from Deddington and he had to re-roof the barns and construct a dutch barn at the request of the War Agricultural Committee.

Mr Rudge proceeded to sell all of his land north of the old coach road. This left him a compact holding of approximately 60 acres still with good access. Land bordering Radbone Hill was sold for building land. 'The Lindens' was built for Mr Tom Rudge in 1967. Houses named St. Clair, Witts End (an appropriate name!) Gables, Fairwinds and Woodside followed with the last four being built by the late Mr Ray Pashley.

Mr Rudge gave the remains of the farm to his daughter Dorothy and son Tom who still own it (1999). They being conservation minded planted a five-acre coppice in 1993

> a woodland mixture of evergreen and deciduous trees which on the whole are thriving. The scrub oak is not doing so well.

Some damage to the trees is being caused by deer and the smaller muntjac which de-bark them; hares cause damage too. The rest of the land, the 'Square Grounds', (arable ground) at this time (1999) is under set-a-side whereby it has to be 'topped' [cut] twice a year and may be used for grazing horses or for making hay for horses. (Conditions regarding set-a-side vary.)

In 1992 Dorothy and Tom Rudge sold the huge – six bedrooms, four attics – farmhouse. It is now named Witts House and is a separate unit from the farm.

It had been expected that the late Paul Rudge, son of Tom and Mavis Rudge and nephew of Dorothy Rudge, would inherit the farm but sadly he died after many years of ill-health, at the age of 43, in May 1997. The Rudge family devoted their lives to looking after him throughout this period.

Many tributes have been paid to Paul. Tom Hall, when doing building work for the Rudges, often worked alongside Paul and is one of many who remembers him for his pleasant personality, his bright cheerful manner, and for his great skills in working on agricultural machinery. Tom Hall also treasures memories of Paul when he would visit Tom's workshop wanting to learn the skills of wood-turning.

Paul lived at Springfield House, part of a barn conversion at Witts Farm, until his illness.

The shape of the front range of Witts House can be clearly seen on the Dawkins Estate Map 1770. This part of the building is late 17th, early 18th century. The second range, added behind, was possibly built about 1800. Five blocked narrow windows can be seen on the front of the house today (1999) which have been replaced by sash-windows. (At Heythrop in 1805 sash windows were installed in the old manor house.) A great restoration plan of Witts House has been carried out by the new owner. A 'blocked in' stone mullioned window has been discovered in a former outside wall and also an earlier fireplace in the former dining room. There are splendid vaulted cellars newly restored which have the original stone- mullioned windows. On the 1770 map can be seen an L-shaped building behind the house which is now (1999) being converted into living accommodation. The house was listed grade 2 in 1986 as being of historical importance.

Mr Archibald Fitt of Little Tew, mentioned by Dorothy Rudge as the supplier of their tractors, traded at first under the name of A.V. Fitt, North Oxford Tractor Services and after 1950 as 'A.V. Fitt Ltd.' He was an agent for Ford tractors and started trading in 1928 and at the firm's peak employed thirty-five men, two of whom were from Over Norton. Mr Fitt owned two sets of threshing machinery and did a lot of work with them in Over Norton up to the second World War after which time combine harvesters had become established. He continued with other contract work in Over Norton – ploughing, but not planting up – until the 1960s. Mr David Fitt, his son, gave names of farms where they worked as: Mr Dawkins' land in Over Norton Park – including land at Hit or Miss Farm just outside Over Norton Boundary – Witts Farm, The Cleeves and Choicehill Farm.

Mr Fitt is remembered as an excellent employer by his former employees.

Firs Farm

The Firs (house) Tenant Hippolyte and Dora Langlois ?1899-1908

Firs Farm	Tenant Weale	1909 - 1912
	Tenant Roper	1912/13 - 1916
	Tenant Stanbra	1916 -?
	Tenant Hall	by 1921 and still tenants in 1925
	Tenant Cambray	1927 - 1971
	Owner Pearman	1972 - present day

Hippolyte Langlois (born 1851 d. 1923) stage name H.A. Lonsdell, actor, elocutionist and entertainer with his second wife, Dora Langlois (née Knight), actress and author came to live at The Firs, Over Norton with their four children Olive Mary Suzellie (1884-1946), Charles John (d. 1945), Augustine (Little Tina) and Jeanne from about 1899 when Hippolyte is mentioned in *Kelly's Directory* of that date. Hippolyte used his birth name for the greater part of his acting and repertory company managing career, especially when playing the giant. He used the stage name H.A. Lonsdell when he and Dora, often with others of the family, were playing at Music Halls during the early 1900s. As said before (chapter I), Hippolyte's family thought that he took out a patent for a mechanical giant. Robert Moulder who researched this point for me at the Patent Library, Chancery Lane, London, reported:

> The patents are in a series of printed volumes – one volume for each year – and consulting them couldn't be easier ... I checked every year between 1875 and the year of his death, looking under both Langlois and Lonsdale and although there were several [under] Langlois, Hippolyte and his invention were not among them.

It is known from 'The Times' that Hippolyte played the part of a giant in many pantomimes:

> Mr Lonsdell played admirably as the Giant. We cannot conceive how any human being can elongate himself to a height of twelve feet and still manage to move his arms and legs in a perfectly natural manner.

Hippolyte was also an accomplished artist and exhibited twenty-one times – in Northern Municipal Art Galleries. He did a painting of the centre of Over Norton which hangs in the Hampshire home of Beatrice Langlois' daughter.

Hippolyte was French and in 1870 took part in the Franco German war; he carried a German bullet near his heart for life. He was one of the three hundred who defended Vendome when attacked by the communists in March 1871. Back in England his first stage success was with a Brinsley Sheridan play in 1874. He was also leading actor when on tour with a Shakespearean Company.

Hippolyte did political work 1920/23 and earlier had run recruiting campaigns for World War I at the Mansion House. He died at Ilford on 7th May 1923, whilst making calls for the Conservative Party and was buried there.

Dora Langlois (née Knight) eldest daughter of Lt Colonel R.D. Knight was born at Leamington in 1865. Her family was distinguished for military service. Dora, educated by her father, was at thirteen considered to be one of the cleverest child mathematicians in the country. Her father became ill and she began an acting career hoping to help pay her younger brother's fees for Rugby School. After marriage in 1884 she continued her acting career alongside her husband, Hippolyte. Dora was a well known writer of magazine columns, sketches and serials. She won much praise for her book 'In the Shadow of Pa-Menkh' printed by W.C. Hayes of Chipping Norton: '... a stirring narrative of mystery and adventure...'.

Dora wrote a fourteen stanza poem entitled 'The Relief of Mafeking' which she was engaged to recite in London and sales of it went to aid those who had suffered in the Boer War.

By the Great War the Langlois family had moved to the outer London area. Eric (Little Tina's son) writes from Australia:

> My memories of grandmother (Dora) while living with us at Middlesbrough are of a spritely white-haired lady much given to smoking De Reske ivory tipped cigarettes ... [and] pounding away on an ancient typewriter ... [and of her] wonderful furniture and artifacts she brought with her. The large mirror-door armoire ... her wonderful French bed with its strange wooden sided sensitively sprung mattress and Buhl cabinet ... special mantel lamps and several items of obvious Indian background, including a beautifully decorated pencil box reputedly made with camel dung.

Dora died in 1940.

Knowledge of this family came to me in a very surprising way. A few years ago I was given (by Alan Brain) three letters headed The Firs, Over Norton, written in early 1900 to Mr Warne, a school master, and signed Dora Langlois. Mr Warne advertised his school in J.O.J. Sept 10th 1899:

> Chipping Norton Grammar School
> Excellent inexpensive School for Boarders and Day Scholars. Modern subjects taught. Very healthy good home. Apply William Warne, Headmaster

Dora Langlois had written to Mr Warne asking if he would admit her daughter Suzie – 'her arithmetic is very uncertain and her spelling truly surprising and original' – who had been educated in France at 'great expense £30 a year from her fourth birthday to her thirteenth one'. Suzie and brother Charlie were both given places at Mr Warne's school.

An unexpected telephone call was received one day from a young woman living near Rugby. She asked if I had any knowledge of her great great ? grandmother Dora Langlois whom she believed once lived at Firs Farm. She was astounded to hear that I had the original letters written in her relative's hand. Subsequently a meeting was arranged and together we walked the routes which Dora Langlois and her family had followed.

Mr William John Weale was at Firs Farm approximately from 1909 to 1912.

Communication with Mr Ambrose Weale of Willow Mead, Little Tew, brought information about his family when at Firs Farm. Mr Weale's father, William John, who was a wheelwright in Chipping Norton moved to Firs Farm, renting it from Mr Walford and he carried on the wheelwright's work as well as farming (see Chapter 3 1911). Mr and Mrs W.J. Weale had two daughters, Violet Rose who was a baby when they came to Over Norton and Primrose who was born April 1909 at Over Norton. In conversation with Mrs Primrose Chandler (née Weale) now living in Dartmouth, she remembered two little boys coming to tea – Percy and Johnny. I wonder what their surname was! Primrose remembered her mother buying presents from the newly opened Woolworths Store in Oxford for the three children.

Each item was priced at 6d. Primrose received a dictionary, the inscription being, 'A present from Mother on the opening of Woolworths' showing what a tremendous impact these new style stores were having. The first Woolworths opened in 1909 in Liverpool, Oxford's store opened a few years later. Ambrose Weale was born after the family left Over Norton so they probably had their presents at a later time than when living at Firs Farm.

Primrose recalled her father making a little cart so that they could harness their dog Rover to it to pull her along.

At the end of the Daly's tenancy of Over Norton House, a sale was held, at which Ambrose Weale bought the iron bungalow which had housed members of the domestic staff. He also learned that day from a former domestic help at the big house, that his father, William John Weale, used to leave a trap wheel, plus axle, on the Village Green. Children would swing round and round on this, only to be chased away by the wheelwright, whip in hand. (See Chapter 1)

Mr Ambrose Weale farmed for fifty years at Wychford Lodge.

From Harry Barnes:

> Mr Weale senior was a bass singer in Chipping Norton Church choir. I was at school with Ambrose.

Mr and Mrs Roper were at Firs Farm from approximately 1912/13 to 1916.

Mrs D. Roper (who married Frank Roper) helped to trace the part of the family who were at Firs Farm. From her I discovered that the late Mrs Marjorie Sale of Kingham – whom my family had known for years, first in the business world through her husband, Reg, an accountant – was the daughter of Mr and Mrs Roper of Firs Farm. Mrs Sale's paternal grandfather (born 1917), Thomas Roper, farmed Priory Farm. He bred shire horses there. After Thomas Roper died, his son William (Mrs Sale's father) stayed on to run the farm as the younger son Charles could not take charge as he was under twenty-one.

Mrs Sale recalls that her grandfather told her that three skeletons were found under a wall in Priory Farm House. (See Mr Pitts Chapter 4)

(Mr Jim Wiggins, owner of Priory Farm (1999) told me that it was a tenancy condition in the past that walnut trees and ash trees should be planted there, as an investment I suppose. In 1906 there were twenty walnut trees growing on Priory Farm.)

Priory Farm House (sold away from the farm) has recently been surveyed (March 1998) by John Steane and a group of his students and their report is published in the Oxon Recorder Issue I September 1999, published by the Oxfordshire Architectural and Historical Society (Listed Buildings Sub-committee).

William and Clara Roper rented Firs Farm for a few years. Clara hated living there, saying that the house was cold and damp. The Ropers had a very distressing time whilst there as three little sons died. Clara Roper (née Keen) had come from Enstone – her father being the publican of the Litchfield Arms.

After a very short period spent at Firs Farm William and Clara Roper moved on to College Farm, Kingham in about 1916 where they experienced happier times with the births of their two daughters

Marjorie and Eileen. They subsequently bought College Farm and it is still in the hands of the Roper Family.

Marjorie Sale (née Roper) and her husband Reg were actively engaged in working for the good of the mentally disabled. They did so for at least ten years in Gloucester and for a further twenty in north-west Oxfordshire.

Mr Thomas Stanbra, who married the sister of John Cambray of Home Farm, followed the Roper's tenancy at Firs Farm. He is featured on the 1916 photograph of the threshing operations. The threshing machine was owned by William Knight of Chapel House. Doris Knight,

> That is my grand-dad standing on top in charge. He lived at Chapel House and also had a grocery shop where the present [1999] French Restaurant is in Horsefair, Chipping Norton.

The Hall family were at Firs Farm by 1921 as they were mentioned by Mrs Minnie Padbury. (See Schools Chapter) They were tenants at the time of the Dawkins' sale 1925.

Harry Barnes:
> The Halls came from Nill Farm. There were twelve children and the girls worked on the farm alongside the boys.

The Cambray family were at Firs Farm from 1927 to 1971. Mr Don Cambray said,

> My father Jack took over the Firs Farm in 1927 on his marriage to my mother Kathleen Verda Lewis. [There were four children Pat, Josephine, Gillian (a Petty Officer in W.R.N.S.) and Don.] My grandfather, John Cambray, was at Home Farm. [see Home Farm] After grandfather's death my father Jack continued to rent Firs Farm – one hundred and five acres.

Mr Jack Cambray died in July 1970 a few months after his wife.

Don and his wife Maretta left Firs Farm in 1971 following Jack Cambray's death. Although Don had worked on the farm since teenage years he forged a new and very successful career in the Civil Service.

The Home Farm and Firs Farm were put up for auction in 1926 by the Over Norton Estate. I believe that Mr A.P. Walford bought them. Firs Farm later became the property of Mr Hancock of Tysoe and then in 1948 it was bought by Mr Rose – for about £4000 – of the Crown and Cushion, Chipping Norton. Mr Woolliams bought Home Farm from Mr A.P. Walford in 1938.

During the Cambrays tenancy of Firs Farm, Mrs Pat Randall (née Cambray) worked with Don, her brother, at harvesting the corn with a binder. To aid communication between them – Don driving with Pat at the back – they had a length of cord tied round Don's middle so that Pat could pull it when the machine 'was throwing out loose' – i.e. corn not tied into sheaves with binder twine. Replacement rolls of binder twine – commonly called 'bag-tie' – were bought from Hartwells.

It was difficult to move Cambrays' iron wheeled Fordson tractor by road, because it had spade lugs for gripping, so Jack Cambray made a contraption of wood and tyres to fix round the wheels so that it could be driven on the road.

One disadvantage for the Cambrays was that their ground, towards Choicehill Farm, was a considerable distance from the farmhouse, yard and buildings. Their cows were not brought down for milking in summer to avoid causing them distress. Cambrays had a corrugated iron hovel built for their animals, by the owner of the farm, which was situated in the far pasture land. Pat recalls taking a cow to forage on the grass verges around the village. She was quite nervous when she came upon American Service Men guarding the stock pile of bombs, which for part of the Second World War were stored at the roadside.

Villagers collected milk in jugs from the kitchen door. Cambrays employed Land Army girls for thistle cutting. German prisoners of war were detained at The Kennels and Greystones, Chipping Norton. Farmers could apply to use them as labourers.

At the Standlake Museum Store Jack Cambray's 'Breaking Harness' (early 20th century), which was used to train horses, can be seen. This was donated by his daughters Mrs P. Randall and Mrs J. Wilson.

There was some support between farms e.g. Cambrays lent Rudges their elevator. One of the many pleasant things one notices about the senior inhabitants of Over Norton is the long-lasting friendships which still exist from their schooldays – both for men and women. There is also a tremendous loyalty shown to each other.

Today, Ian and Rebecca Pearman and their four children live at Firs Farm, having moved there after their marriage in 1972.

The farmhouse, listed Grade 2, is huge and is late 17th century with late 18th and early 19th century additions. A farm building converted to domestic use to the right of the front elevation can be seen in its original form in the 1916 threshing photograph mentioned earlier. Other farm buildings in the yard which had been used for cow pens, pigs and turkeys were converted to business premises in 1986, the work being done by Albert Benfield. This conversion – now a village shop – won an award in a Country Landowners Association national competition in 1987. More recently a conversion of part of the farm buildings to a cottage was completed and subsequently let as a holiday home.

During the 1980s, when there was fear of nuclear fallout, the cellar at Firs Farm was designated as a safe haven for villagers. Ian Pearman used to attend meetings in Witney for briefings.

Ian and Rebecca Pearman (Ian being David Pearman's son) are part of D.H. Pearman and Sons Over Norton Ltd 1975. (See Sandfields Farm) Ian is also a director of Abbott and Company Wessex Ltd dealing in hay and straw. Ian and Rebecca are both directors of I.C. Pearman Haulage Ltd. Ian's brother Glyn, is a pheasant farmer at Chipping Norton and his sister Rosalyn and her husband, Keith Millard, run a skip hire firm in Over Norton. (See Sandfields farm regarding Firs Farm land.)

Sandfields Farm
Sandfields Farmhouse was built in 1959 for David Pearman and his wife Phyllis (née Pinfold). Phyllis' father had bought the land some years earlier and had built a retirement bungalow there. At the time of the marriage of David and Phyllis in 1947 the Pinfold family were farming 'The Larches' at Salford. Before moving to Sandfields, David and Phyllis lived at Little Meadows, near Choicehill Farm.

Jack Cambray had willingly agreed to surrender two acres of The Firs land in 1950 which he tenanted, so that a bungalow could be built on it for the Pearmans. At this time Mr Rose owned the land.

The land farmed by D.H. Pearman and Sons Over Norton Ltd is scattered. It consists of the field in which the farmhouse and bungalow are built; Guys Ground, now called Pheasant Field situated opposite the farmhouse; the old Firs Farm land of one hundred and five acres, all of which are owned by Mr David Pearman. The fifty-five acres of Over Norton Common and a further ten acres belonging to Mr Richard Woolliams, are rented.

Mr Ian Pearman bought three fields, Lower Smartway, Middle Smartway and Top Smartway totalling thirty-eight and a half acres, from Richard Woolliams of Home Farm. Although this land adjoins the old Firs Farm land it is a separate holding.

Guys Ground (1999 Pheasant Field) was bought from Mr Rudge of Witts Farm.

At this time (1999) the Pearmans have eighty per cent of their land as arable, growing wheat, barley and linseed. Ten per cent is permanent set-aside but can be grazed by cattle from the beginning of September to the end of December. The remaining land is used for grazing. Their cattle are all cross bred but having Friesan mothers right through: twelve Simmental steers; one Blond D'Aquitaine; two Limousin and four Hereford X calves.

One hundred and ten breeding sows with eight hundred progeny are predominantly Large White and Landrace with some Duroc and are housed at Sandfields.

Twenty years ago it took the Pearmans from the end of July to the end of August to bring in the harvest with up to five men working. Now it is completed in five days by contractors. Small farmers no longer find it financially viable to buy their own combine-harvester. Farm machinery owned by the Pearmans include four tractors, a drill, a baler and a four furrow reversible plough. One farm worker is employed now.

Walk Farm

Walk Farm probably got its name from the sheep walks. The V.C.H. vol XI p.132 states that it was

> not marked on a 1767 map but was referred to as the new house homestead in 1790 .

The farmhouse is a Grade 2 listed building. Mr Woolliams (later at Home Farm) farmed Walk Farm in the 1930s. Mr Tom Hall (born 1919) worked for Mr Woolliams. Tom lived at Furze Cottage, Dunthrop (later burned down) and recalls that five men were employed on the farm including a cowman and under cowman. Flocks of sheep – about one hundred and fifty – used to be walked from Walk Farm to Adlestrop (8.6 miles) by Tom Hall and one other man. Great reliance was placed on a sheep dog which was as 'good as four men'. The route taken was N.E. of Walk Farm going under the railway bridge and left up Sandy Lane to Rollright Heath Farm. A left turn took them into Great Rollright and from there they followed a direct line passing the Rollright Stones and on to the Cross Hands public house. Adlestrop is situated just off the main Stow-on-theWold road. Mr Woolliams' twin brother farmed Lower Farm Adlestrop and the Evenlode Grounds Farm there is now (1999) run by Mr Richard Woolliams' nephew. In earlier times flocks of sheep had been 'walked' to London from Dunthrop and Heythrop.

Tom recalls delivering milk to a collection point near the present (1999) Midland Shires business at Chapel House. On one occasion when Mr Woolliams, the carter and Tom were delivering churns containing fifty gallons of milk by horse and trap the carter was instructed to 'touch up' the horse, whereupon it bolted. The churns fell off, the milk was wasted and the horse was not under control until they reached Chipping Norton! It had been the practice to add 'oil of vitriol' or 'spirits of salts' to the horses' food to liven them up. 'My, they were frisky', laughed Tom.

Tom Hall's other duties included looking after the heavy horses – Darky, Prince, Colonel and Blossom – two, or perhaps three were harnessed for pulling a double plough and water had to be collected from the River Swere at Priory Mill – six ten-gallon churns were filled by using a bucket on a rope and transported by pony and float.

The Gelf family were at Priory Mill and Tom was sent to help at hay making time and he also delivered corn there.

Tom, when reliving this part of his life said with great enthusiasm, 'I loved it!'

Mr Woolliams sold Walk Farm to Mr Peck of fish-paste fame in 1938 and moved to Home Farm in the centre of Over Norton village.

The Residential Freehold Property known as Walk Farm, with sixty-one acres plus three cottages, was put up for auction in October 1960 by Nancibel Gregory and Viola Margaret Sumner of Dunthrop, Heythrop, Oxon. The vendors agreed to supply water to Walk Farm at 2s.6d. per thousand gallons and to the three cottages at £3 per cottage per annum. Following this sale the O.N.P.C. had to deal with a planning application for a change of use of the farm buildings; they were converted to a fertilizer store and accommodation for a haulage business. The Wallington family bought the property in 1961. Today (1999) Mr Brian Michael Wallington owns the farmhouse, buildings and approximately 10 acres of rough pasture. The buildings are used for storage. Two of the three farm cottages opposite are owned by members of the Wallington family. The water supply to Walk Farm is provided by a wind pump which is situated on Mr Kettlewell's land. A wind pump was supplied by Rowells of Chipping Norton in 1936.

Home Farm

Mr John Cambray came to Home Farm in 1926. Previously he had farmed Cold Harbour Farm. David Pearman, John Cambray's grandson, and Mrs Pearman, David's mother, were living with him at Home Farm. Sadly Mr John Cambray died a few years afterwards of a heart attack. David, aged seven, having suffered the loss of a beloved grandfather, had to drive their cattle to a new owner, Herbert Hall, at 'Tew Meetings'. No other boy was available to accompany him and so his mother did so as he was feeling too nervous to go alone. He was rewarded with sixpence. David and his mother and an aunt moved to a cottage opposite the farm. (This is now part of Three Chimneys) When the Fox family moved from the adjoining cottage both cottages were made into one for the Pearmans.

David Pearman was encouraged by his family to find a profession outside farming due to the difficulties presented to farmers in the early 1930s so he trained as a Technical Teacher at Loughborough. David enjoyed his teaching career and the last post he held was at Shipston-on-Stour and since early retirement he has made a full-time career of farming Sandfields Farm.

Home Farm was sold by Mr A.P. Walford to Mr Woolliams in 1938. Mr & Mrs Woolliams had two children Audrey and Richard. Richard still owns the farmhouse situated in Main Street, next to Witts House, and ten acres of land behind the house. Home Farmhouse is probably the most attractive house in the village, built in the early 18th century of coursed limestone with ashlar dressings.

Richard Woolliams:

> When we arrived there were about fifteen cows, 'Dairy Shorthorns' – no corn – just grass – we sold the milk wholesale. [Same system as the Rudges]
>
> My mother supplied accommodation for paying guests. Sometimes she took extra rooms in the village – at Dolly Trace's house.

Mrs Woolliams advertised in a tourist guide and offered:

> Home Produce and Good Cooking   Lovely Views   Terms Moderate and a Garage.

Her charges were not listed but at that time The White Hart Hotel, Fairford, charged Single Bed and Breakfast 5s.6d; Double 10s.0d; Lunch 2s.0d. hot; and 1s.9d. cold.

Cleeves Farm

Mr John Lamb and his wife Hilary bought three hundred and five acres made up of the Cleeves land, Elmsfield Farm and part of the Primsdown from Mr Edwyn Stobart in the early 1990s. Since then a further forty acres have been acquired in Chipping Norton parish. In total John Lamb farms over sixteen hundred acres of arable land, some of this being rented or share-farmed. Part of this is in Heythrop parish.

The Lambs built their farmhouse just out of Over Norton Village on the Salford bridleway and it was ready for occupation on the 7th July 1994. It bears a date-stone which will be helpful to future historians.

Choicehill Farm

Mr George Fawdry of Village Farm, Salford allowed me to read family documents relating to Choicehill Farm, Over Norton. In 1871 at the early age of twenty-two William Albert Fawdry was farming 214 acres there and was employing five men and three boys. By 1881 the acreage had increased to 256.

William Albert was born at Cornwell Hill, Oxon and his wife Susan was from Over Norton. They had six children: Mary Elizabeth (later Mrs Jefferies), Catherine, William George, John, Violet and Daisy. In 1891 they had a Farm Bailiff, Thomas Stratford, aged 40 (born at Heythrop) living in and one female servant whose name is unclear on the census return possibly ?Mildred ?Mary ?Rollings. William Albert Fawdry died 15th June 1908 aged 59 years.

A. Rowell and Sons' (High Street, Chipping Norton) bill dated Xmas 1908, addressed to Mr J.H. Fawdry, includes repairs to a pump. This may have been the ram pump which was situated N.E. of the farm buildings near to the Stratford Road and was, presumably, pumping from the Rollright Brook. A further record shows a receipt for the Poor Rate totalling £16.11s.7d. dated November 1909.

In 1876 when John Lyne was renting the farm from Mr Fawdry 9a 2r 37p were sold to the Banbury and Cheltenham Direct Railway Co. for £2,200.

Although the Fawdrys owned the land there was a fixed rent charge of £62 per annum payable to the Chipping Norton Vicar which had to be paid by the tenants of the farm. This was not a tithe rent but came about on 29th April 1858 when

> The Dean and Chapter of Gloucester conveyed their land to Thos. Huckvale subject to the annual charge; and this does not vary with the price of corn ... and, would not be liable for any local rates. [An explanation from the Vicar to the tenant.]

Thomas Huckvale aged 49, with wife Mary, was farming 213 acres at Choicehill Farm in 1851. He employed nine labourers. (1851 census)

Correspondence from Revd. Godfrey Littledale, Vicar of St. Mary's Church, Chipping Norton to Mrs Rainbow, tenant of Choicehill Farm included:

Total due from Choicehill £62. 0s. 0d. per annum
Less payment by G.W.R. £ 2.13s. 8d.
£59. 6s. 4d.
Deduct Income Tax at 13s.2d. £ 3. 9s. 5d.
£55. 9s. 5d.

The informality of the final statement in the letter is rather amusing.

I shall be glad to knock off the odd shillings and say £55.0s.0d.

Choicehill Farm remained in the hands of the Fawdry family until the death of George Fawdry's (of Village Farm, Salford) grandfather when it was sold to Mr Cooper in 1946. He bought extra land from Mr Rudge of Witts Farm. This was made up of fields bordering the old coach road – the north side of it. When the Coopers left Over Norton they went to Ireland and many people have related the story of how they drove their tractors to the ferry.

Mr Cooper sold the farm to Mr Reed in 1974. Today (1999) the farm consists of 340 acres of arable land in Over Norton Parish still owned by Mr Reed and under the management of Mr Peter Green of Little Rollright. In 1910 approximately 88 acres were pasture out of a total of 204 acres.

The Choicehill Farmhouse, a 17th century grade two listed building with eleven acres was offered for sale in August 1998. Included in the sale were many outbuildings, an early 18th century barn and a three bedroom cottage. The price guide was £650,000. The new owner is seeking planning permission for an extensive programme of restoration.

Halt Farm
Presumably its name comes from the Rollright railway halt which opened 12th December 1906. The present Halt Farmhouse was converted from two cottages.

Lime Kiln House, on the opposite side of the road to Halt Farmhouse and just inside Great Rollright parish, is thought to have been the original farmhouse but I have no firm data on this. Harry Barnes recalls,

> About seventy odd years ago, when I was ten or twelve years old, I used to get a bushel of lime from Daniel Hopkins who lived at Limekiln House, just beyond The Halt. He had a limekiln at the back of his house. I used my home made wooden truck to transport the lime back to Over Norton. We kept chickens at that time and it was used in the chicken houses.

A John Bradley announced in the *J.O.J.* 11th June 1774 that he had

> a new Lime Kiln built in the Parish of Great Rollright ... burnt with Furze.

The following information comes from Mrs Kathleen Brown, wife of the late Thomas Brown:

> Halt Farm was bought by my husband's mother in the 1940s for £2,500.

It is still (1999) owned by the Brown family with Peter Brown (Kathleen's son), farming 834 acres of which 119 acres are in Over Norton Parish, 140 acres are rented and the balance of 575 acres is share farmed. No animals are kept at Halt Farm now (1999) as all of the land is under arable cultivation.

Hull Farm and Priory Mill

Hull Farm, when owned by Henry Dawkins in 1770, was named New Farm (see chapter 8).

In 1897 William Gregory Dawkins advertised the Hull Farm for sale (426a) with the house and buildings.

In 1952 Mr and Mrs Illingworth bought Hull Farm. They came down from the north of England to live there with their two daughters thinking that this area of Oxfordshire would be within easy reach of a wide range of cultural activities for the family.

In June 1960 Priory Mill was added to the Hull Farm when Mr Illingworth bought it from Mr Peck of Walk Farm. Mr Illingworth died in 1962.

Mrs Illingworth was very much involved with Over Norton

parish activities. At one time she was chairman of the O.N.P.C. Her interest in the W.I. is mentioned in the W.I. wall hanging appendix. Mr and Mrs Marriott (née Illingworth) took over the running of the farm.

After leaving Hull Farm Mrs Illingworth lived at Priory Mill for some years but ended her days back at Hull Farm in a very pleasant farm building conversion. Mr & Mrs Marriott now (1998) farm 454 acres at Hull Farm. They chose not to have the farmhouse listed. Mrs Marriott believes that part of the house is 1600s but with many subsequent alterations.

At the approach to the farmhouse there are two bungalows: No. 1 is of wooden construction and No. 2 was re-built in brick after the original wooden one was burnt down in about 1996. Near the farmhouse is Barretts Cottage, occupied by Mr Philip Haslum, a tractor driver (1998). This was formerly known as the Bailiff's House. Three farm workers' cottages, known as the Caroline Colyear cottages, were built in 1866 by the Dawkins family and have been sold away from Hull Farm and been made into one house. On each gable Caroline Colyear has been inscribed within a diamond shape.

Today (1999) Mrs S.E. Bannister (née Illingworth) owns Priory Mill House and thirty acres of land which includes the Priory Field (now under set-aside).

Mr Bannister allowed me to copy an interesting sale catalogue showing that Priory Mill, the Mill House, Farm Buildings and 35a 0r 10p – described as an 'Excellent Small Holding' – were to be put up for auction on 3rd October 1923 at the Crown Hotel, Chipping Norton.

The sale particulars included:

> Also will be sold: 32 Acres of Lattermath Grass Keeping. [The term Lattermath means the second crop.]

The Bannisters found a 1937 cash book at the mill showing that it was still operating at that time. The mill stones are still on site.

Mrs Bannister was told by a visiting archaeologist that a Roman carp pond had existed on the site. She had also been told that two cottages, now disappeared, had been situated to the south of the present house. The approach road to the mill from the Hook Norton road is recent. The original track crossed from Walk Farm.

The following extract is from Transactions of the Archaeological Society of North Oxfordshire AD1853-1855:

> One mile and a quarter north of Priory Farm is Priory Mill, a small building still used as a mill, and having been formerly part of the possessions of the Prior and Canons of Cold Norton. This mill stands upon the infant stream of the river Swere, which rises at a short distance southward of it, and after passing the mill turns eastward on its course to the Cherwell.

Chapel House Farm

The Brown family have owned this farm for approximately fifty years. Robert Brown, cousin to Peter Brown of Halt Farm, runs the farm which consists of approximately 107 acres, some in Over Norton Parish plus the land east of the old woolway as far as Southcombe and bordered by the A3400 and the Chipping Norton London Road. (See parish map)

Robert's mother was born at Hull Farm, Over Norton. (See also chapter 4)

Merryweather Farm, Hook Norton road

This was formerly known as Merryweather Gardens – market gardens. The house was built in 1946. The present owners are Mr and Mrs K.F. Nash having inherited the property from Mrs Nash's father. The ground is divided into two areas with $3_{1/2}$ acres behind the house and 5 acres (N.E.) bordering the Hook Norton road. Sheep are kept on the latter piece of ground.

Wynmere Farm, Hook Norton road

This property, including the house and 10 acres of land was bought by Mr Clifford about twenty years ago.

Shepherd's Dene Farm

This 18 acre farm situated on the Banbury Road was bought by Mr Fred Goodey in 1990.

Fred's parents were well known farmers at Lidstone, also owning Lidstone Mill (now demolished), Mill house and cottage.

An earlier name for Shepherd's Dene Farm was Four Elms – but sadly these trees succumbed to the Dutch Elm disease.

Elmsfield Farm

This is no longer a working farm but an industrial site owned by Mr Edwyn Stobart. Although in Over Norton Parish it can only be reached off the Worcester Road in Chipping Norton. Four houses have been built on this site and are completed ready for sale, March 2000.

Dawkins Involvement in Over Norton from 1950 (all provided by Mr C.J. Dawkins)

The last male descendant of Henry and Emma Dawkins (see chapter 6) was Hereward who died in 1946. He willed Over Norton to Clinton John Dawkins (m Jean) who is the great- grandson of Clinton George Augustus Dawkins (1808-71, brother of Henry). Clinton John was then serving in the Colonial Agricultural Service in Nyasaland (now Malawi) in East Africa and had never been to Over Norton! His father C.G.E. Dawkins (b.1882) was excluded from the bequest, being considerably older than Hereward.

> The Dalys occupied about half of the Park with their horses, and the rest was let to farmers: Hit or Miss to Thornett, the Nursery Gardens to Stonebridge and most of the rest to Cyril Moulder. [As mentioned before] the fifteen or so huts in the ex-Prisoner-of-War camp were let by the west Oxfordshire District Council to various 'displaced persons'. [It was the existence of the prisoners' camp which brought the late Ray Pashley to Over Norton; he then was in the army and came to guard them. Mrs Pashley, his wife, describes his work as 'looking after them' – that I think is very pleasing terminology.]
>
> At Mrs Daly's death (Clinton) John and Jean Dawkins took over the running of the Over Norton Estate from 1st January 1950, living for a year in the big house while Alfred Groves of Burford converted the two lodge cottages into a single house for them and their two children. These were Richard, then aged nine, and Sarah, aged five-and-a-half. Richard is now (1999) Professor of The Public Understanding of Science at Oxford and author of several books enlarging on Darwin's writings about Evolution. He has one daughter, Juliet. His wife is the Hon. Lalla Ward of Dr.Who and other acting fame.

Sarah married Mr Michael Kettlewell, a senior Consultant Surgeon at the John Radcliffe Hospital (1999) and founding Fellow of Green College in Oxford.

Sarah and Michael have two sons, Nicholas and Peter, and one daughter, Jo. Nicholas (Farm Manager since 1991) and Emma have three children and live in Over Norton Park. Peter and Kate, both Veterinary Surgeons, have two children. (Nicholas and Peter are grandsons of the late Mr Kettlewell who lived in Orchard Close, Over Norton.)

> The large Victorian house (1875-79), as mentioned, was divided into self-contained flats in 1950, by Alfred Groves and they were mostly occupied by friends from Africa on home- leave but now (1999) let on long-term tenancies. (C.J.D.)
>
> John and Jean farmed the land (170 acres) organically till 1991, under their farm company name Over Norton Park Ltd, mainly with pigs and Jersey cattle, distributing Jersey cream up to thirty miles around. Two first prizes were won for cream at the London Dairy Show. They are very proud of a reference from the Head Chef of University College: "I have never used a better cream than that supplied by Mr C.J. Dawkins of Over Norton; ... not only myself but other people of high rank have nothing but high praise. I have served it twice on royal occasions." The cream company and round were sold in 1982 together with the name Upper Norton Jersey Cream Co Ltd, and the arable was then share-farmed with Nigel, the farming son of Richard Adams (and Peggy), our pigs manager from 1957 till 1984.
>
> John Dawkins gave up ownership of the Over Norton Park Estate by gift of the woods and farmland and buildings to son Richard in 1977, and of the big house and garden to daughter Sarah Kettlewell. Sarah and Michael later (1997) bought about half the land from Richard, and set up beef farming with South Devon cattle, their son Nicholas Kettlewell, continuing to manage the family farming company on the rest of the farm. But current euro and indeed world, economics and politics are casting clouds over the farming prospects in Over Norton Park. (C.J.D.) [C. John and Jean Dawkins still live in the house which was renovated for them in 1950.]

The present (1999) 'Dawkins-Kettlewell farming partnership' will not find themselves presented with the same problem as their ancestor James Dawkins who at the 1735 Easter 5 Quarter Sessions, with Jonathan Huckvale and William Clarke, was ordered to carry baggage to Stratford – three teams on 12th March 1735. I could find nothing about payment for this in the Chamberlains' (1730 to 1750) accounts, receipts, and vouchers at Stratford- upon-Avon's' record office but entries in the *'Wiggington Constables Book'* 1691-1836, edited by F.D. Price and published by Phillimore for the Banbury Historical Society, vol. 22, give a likely explanation.

Extracts from the above:

1739 (p.54 f.39)
Charge drawing the kings carrige [sic] from
Banbury to Woodstock   £1.10s.0d.

1741 (p.55 f.40)
Charge with the soldeirs [sic] carriage from
Banbury to Woodstock   £1. 1s.0d.

The soldeirs [sic] carriage from Banbury to
Chippingnorton [as written]   12s.0d.

It is also explained that payment was claimed from the military authorities and any extra costs came from the county rate fund.

Rose Cottage, Old School Yard

Witts House (1770 Middle Farm)

Above: Walk Farm House (Courtesy of Mrs Wallington)

Below: Cleevestones (1770 West Farm and later Hill View Farm)

Above: Home Farm House

Below: Sunnyside

Above: Three Chimneys (Dame School)

Below: L/r No.1A, Nos.1-4 The Green and the Old Post Office.

Above: L/R Springfield House, Well House and Endalls (all part of Witts Farm)

Below: Over Norton House demolished c.1875.

Over Norton House built for William Gregory Dawkins 1875-79.

Coach House and Stable Block (part of the original Over Norton House property. The left end is being converted to living accommodation 2000.)

Restoration of the Dawkins' fountain 1985 by Robert Warner, Builder. Dennis Beaucham, Robert Warner and son Terry.

Samuel Moulder wearing a fur cap purportedly worn by the Colonel during the Crimean War. Painting W.G.D (Chapter 6).

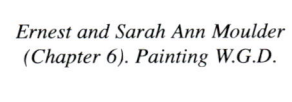

Ernest and Sarah Ann Moulder (Chapter 6). Painting W.G.D.

*Roy Worvill's father Bernard.
Painting W.G.D. c.1887*

*Bill Giles. W.G.D.
painting (Chapter 6)*

Over Norton Park showing the deep valley of the Cleeves stream.

Ridge-and-furrow can be seen from footpath 29.

Priory Farm – bluebells and furze.

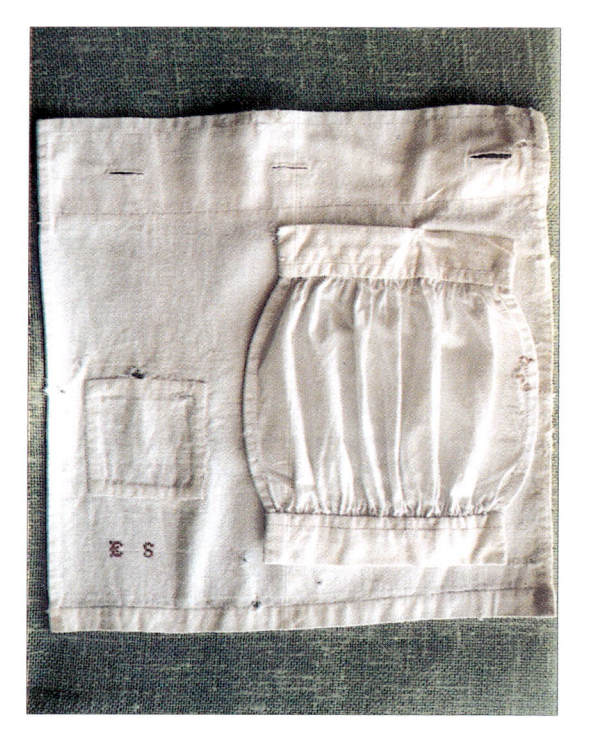

Child's sampler. (Possibly ? Smith, of Chipping Norton.)

Len Cox unlocking the new Village Hall 1980.

Sculpture made from used metals by Sophie Thompson and exhibited during County Art Week 1999.

Wall-hanging to mark O.N.W.I. Diamond Anniversary (see appendices).

Left: Doris Knight at No.8 Main Street.

Below: Model traction engine made by John Benfield and exhibited at the Caperbility event 1987.

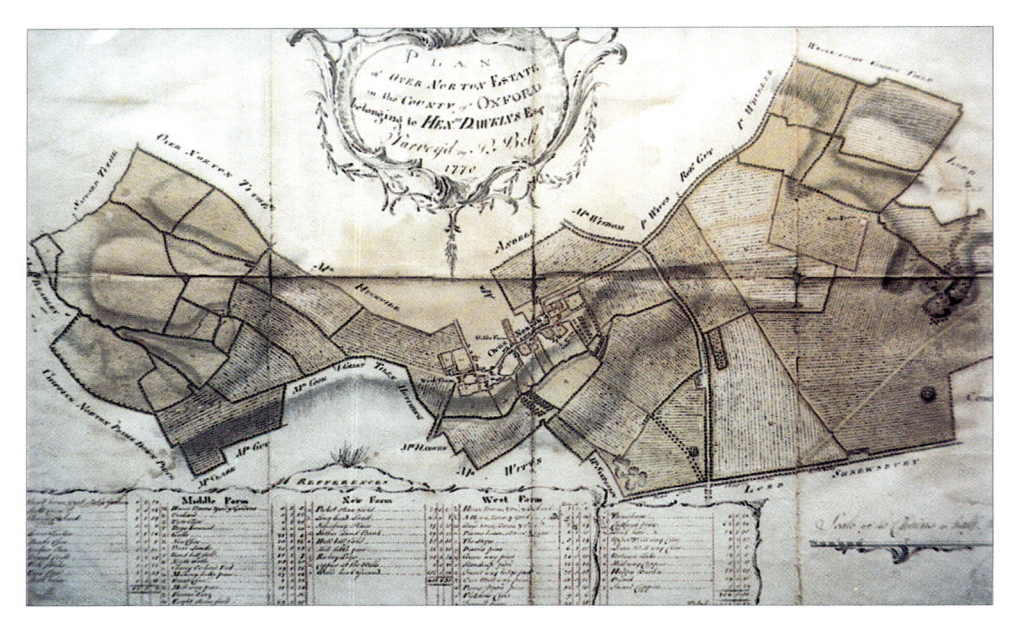

Above: Map No.1 (Chapter 8) Henry Dawkins' Over Norton Estate 1770.

Below: Map No.2 (Chapter 8)

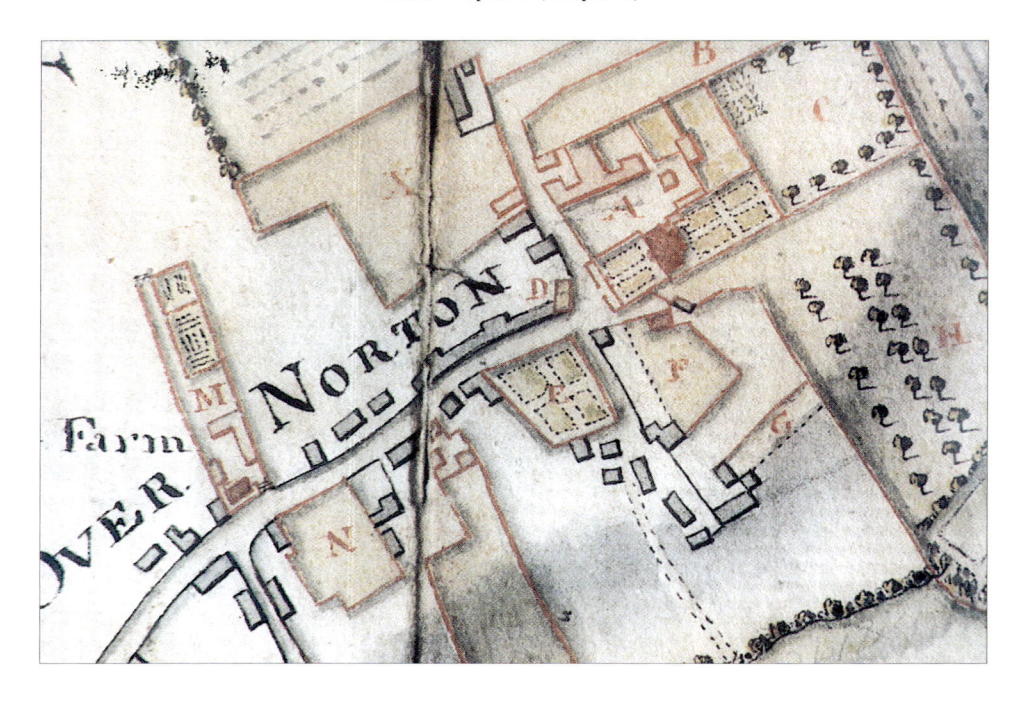

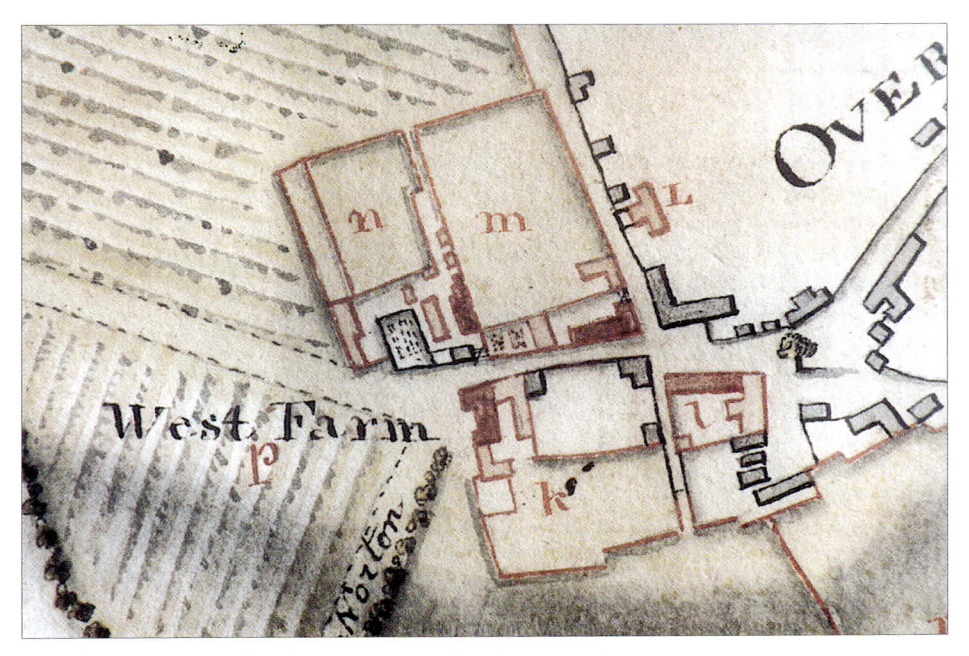

Above: Map No.3A (Chapter 8)

Below: Map No.3B (Chapter 8)

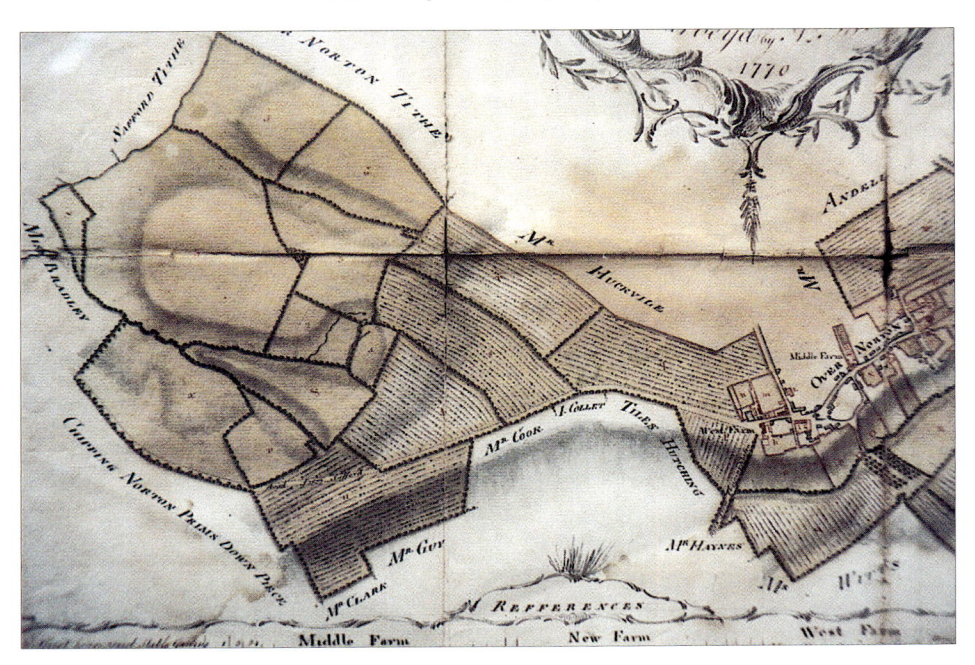

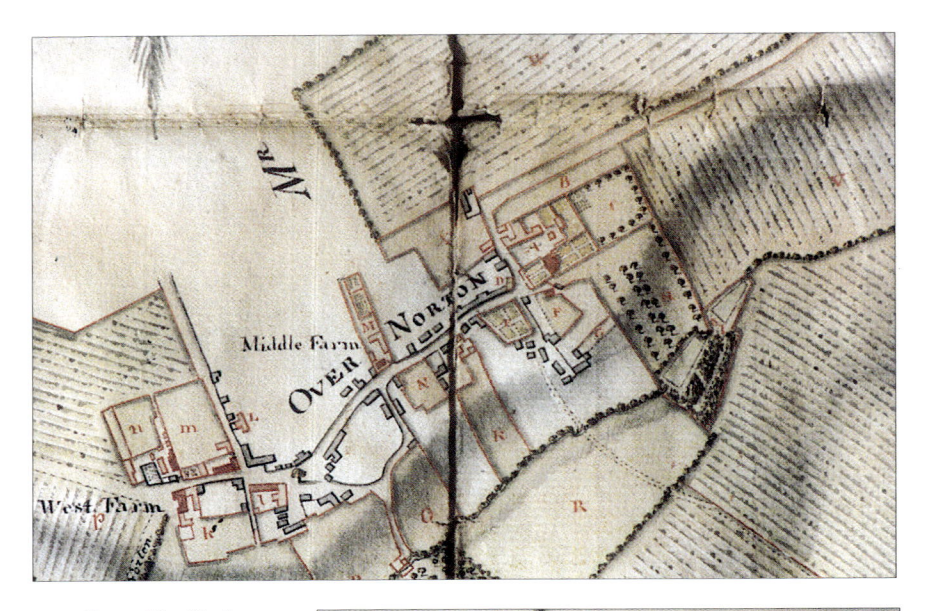

Above: Map No.4 (Chapter 8)

Right: Map No.5 (Chapter 8)

CHAPTER 15

Wilmot Poole Walford—Nos. 1-4 The Green—Laburnum Cottage—Sunnyside—Broadclose and Shanlee   Joe Benfield—Post-war housing—Joe Roughton (Men's Club and Cricket Team)—Motor Bike Scrambles—Public Houses—Coronation 1953—St James' Chapel Group—Sunday School—The Cemetery—Cub Pack—Silver Jubilee 1977—New Village Hall—County Art Week—Youth Club—Play Areas—Caring for the Village—The Allotments-German Band and Goats—Millennium Bells

Wilmot Poole Walford of Home Farm, Over Norton was a generous benefactor giving Hill Lodge, Chipping Norton to be used as the War Memorial Hospital:

> a ... Public Memorial to our fallen soldiers and sailors in the Great War – (see Chapter 11)

... and £1000 to help support it.

In 1911 Mr W.P. Walford had offered £1000 towards the cost of a proposed recreation ground in Chipping Norton which was to have been a memorial of the coronation of George V. He withdrew his offer when the plans were changed. (Full details of this are included in John Grantham's book, *The Regulated Pasture* pub. 1997.)

Mr W.P. Walford was interested in the old Over Norton School (St. James' Chapel site). His visits were recorded in the school log book:

> 1900 30th July
> Mr Walford visited the school just as we were dismissing. He desired to place before the children a scheme for assisting to place a bed in "Princess Christian's" Home at Bisley. [Many families would not have been in a position to subscribe to this.]

and another entry dated

> 1900 25th September
> Registers checked and found correct.
>   W.P. Walford

The 1891 Over Norton census return gave W.P. Walford's address as 'The Village', his age as 49, occupation farmer, and born in Hook Norton. His wife Mary was 66 (not clear) and born in Over Norton.

In 1907 Mr Walford offered his newly-built row of cottages, numbers 1 to 4 The Green, Over Norton to Albert Saunders for £300. Albert declined the offer. He did in fact become a beneficiary in Mr Walford's will when he was left £200. These four cottages were built between Laburnum Cottage and the Post Office. (See photograph prior 1907). Mrs Harris (née Saunders) told her son George Harris that as a young girl she drew beer from their cellar to take to the men who were building the cottages. The chimney pots were added about two years after completion of the cottages. The staircases had been delivered ready-made and this being such an important innovation the details were passed down in oral tradition to Mrs Margaret Howse.

Many residents of Over Norton say that Sam Moulder, employed as estate foreman by the Dawkins family, helped to demolish fifty houses in his time. I discovered in his ledger that on 4th, 5th and 6th August 1910 he was pulling down old buildings and likewise on 17th February 1912.

Numbers 1 to 4 The Green later became part of the Dawkins' estate and were put up for auction as part of a sale to close the estate in 1926. They were described as 'newly erected' and produced £33.16s.0d. per annum and were tenanted by Miss Jarvis on a quarterly tenancy, Mrs E. Thornton a monthly tenancy, Mr Charles Heath weekly and Mr W.H. Creek or his sub-tenant, yearly. Each house had a living room, kitchen with copper, coal hole, four bedrooms and an earth closet plus a garden measuring nine poles. Two of the houses had a pantry each. There were three scales of rent: Miss Jarvis, a former servant of Brasseys at Heythrop paid £7.16s.0d., two were set at £8.9s.0d. and one at £9.2s.0d. per annum.

As mentioned in Chapter 14, the sitting tenant at the Post Office, Albert Saunders, bought his house (made from two cottages), a piece of land named Broadclose (2 acres 35 perches) plus the lower end of a barn attached to Home Farm property.

At the same time,

> Laburnum Cottage with Bakehouse and Buildings suitable for Business Purposes

was for sale. (Dawkins Estate Sale) It was occupied by Herbert William Clarke at that time on a quarterly tenancy, the rent being £14 per annum. Villagers took food to be cooked there. (See Mrs Joyce Thomson Chapter 9). Hook Norton beer was sold from these premises and a member of the Clarke family at the brewery did confirm this with Mr John Howse. Mrs W. Jasmund, née Sheffield, writing from U.S.A. says,

> Where Molly Clarke lived it used to be a brewery but she used it as a wash house . (Now 1999, 1A The Green)

The main part of the building was the off-licence and the lower section was the bakehouse and the rest of the building linked up to present day (1999) No. 1A. A well was situated close to the front of the house.

Margaret and John Howse, newly married, moved to No. 2 The Green, Over Norton in November 1953 having bought the row of cottages, numbers 1 to 4, from Mr Davis of No. 2. In 1971 John and Margaret bought Laburnum Cottage from the trustees of Mrs Vera Clarke. At this time the frontage of the old oven, including the oven door, was still there. The thatched stabling had collapsed. This building had been bought by the Howses in 1954. Twenty-eight tractor loads of human waste and ashes were taken away by a local farmer who charged 5s.0d. per load.

At one time there was a rotating summer-house type building in the garden of Laburnum cottage to accommodate a patient suffering from tuberculosis. This open-air treatment was believed to be beneficial and was practised by hospitals too.

In 1968 John and Margaret Howse bought a cottage named Sunnyside from Mr Haney who was landlord of the Butcher's Arms in Milton-under-Wychwood and brother to Mrs Aubrey Buckingham of Over Norton. Sunnyside is an interesting property, a 17th century, Grade 2 listed house, which along with the old Post Office, Rose

Cottage, School Yard and Cleevestones, is one of the oldest buildings in the village. It is believed to have housed a bakery in the western half and an ale house in the eastern half under which a cellar still exists. (Source: John Howse)

Margaret Howse has been a staunch supporter of the W.I. at Over Norton. She was secretary for many years and it is due to her care that many W.I. documents have been preserved.

There had been changes in Main Street in 1934 when Jack Joines and his wife Grace had their semi-detached house, Broadclose, built by Harry Sandels for a cost of £340. The building site was bought from Albert Saunders for £22. (i.e. £1 per chain). The mortgage repayment to 'The Leeds' was 10s.6d. per week plus 6d. for rates. There were very few bathrooms in Over Norton at this time so many brides to be, prior to their wedding day, were pleased to use the bathroom at the newly-built Broadclose.

Joe Benfield had the adjoining house built, now called Shanlee. During the second World War he drove a Queen Mary transporter all over Great Britain to collect crashed aeroplanes for repair. Driving conditions were hazardous due to black-out restrictions when metal covers were placed over the head lamps with only a small slit allowed for light. He drove long hours without proper rest and meals.

After leaving Over Norton Joe ran an antique shop and upholstery business in Market Street, Chipping Norton, at one time extending into the Citadel (now the theatre). Second-hand carpets used to hang from the balcony there. Joe was a school governor, a town councillor and a very great supporter of Chipping Norton Cricket Club a kind and generous man who would help anyone. John Benfield, his son, lives in Over Norton now. (See later)

Post-war housing
The first request for post-war housing was minuted by O.N.P.C. in March 1943 and R.D.C. plans for sixteen houses off Choicehill Road were put before them in May and November of 1945. By 1947 tenants were moving in. Further development continued and in 1969 Minns of Oxford completed another fifteen houses and eight bungalows at Cleeves Corner – some bungalows having been converted

from old farm buildings. (Hill View Farm). In recent years the huge barn has been converted into four houses – a private development. Recently one of them, described as a Grade 2 listed semi-detached property with two acres, was for sale with offers around £229,000 freehold requested.

During the early stages of planning for the R.D.C.'s new housing scheme there were many complaints regarding lack of facilities:

> built without shops or even a public house!

Within living memory there have been shops in the Choicehill Road, the most recent being at Kings House, where Mrs Joe Roughton ran a general grocery shop (after 1947) and residents now in their seventies recall shopping at Messengers in Paynes Square (now derelict red brick and stone building). Mr John West remembers the shop at Rose Cottage, Choicehill Road kept by Mrs Adeline Stanley and recalls the sticky condition of the chocolate bars which were displayed in the window, facing the afternoon sun. At the latter shop customers were served through a half-opened stable type door. On one occasion – during darkness – some boys were tempted to steal what they thought were some large bananas from the van delivering to the shop. A chase ensued and the boys took refuge in the old beer house, lying along the beams so they were unseen when the driver opened the door. When they inspected their booty it was a great disappointment to find that they were left holding cucumbers. Bananas were unobtainable during the war years.

As regards wanting a public house, that was a pipe dream but Joe Roughton started a men's club about 1947 which was held in the old wooden village hall. There were about fifteen members meeting twice a week. They had a drinks licence and so could sell bottled beer. Joe formed a cricket team too which played in Rudge's field and Mrs Roughton prepared teas for them at Kings House.

Men and boys enjoyed the motor bike scrambles which were held in Ewe Cub Hovel Ground by kind permission of Mr Rudge of Witts Farm – W.I. members enjoyed this sport too.

The W.I. bought curtains and an electric urn for the old village hall from the profits on teas we served at motor bike scrambles on Mr Rudge's farm, and transport was provided for us by Murray Major in his little van. Admittedly we were packed in like sardines and some of us were right at the back, our legs dangling, but looking back one wonders why we had to scream like a lot of Beatles fans when we swerved round the corner by the Church [Chapel]. Passing thought, the Beatles were wearing nappies then! [K.V.C.]

It has been a long time since Over Norton had a pub (see Horse & Groom earlier) but from oral sources (Virginia Gilbert and John Howse) three different names have been given for the public house (or ale-house) which operated in the present Old School House next to St. James' Chapel: The Unicorn, The White Horse and The Sergeant Major. A bench from this pub ended its days at The Unicorn, Great Rollright. Rosalynd Garrod, née Adams, wrote that this pub was operating in the 1840s but was closed by Colonel Dawkins in the 1860s. It is thought that local people were then offered the use of the beer-house (malt-house on 1770 map) in Choicehill Road. None of the pub names just mentioned appears on the 1851 or 1861 census.

A baby, John Heath William Bull, baptised 15th December 1835 was registered at St. Mary's Church, Chipping Norton, a son of William and Charlotte Bull, Innkeeper of Over Norton. Charles Bull, brother of John was baptised 16th April 1837.

In the 1930s and 1940s, Harry Barnes and friends used 'The Three Tuns' public house in Horsefair, Chipping Norton. The name was changed in November 1942 when a one shilling fee was paid to amend the Register of Licensees and it became 'The Oxford House'. It is still there today near the hospital. The name 'Three Tuns' is more expressive as a tun was a liquid measure of 216 gallons of ale, or 252 gallons of wine. (Tun measure now obsolete. Chambers 1994)

Coronation 1953
Celebrations to mark the Coronation of Queen Elizabeth II were held in Over Norton. Prizes of £2, £1 and 10s.0d. were awarded for the three best decorated houses. A comprehensive sports programme was held in Mr Cambray's field opposite the allotments. A tea party and dancing on the lawn was held at Cleevestones, the home of Mr and Mrs Blellock :

prams are to be parked just to the right inside the gate.

A television was lent by Mr and Mrs Buckingham and installed by Mr Dawkins in the village hall so that the Coronation ceremony could be seen, for very few families had television at that time. The Coronation Fund, to pay for all these events, stood at £113.

Cleevestones, a 17th century property as mentioned earlier, has been the centre for many village events and appeared in the local press when Stanley Mansell, a builder, discovered a fan-controlled spit (1969) which extended through three floors. This type of spit is believed to have been in use from the 17th to early 19th centuries. Mr Walter, the owner, had a bedroom hearth removed and replaced with a glass cover. It was an impressive sight to be able to look down and see the mechanism.

During the 1999 Cleevestones restoration work a letter, dated 9th January 1927, was found under the floor boards. It had been delivered to Mr Fred Lewis, well-known Chipping Norton builder and father of Mrs K.V. Cambray, asking him for help:

> Can you come and put new tap on at Dr. Robertson's after dinner. There is a pipe Blocked as well. Coffin plate to write also. Let bearer know about coming down please.
>
> [Signed] P.H.

St James' Chapel Group

The Misses Irene and Gladys McDonald retired to this village. They set up an ecumenical St. James' Chapel discussion group which was led by Irene until her death in 1990 and then her sister Gladys undertook the role.

The group supported Action Aid, the purpose of which was to help educate an African child and to encourage self sufficiency within African villages. Committed members for at least twenty years have been Mr and Mrs Len Cox, Mrs Mary Brearley and Miss Virginia Gilbert. Mrs Margaret Lewry, and the late Mrs Winifred Manning, were also members. During 1999 due to removals and illness, only two members have continued to meet, doing so by linking up with the Alpha scheme in Chipping Norton.

Dr. Leslie and Mrs Brearley (Mary) came to live in Over Norton in 1973 where they did much to help many village projects. The late Leslie Brearley was the Medical Officer of Health for Oxfordshire. Mary was a W.I. treasurer for many years and also for the new village hall through the years when interest in it was at a low ebb. During this period Pat Prowse (of Cleevestones) was secretary and together they made a dedicated team.

Sunday School

For many years there was a very strong Sunday School in Over Norton. The teachers over the years being: Miss Tombs of Kings House; Mrs Franklin a district nurse who held her classes in the old village hall; Miss Doris Knight and Mrs Cox, and about 1994 Polyanna Pearman ran classes for some time before going to university. People in their seventies still treasure their books of Sunday School stamps which they collected each week.

Doris Knight carried out many duties at the chapel throughout her life, having always lived just a few yards away. She played the harmonium and later the electric organ for chapel services until a few weeks before her death in 1999.

The Cemetery, Chipping Norton

In 1999, at O.N.P.C.'s A.G.M. a request came from the floor asking for consideration to be given to the possibility of having a cemetery in Over Norton. Elderly residents, without their own transport, wishing to visit their loved ones graves, are unable to walk to Chipping Norton cemetery which is over two miles away.

Posters concerning the Public Health (Interments) Act 1879, relating to Chipping Norton and Over Norton were displayed. William Bliss gave $3_{1/2}$ acres for a new cemetery in 1881. (See John Grantham's *The Regulated Pasture*, published 1997, for more information on this matter.)

Cubs

Mr Jackson of Slad Cottage ran a cub pack (formed 1961) and although it only lasted for a few years the boys enjoyed it as reported:

> We had some lovely times tracking in the trees, around the Slad and by the stream.

Silver Jubilee

There was a great surge of activity in the village in 1977 when Over Norton's Silver Jubilee Event was staged to raise money for a new village hall. In September of that year 'A Cotswold Caper' took place – a descriptive title taking its name from a Morris Dance. The Chadlington Morris Men and Maidens performed their dances in Over Norton that day.

Fuelled by the success of the 1977 event the following year a 'Cotswold Caperbility' was arranged. [A]'bility' had been added to Caper of 1977 and so a spectacular exhibition of 'Art and Skill', the caperbility of Over Nortonians was set up in Over Norton Park.

Mr John Black, of Wolcot House, Over Norton was chairman of the proposed new village hall committee and in a letter sent out to householders he wrote in May 1980:

> The progress of the building, as you may have seen, has been considerable. This has been due to the able management of the site by Ray Pashley, working in close communication with Lance Cartwright and Robin Thompson.

John Black also requested help from 'the villagers of Over Norton' which included such items as 'felting, battening and tiling the main roof' to 'fixing coat hooks' and 'planting shrubs'.

The late Mrs Boyce and Mrs Mary Ashby, both W.I. members, made the curtains for the new hall. When making the stage curtains Mrs Ashby recalls working with a huge expanse of fabric spread out on her sitting room floor. Mrs Boyce helped to raise money for the project by running whist drives.

Mr Mike Barfield, then at Fountain Cottage, was treasurer of the new village hall fund.

A new constitution was approved by the Charity Commissioners and Mr Len Cox was voted chairman of the new management committee with Mrs Rebecca Pearman as secretary. Mr Cox worked very hard to make this new venture a success. It was hoped that a social club would thrive in this new building with people dropping in for a pint in the evenings. It seems that this idea did not work out in practice. A tremendous amount of voluntary labour would have been needed which could not be provided from such a small community. However, a mother and toddler group thrived for quite a while.

There have always been many exceptionally creative people living in Over Norton and this is still true of 1999. This was shown at the County Art Week in Over Norton Park with examples of four Over Norton artists work on show, which included Sophie Thompson's dramatic and highly individual metal animal sculptures, the raw materials coming from redundant farm machinery and other scrap. I believe she found a rich source for these at the late Tommy Aldridge's yard (died 2000). Some of Sophie's work has been sold on the international market.

Youth Club
When the new village hall was built in 1980 Mr Vince Pashley started a Youth Club there. He was followed by Mr Bernard Hughes as youth leader – both of them lived in Over Norton. Since a residential International Work Camp was held in the village hall (August 1988) Mr Glen Pashley and his wife Pam have been running the Youth Club with Ms Krista Du Boisson as a helper at the present time (1999).

The Youth Club's significant achievements have included reaching the national finals in pool and they have also done very well in darts and five-a-side football. (Dates are unavailable).

Mrs Pashley and her late husband Ray (parents of Vince and Glen) were also great workers for the village hall before and after its completion.

During the Second World War a youth club was held in the old wooden village hall. Some teenagers joined the Young Farmers Club at Enstone. Dorothy Rudge and Pat Cambray were members of this and also Margaret Howse who was from a Chipping Norton farming family.

Playing Field
This piece of land is owned by Mr Edwyn Stobart who kindly leases it to the O.N.P.C.

Playground
The play area in Quarhill Close has recently been refurbished (1999) and provides a safe area for young children with a slide and swings.

Caring for the Village
In the past John West's father, Harold, was employed by the council as a lengthman in Over Norton. The area for which he was responsible included: the road track to Salford – maintaining the fifteen feet width as described in the 1770 Inclosure Act; Choicehill Road to the old toll house (where it meets the ridgeway leading to the Rollright Stones); scything the grass verge leading to the stones; and from the bottom of Over Norton hill through to the Stratford Road. Saturday mornings were reserved for working in the centre of the village. Lengthmen's duties included sweeping the road, clearing drains and ditches and cutting and edging the grass. Today (1999) machines are used to cut the grass with the cuttings left to block the drains! No modern machines do the work as well as the former lengthmen who took a pride in their work. John West did not follow in his father's footsteps except that he too takes a pride in looking after his garden and surroundings.

John worked for a short time at Bliss' Tweed Mill until he joined the Oxford and Bucks Light Infantry. During the Second World War he served for two years in Egypt, Palestine and Cyprus. After service he qualified as an electrician and worked in this capacity for the Co-operative Society at Cheltenham and Gloucester for forty-four years with not one day's absence.

Some areas in Over Norton village are well maintained. Mr Ian Pearman, Chairman of O.N.P.C., mows the village green on a regular basis and this makes a pleasant setting for the houses grouped around it.

Daffodils have been planted on the Over Norton Hill grass verge in memory of Albert Benfield and his sister-in-law Doris Knight (d.1999). Earlier plantings on Choicehill Road approaching the village hall are in memory of Albert's wife, Edna (née Knight). (See W.I. wall hanging appendix)

Mr Gordon McCrae, a parish councillor for eight years, checks the work done by groups working under Community Service court orders in collaboration with the Probationary Service. Some valuable maintenance work has been done by these groups which has included painting the railings round the fountain, cleaning footpaths and decorating the interior of the village hall.

The present village hall committee (Krista Du Boisson, Dave Pratt (treasurer), Gordon McCrae and Glen Pashley) and O.N.P.C. have been making great efforts to improve the interior of the hall. The kitchen was refurbished in 1999. Residents of the Over Norton Parish are allowed free use of the hall for family parties. The hall is used by the Women's Institute for meetings and for providing teas for coach parties and the Over Norton History Group has monthly meetings there, except through the summer.

The Allotments 1999 (information from John Benfield)

The Over Norton Common (designated for the Poor 1770) which is situated along the Banbury Road, used to be divided into allotments of half-an-acre each for Over Norton parishioners.

John Benfield:

> My grandfather had one. At least eighty years ago an alternative piece of ground for allotments was provided by the Dawkins family at the top of Choicehill Road. This is much nearer to the houses and so more convenient. Now in 1999 the ground is divided into thirty-one cuts of quarter of an acre each: the annual rent being £5 per year with the rent due on Lady Day and Michaelmas Day. Some people rent more than one cut, whilst others rent half a cut.

Gradually there has been less call for people wanting to work an allotment. In 1999 about ten people are doing so. John Benfield collects the rents for Mr Dawkins.

Mrs Christine Clifton does a great deal for the conservation of wild-life by providing a rich habitat in which birds and butterflies thrive, both on her large allotment area and in her garden. Christine's garden can be recognised by the bunches of teazles hanging in it during autumn!

Many people have a high standard of care for their surroundings and in this context I wish to mention two young men. Mr Gary Hughes of Penfield – just bordering the Penn footpath – keeps up a consistently high standard of gardening carefully blending the needs of his young children and a pet rabbit! Gary's delightful water feature would have been unheard of in the past except in the gardens of huge land owners. Mr Alan Lewis of The Orchard, Main Street has a beautifully balanced garden, very much in scale with its surroundings. These young men will be remembered in the future as are Mrs Barnes' flowers (Chapter 9) and Wilmot's dahlias from the past. (See Fred Sole Chapter 9)

As this book began with stories about the focal point of the viliage, The Green, it seems right to add another story in conclusion.

> Every so often we used to have a band come – a German band used to stand under the old elm tree on the village green and we kids used to stand round and listen – it was always German men who were playing the instruments. [Elm tree felled 1914]
>
> My family used to tell me tales about when they used to bring a herd of goats through here and stand under the big elm tree ... they used to be able to have milk from these goats but they never came that I can remember.
> [Source: Mrs Joines from Garrod tape recording. See Chapter 10]

For almost fifty years John Benfield of Workhouse Row, Over Norton, has been a bell- ringer at St. Mary's Church, Chipping Norton.

On New Year's Eve 1999 a team rang in the new Millennium. Standing in my garden at Over Norton I could hear the bells clearly and I pondered on the words of Kierkegaard, the Danish philosopher and theologian (1813-55):

> Life can only be understood backwards but has to be lived forwards .

APPENDICES

Appendix (i) to Chapter 5
1765-66 The following window tax rates were levied:
    7 windows and no more 2d each
    8 windows and no more 6d each
    increasing by 2d per window
    up to
    13 windows   1s.4d. each
    14 to 19 windows   1s.6d. each
    increasing by 1d per window
    up to
    25 windows and upwards 2s.0d. each

Charges were made on windows in 'kitchen, scullery, buttery, pantry, larder, wash-house, laundry, bakehouse, brewhouse and lodging room' but dairies were exempt. At the Manor Farm Museum, Cogges, Witney, the dairy has a painted wooden sign over it – DAIRY – a reminder to the tax collectors that nothing was due on that building. Some householders blocked up windows to avoid payment but this had to be done with stone or brick or 'plaister upon lath'.

Twice a year the assessors were allowed to pass through any house and also to check all round it externally. Collectors were paid 3d in the pound; the receiver 2d in the pound.

There was a case when assessors and collectors cheated by 'assessing some too high ... omitted others ... yet levied the money ... and put it in their own pockets'. The judgement passed considered that 'the crime was not of an infamous nature' so no corporal punishmentto be inflicted but they were 'adjudged to the pillory'. (An upright wooden frame with holes through which head and hands were put   abolished in 1837.)

Dog Tax (1796 to 1882) – levied on the keeping of a dog.
The 1796 return for Over Norton shows that four people each paid 2s.3d: Jane Wallington; William Carpetner; Thomas Roach; John Endall.

Cart Tax
In 1790 John Endall paid 2s.0d. cart tax and in 1796 Sarah Witt and Samuel Huckvale paid 10s.0d. each for cart tax. Sarah did not appear to own a horse.

Waggon Tax
The 1790 return shows nine entries for the payment of 4s.0d. waggon tax but none in 1796.

Horse Tax
In 1796 taxes were collected on 93 horses. John Endall owned 27 the largest number. One woman was listed as a horse owner, Jane Wallington, having ten. The tax rates were 10s.0d. Old Duty, 10s.0d. New Duty on the first horse and 2s.0d. per horse for more.

Carriage Tax (paid by two households only)
A note of caution is required when stating the dates of the various taxes. One source gives the carriage tax dates as 1747 to 1782 but the Over Norton returns show that Henry Dawkins Jun Esq. was paying carriage tax in 1796:

[1796] Henry Dawkins Jun.' Esq.' [Over Norton House]

	£	s	d
Window New duty or Commutation Tax	6	10	0
D.° ... Old duty	5	3	0
Inhabited House Tax	0	7	6
Male Servants ... D° ...	6	0	0
Old duty on Horses 24th Geo. 3rd [1783-84]	2	0	0
Add¹ .. duty on D° .. 29th Do [1788-89]	1	2	6
further Add¹ duty on D° 36th Do [1795-96]	3	2	6
Duty on Carriage with 4 Wheels	7	0	0
Additional .. duty on D° ...	1	0	0
Duty on Carriage with 2 Wheels	3	10	0
Old Ten P' Centum Duty ...	2	12	4
New Ten P' Centum Do ...	2	19	1
	£41	6	11

£ s d
20 13 5½ [for Half-Year]

Appendix (ii) to Chapter 12

Over Norton Women's Institute Wall Hanging was completed in 1997 and first hung on Saturday 1st March 1997 in Over Norton Village Hall

This Wall Hanging was designed by Pamela Foxall to mark the 'Diamond Jubilee of Over Norton Women's Institute' which was formed 16th February 1933. It is worked in cross stitch on sixty, six-inch squares of canvas. (See photo section between pages 272–273)

The Wall Hanging was partly funded by a legacy left to Over Norton Women's Institute by Mrs Illingworth of Hull Farm, former County Chairman of Oxfordshire Federation of Women's Institutes and a member of Over Norton Women's Institute.

Top Row, Left to Right

1. *W.I. MARKETS' BADGE* (Olive Baker)
The W.I. Markets were started in 1919 to help the unemployed and disabled service-men.
   There is a W.I. market at Chipping Norton on Fridays. [1999]

2. *DARTS* (Jane Runacres)
Playing in a darts league is one of the many social activities available to W.I. members.

3. *RAPE FIELDS* (Phyllis Pearman)
The growing of rape seed in this area has increased considerably over the last few years.

4. *SNOW SCENE, MAIN STREET, OVER NORTON* (Olive Baker)
   Looking from the Post Office along Main Street to Chesterton's Cottage.

5. *ST. JAMES' CHAPEL* (Peggy Adams)
Formerly used as a school, Parish room and Mission room. The school closed in November 1901 when the new school opened in Choicehill Road.

6. *FLORENTINE STITCH* (Peggy Adams)
Chosen to represent one of the many crafts taught in the old wooden Village Hall.

7. *WILD ORCHIDS* grow in the village (Olive Baker)

8. *SWIFT* (Virginia Gilbert)
Many swifts are seen swooping over Over Norton Park during high summer. They nest around the Village Green.

9. *COMMON BLUE BUTTERFLY* (Virginia Gilbert)

10. *BASKET MAKING* (Rhona Arthur)
A day's class in willow basket making was held in the Pearman's barn at Sandfields Farm in 1993.

Second Row, Left to Right

11. *MAYPOLE DANCING* on the Village Green (Rhona Arthur)
Mrs Cambray revived May Day celebrations in 1934 and they continued each May until 1939.

12. *ROSEHIPS* (Olive Baker)
Rosehips were collected by Women's Institutes during the Second World War to be made into rosehip syrup.

> **From W.I. records**
> Aug. 1943: collection of rosehips; children involved   give them 1d per lb
> Sept 1945: children offered 3d per lb

13. *OLD POST OFFICE* (Olive Baker)
Letter dated 2nd August 1960 from Her Majesty's Postmaster General to Mrs Lizzie Saunders (George Harris' grandmother).

> "Mrs Lizzie Saunders Sub. Postmistress at Over Norton from 9th May 1938, and with service as assistant to husband (previous sub-postmaster), you have given 53 years service to the Post Office." (Reginald Bevans, Her Majesty's Postmaster General).

14. *COUNTY BADGE* introduced 1987 (Olive Baker)
Featuring the fritillary flower which is of great importance in Oxfordshire.

15. *DAFFODILS* (Olive Baker)
Daffodils have been planted leading to the Village Hall in memory of Mrs Edna Benfield, a founder member of the Over Norton W.I.

16. *FRIESIAN COW* (Shelley Smith from Australia)
To represent farming interests. Embroidered by Shelly Smith, from Australia, who was here to nurse a dear, elderly gentleman until he died (Mr Kettlewell).

17. *NATIONAL BADGE* (Rhona Arthur)

18. *SCHOOL* (Mary Deering) opened 11th November 1901. Closed 12th April 1933 (Now Houlahan's Dairy and converted to three houses 1999.)

19. *SNOWDROPS* (Olive Baker)
Many areas of Over Norton Park are covered with snowdrops Chapter 6.

20. *BUCKINGHAM PALACE GARDEN PARTY* 1965 (Olive Baker)
Mrs Joan Illingworth, Executive Committee Member O.F.W.I., also member of Over Norton W.I., and Mrs Peggy Roughton, member of Over Norton W.I. were guests at the Royal Garden Party to mark the Golden Jubilee of the National Federation of Women's Institutes.

Third Row, Left to Right

21. *W.I. BANNER* (Rhona Arthur)
being escorted to a new home after the Grenadier Guards had requisitioned the old Village Hall. Design from a drawing by Dennis Hudson, who was an evacuee at Over Norton.

22. *HOME FARM* (Rhona Arthur)
W.I. Committee Meetings were held here.

23. *LABURNUM TREE* (Rhona Arthur)
Laburnum trees were provided by Mr & Mrs C.J. Dawkins for the village gardens, to mark Queen Elizabeth II's Coronation 1953.

24. *THE SHED* (Virginia Gilbert)
There was a lean-to shed, Stonesfield slated, on the house at the corner of Choicehill Road. It was a meeting place for villagers and believed to be a shelter for drovers in days gone by.

25 & 26. *CENTRE PIECE* (Oliver Baker)

27. *APPLES* (Olive Baker)
Apples to remind us of the war-time canning operations by Mrs Joines, which took place in the old Village Hall.

28. *OVER NORTON HOUSE 1875* (Margaret Howse)
Over Norton Park has been the home of the Dawkins family since James Dawkins came from Jamaica in 1726.

29. *HOUSE MARTIN* (Jane Runacres)
Hundreds of house martins meet up on the telephone wires and on the roof of Pony Close during the latter part of August each year.

30. *DRAMA* (Olive Baker)
The Over Norton Women's Institute had a thriving Drama group for many years.

4th Row, Left to Right

31. *THE ORANGERY, OVER NORTON PARK* (Virginia Gilbert)
The Orangery was contemporary with the first great house in Over Norton Park.. W.I. meetings were held in The Orangery at one time. (The Dalys used it as a play room.)

32. *W.I. MEETING* (Margaret Howse)
Meetings were held monthly.

33. *YELLOW BRIMSTONE BUTTERFLY* (Caroline Jennings)
Recorded in Margaret Howse's garden.

34. *GREAT SPOTTED WOODPECKER* (Olive Baker)
This bird is a common sight at Pony Close.

35 &
36. *CENTRE PIECES* (Olive Baker)

37. *HARVARD AEROPLANE* (Margaret Howse)
These training planes were often seen over the village during the 1939 war years.

38. *THE FOUNTAIN* (Rhona Arthur)
It was erected in memory of Colonel Henry Dawkins and Emma, Mrs Dawkins 1864 by their four surviving children.

39. *OLD VILLAGE HALL* (Jane Runacres)
It was opened on 10th December 1934. Mr Dawkins gave the land. W.I. meetings were held there from 1934 until the new village hall was built in 1980.

40. *THE ROYAL ALBERT HALL* (Margaret Howse)
The Women's Institute Annual General Meeting was held there.

5th Row, Left to Right

41. *POPPIES* (Jane Runacres)
A joy to be seen!

42. *CROCUS* (Olive Baker)

43. *SHEEP* (Olive Baker)

44. *COUNTY BADGE* introduced 1969 (Jane Runacres)

45. *THREE CHIMNEYS* (Rhona Arthur)
Part of the cottage named Three Chimneys was used as a 'Dame School'.

46. *H.R.H. THE QUEEN* (Olive Baker)

47. *W.I. COUNTY BADGE* introduced in the early days of W.I. (Jane Runacres)

48. *TRACTOR* (Margaret Howse)

49. *DENMAN COLLEGE* (Olive Baker)
The college was opened in 1948. It is the Women's Institute's residential life-long learning centre.

50. *COACH TEA PARTY* (Margaret Howse)
O.N.W.I. raised funds by serving teas to coach parties.

6th Row, Left to Right

51. *A PAGEANT OF SEVENTEENTH CENTURY OXFORDSHIRE BLENHEIM PARK, 21st July 1951* (Mary Deering)
Over Norton W.I. took part and had great fun pelting the Puritans with turnips.

52. *PIG* (Phyllis Pearman)
To represent farming interest.

53. *PLANTING THE TREE ON VILLAGE GREEN* (Rebecca Pearman)
This was to commemorate George VI's Coronation 1937.

54. *OVER NORTON VILLAGE HALL* (Rhona Arthur)
The present village hall was completed in 1980. Building commenced in 1977, the Queen's Silver Jubilee year, and a large part of the work was done voluntarily by the villagers.

55. *PUBLIC SEAT VILLAGE GREEN* (Olive Baker)
O.N.W.I. gave a public seat to the village to commemorate the Golden Jubilee of the W.I. movement 1965. Its replacement is featured in the wall-hanging.

56. *THE SETT, CHOICEHILL ROAD* (Olive Baker)
An excellent, well cared for example of part of a modern development in the village.

57. *SKYLARK* (Olive Baker)
Mrs D. Pashley senior has reported hearing, since early childhood, the songs of the skylarks, which nested on her father's allotment.

58. *CHRISTMAS PARTY* (Rhona Arthur)
>From the W.I. records:
November 1946 Christmas Party to be Fancy Dress.

59. *REMEMBRANCE POPPY* (Jane Runacres)
In memory of those Over Norton men who lost their lives in two World Wars.

60. *FOXGLOVES* (Olive Baker)
W.I. members grew foxgloves during the war from which digitalis was extracted for its medicinal purposes.

Designs were by Pamela Foxall, except for no 59 Remembrance Poppy and the tree logo (centre) which were by Jane Runacres.

Photographs (basis of designs) from archives of O.N.W.I. and O.N.H.G., eleven were by Mr J. Arthur, two by Mr C.J. Dawkins.

The wall hanging was stitched by Peggy Adams, Rhona Arthur, Olive Baker, Mary Deering, Virginia Gilbert, Margaret Howse, Caroline Jennings, Rebecca Pearman, Phyllis Pearman, Jane Runacres and Shelley Smith (from Australia).

Olive Baker deserves a special mention, as she embroidered twenty-four squares, all of the straps, and did much of the joining up of the squares.

Mr Eric Runacres handled the publicity well and as a consequence the 'launch day' drew visitors from a wide field: Oxford, Banbury, Deddington and Moreton-in-the-Marsh. The latter's W.I. wall-hanging had been the inspiration behind the project. Mrs S. Rhona Arthur suggested the project and acted as co-ordinator and chairman of the Wall Hanging Group. Originally it was to be hung in Over Norton Village Hall but it has been donated to Chipping Norton Museum where it is on display.

Mr & Mrs E. Runacres have given freely of their time in helping in many ways to seeing the wall hanging through to completion.

The Over Norton Women's Institute was suspended in 1996, not because of lack of interest, but due to the inability of finding enough members willing to be officers. It was reformed in 1998.

Appendix (iii) to Chapter 13

1881 Census – Over Norton Village

Each census enumerator tried to find a clear way of showing the geographical location of the houses in the village a great problem as there was no sequential numbering. Many houses had been demolished, some larger ones had possibly been divided at enclosure time and other small cottages amalgamated. The enumerator of 1881 thought that he had solved the problem by naming the rows of cottages after the first occupant in the row in the cases where there was no other way of defining them.

Farm House	1	Guy Caroline age 42 Farmer, 310 acres
Cottages in Village	4 houses	
Slated Row	4 cottages	Moulder, Fox, Webb and Moberly
Choicehill Road	5 houses	(with a blacksmith and baker)
Payne's Square	no. 1	Harrison-Shadrich & Sarah, General Dealer
	no. 2	George Payne, Beer House Keeper
	no. 3	Jarvis Thomas and Mary Ann
	no. 4	Harrison George and Rhoda
Lower Side	17 houses	
Union Row	10 houses	
Giles' Square	4 houses	(1 uninhabited)
Nash's Row	4 houses	(in one a baker)
Tomkins' Yd	2 houses	
Simms' Row	3 houses	(No. 1 husband, wife and son worked as Tailors)
Woodbine Row	4 houses	(in one a stone mason)
Main Road	7 houses	
Centre Village	1 house	Edwards William J, Farmer age 25
Old Elm Tree	2 houses	
Main Road	3 houses	(in one Harry Huckvale Farmer age 30, 200 acres)
Glovers Hall	1 house	George Bowen and wife Emily
Main Road	1 house	Edwards William W. Farmer age 53
Main Road	1 house	Nurden, Shepherd
Pump Cottage	2 houses	No. 1 Croote a coachman
		No 2 Betterage Thomas
School Square	3 houses	(No .2 uninhabited in use as a school)
Lodge Cottage	2 houses	Messrs Clack and Woodward
Over Stables	1 house	Groom
Over Norton House	1 house	Dawkins

The outlying parts of the parish have not been included here but were of course on the 1881 census.

N.B.: 'The Slated Row' is now called Blue Row. Most of the small cottages were thatched.

Extract from 1871 Census Return

Over Norton's Census return for 1871 began with

> Schedule No. 1 Blif's Lodge (probably near The Mount, Chipping Norton)
> No. 2 The Cot
> No. 3 Folly Farm

Having been derelict for some years 'The Cot' was a meeting place for teenagers through the 1930s and likewise 'Folly Farm' although notices to 'Keep Out' were posted. Children played there and one inhabitant recalls taking cold mashed potato for a picnic.

The Cot Ground – pasture land of just over four acres – plus a two-roomed cottage were sold to Mrs Elizabeth Taylor of Churchill for £400 in January 1885. In 1891 Thomas Pagett and his wife Dorcas aged 58 years were living in The Cot. Earlier occupants in 1861 had been Richard and Dinah Hovard with their three children and in 1871 the Joyner family were there.

Abbreviations

a.r.p.	acre rood perch (See Chapter 8)
C.J.D.	Clinton John Dawkins
C.S.E.	Certificate Secondary Education
H.M.I.	Her Majesty's Inspector
K.V.C.	Kathleen Verda Cambray
L.D.V.	Local Defence Volunteers
N.F.W.I.	National Federation of Women's Institute
O.C.R.O.	Oxfordshire County Record Office
O.F.H.S.	Oxfordshire Family History Society
O.F.W.I.	Oxfordshire Federation of Women's Institute
O.N.P.C.	Over Norton Parish Council
S.E.B.	Southern Electricity Board
V.C.H.	Victoria County History
W.I.	Women's Institute

INDEX

A
A Cotswold Caper 281
A.R.P. 9, 213
acreage 15, 58, 244, 250, 265
Adams, Peggy 227, 271, 289, 295
Adams family 227, 271
Adlestrop 154, 262
Allen, Elizabeth 52
Allen, Frederick 27, 41-42, 114, 117, 138-139, 188
Allen, Kathleen (née Bennett) 220, 235
Allotments Act 1769 4, 17, 48, 97, 118-119, 123, 127, 131, 240, 284
Allotments (Choicehill Road) 15, 165, 240, 273, 284, 285
American 9, 88, 156, 213, 224, 228, 259
Anker, Graham 142
Anker, William 8, 123, 133, 142-147
Arch, Joseph 8, 123, 136-138
Aries, Bernard 38, 208, 243, 249
Arkell,Revd. 169
Arkell, William 149
Arliss, George 164
Arthur, Joe 295
Arthur, Rhona 289-295
Ascott Women 8, 123, 137
Ashby, Mary 281

B
Badminton Hunt 55
Bakehouse 275
Baker, Olive 288-295
Bakewell, Robert 129-130
Banbury 5-9, 14, 22, 24, 32-33, 37, 51, 53, 58, 93, 111-113, 133, 135, 142, 147, 175, 204, 205, 206, 243, 250, 265, 272, 295
Banbury and Cheltenham Direct Railway Co. 265
Banbury Guardian 133, 147
Bannister, Mr & Mrs (née Illingworth) 268
Barfield, Mr & Mrs Michael 95, 281
Barnes, Harry 8, 152, 156, 158, 163-166, 201, 235, 243, 257-258, 267, 278, 285
Barnes, Ernest 243
Barrett, Mr & Mrs A 122, 248,
Barretts Cottage 268
bats 24
Bayliss, Capt. James William 58, 119
Bayliss, WIlliam George 58
Beale, Mr 31
Beck, Ann 236
Beck, Mrs 14, 17, 30, 99, 193
beer-house 278
bell- ringer 285
Benfield, Albert 260, 283
Benfield, Edna (née Knight) 219-220, 246, 290
Benfield, Joe 119, 122, 273, 276
Benfield, John 276, 284
Bennett, Harry 14, 122
Bennett, Mrs 119, 214-215
Bennett, Miss Winifred 199
Betteridge family 26, 187,
Betteridge, Emma & Lucy 235
Bickford, Mrs 213

Billeting Officer 215
Birmingham 17, 54, 136, 196
Bishop of Reading 182-183
Black, John 281
Bliss' Tweed Mill 9, 138, 198, 229, 234-235, 283
Bliss, William 234-235, 280
Blue Row 13, 125, 138, 173, 201, 243, 297
boundary, parish 15-17, 28-30, 33, 97, 170
Bowen family 229-233, 296
Bowler, William 65
Boyce, Mrs 281
Brassey family 23, 135, 152-153, 192, 197-198, 274
Bread Charity 117, 161
Brearley, Mary 279-280
Brearley, Dr. Leslie 280
Brick Kiln Cottages 30
Brigg, Dr. 170
Broadclose 273-274, 276
bronze age flint 45
Brown family 267, 269
Brownrigg, Mr 182, 184
Bruern Abbey 50
Buckingham, Mr & Mrs Aubrey 223, 275, 279
Burbidge & sons 28
Burbidge, Fred 218
Burbidge, Mrs 189
Burtonshaw, Thomas 198
Busby family 5, 7, 58, 60, 62-63, 71-72, 74-81, 100, 134, 149-150, 238
Busbye family 67, 69-70, 72-73

C
Cambray, Don 47, 213-218, 223, 226, 258, 259
Cambray, W.J. (Jack) 214, 215, 216, 228, 251, 253, 258-261, 259
Cambray, Kathleen Verda (née Lewis) 152, 155, 213-218, 222-223, 225-228, 258, 278-279, 289, 298
Campbell, Major 228
Castle Chipping Norton 16-17, 29
Cemetery Chipping Norton 10, 209, 273, 280
Census 13, 25-26, 41, 57, 81, 93, 98, 123, 148, 150, 178-179, 187, 229-230, 234, 237, 265, 274, 278, 296-297
Chamberlayne, Col. 250
Chamberlayne, Thomas 62
Chandler, Primrose (née Weale) 256
Chapel, St. James' 15, 37, 96, 119, 160, 163, 179-180, 273, 279
Chapel House 18, 21, 22, 30-32, 44-45, 49, 53-59, 81, 105, 150, 157, 170, 174, 214, 229, 231, 235-238, 240-242, 258, 269
Chapel House Hotel 58
Chappel on the Heath 18-19, 53
Charities 8, 40, 106, 114-119, 122, 138, 161, 169, 281
Cherwell 16, 269
Chipperfield circus 23
Chipping Norton 4-9, 13-24, 28-30, 33-34, 37, 42-43, 45-49, 53-54, 59, 65, 68, 80-81, 85, 88, 96-105, 107, 114, 116-119, 123, 126, 131-133, 137, 153-154, 157-159, 162-166, 170-175, 177-178, 181-184, 186-188, 190, 193-199, 201-206, 208-209, 212-214, 216-219, 222-224, 226, 229, 233-234, 238, 240, 243, 245-246,

INDEX

250, 254-260, 263-266, 268, 270, 273, 276, 278-280, 282, 285, 288, 295
Chipping Norton Museum 4, 6, 45, 59, 123, 212, 233, 295
Choicehill Farm 5, 15-17, 33, 48, 65, 149, 229, 253, 265-266
Choicehill Road 23-28, 34-38, 47, 124-125, 164-166, 171, 174, 179, 190, 205, 220, 238, 241, 276-278, 283-284, 289, 291, 296
Christmas 114, 122, 156, 158, 160-161, 166, 169, 172, 221, 223, 226, 250, 294
Church Army 174, 202
Clarke, Emily 58
Clarke, Herbert 275
Clarke, Molly 275
Clarke, William 271
Clay Lane 17
Cleeves 15-17, 28, 125-126, 170, 227, 240, 244, 253, 264
Cleeves Farm 240, 244, 253, 264
Cleevestones 38, 43, 142, 213, 219, 225, 227, 276, 278-280
Clifton, Christine 284
Co-op 159, 161, 172-173
coal 20, 34 39, 71, 109, 122, 135, 161, 163, 198, 274
Coke, Thomas 128-129
Cold Norton Priory 45, 48-52, 58, 85
Common 7, 16, 20, 27, 32, 34-36, 48, 76, 159, 185, 196, 261, 284
Cook, Gladys (née Fox) 152, 159-163, 235, 243
Cooper, Mr 266
Coronation 10, 174, 192, 196-197, 273, 278-279, 291, 294
Cotswold Caperbility 281
County Council 4-5, 18, 25-26, 36, 177, 240-241
Courtyard 16, 49, 59
Cox, Mr & Mrs Len 279-282
Cricket team 277
Cropredy 123, 128, 133, 142, 144-145, 147
Cubs 273, 281
D
Daly, Capt.42-43, 106, 119, 152-157
Daly family 98, 100, 122, 152-157, 159-163, 165-166, 169, 191, 256, 270, 292
Daly, Mrs Rose (née Brassey) 23, 135, 152
Dawkins Charity 117
Dawkins, Mr & Mrs Clinton John 32, 36, 81-106, 233, 270-271, 279, 291, 295, 298
Dawkins, Col. Henry 36, 48, 81-106, 123-125, 139-144, 236-237, 267, 287, 292, 295
Dawkins Estate Sale 240-241, 275
Dawkins family 13, 17, 19, 25, 27, 30-32, 36-37, 41-43, 48, 55, 59, 72, 81-91, 93-106, 108, 116-119, 123, 125-127, 131, 139-141, 144, 152, 179, 183-184, 205-206, 233, 236-237, 240-243, 246, 252-253, 258, 267-268, 270-271, 274-275, 278-279, 284, 287, 291-292, 295-296, 298
Dawkins, James 19, 59, 81-106, 291
Dawkins-Kettlewell farming partnership 271
Dawkins, William Gregory 25, 27, 30, 32, 37, 41-43, 72, 81-106, 117, 126, 139, 152, 183-184, 205-206, 237, 242, 246, 267, 278
Dawkins' Old Coach Road 17, 30
Dawkins Pennant, George Hay 87-88, 104
Deering, Mary 290, 294-295
Domesday Book 45-46
Double Diamond 44
Doubles 26-27
Du Boisson, Krista 282, 284
Duke of Wellington 13, 36, 90
Dunkirk 216, 223
Dunstan House 202
Dunthrop 50, 134, 169, 262-263
E
Easter 13, 166, 271
electricity 171, 218, 220, 227-228, 245, 250
elm 13, 107, 160, 285
Elmsfield 9, 16, 240, 264, 270
Elmsfield Farm 16, 264, 270
Empire Day 159, 196
Endall, John 57, 286-287
Endall, William 116
Endoll family 47-48, 115
Endolls Farm 114
Enstone 22, 25, 38, 50-51, 61, 68, 136, 141, 173, 199, 225, 257, 282
Evacuees 9, 213, 214-216
Evenlode 16
F
fair 8, 49, 175, 194-195
Fawdry, George 265-266
Fawdry, J.H. 265
Fawdry, W.A. 114, 149, 265
Fifteen Lands 30
Fire Mark 123, 135
Firs 83
Firs Farm 5, 35, 38, 44, 47, 59. 98, 201, 214, 216, 223, 240, 244, 253, 255-261
Fitt, Archibald 251-253
Fitt, David 253
Flick, Diana and Pauline 203
Flick, Peter 35
Foote, William S 179, 181
Forbes, Eileen 37
Forster's Education Act 177, 181
fountain 13, 95-96, 99, 160, 284
Fountain Cottage 25, 38, 95, 242-243, 281
Fowler, Robert 123, 129-130
Fox, Sydney 157-159, 162, 243
Fox, Thomas 42
Foxall, Pamela 288, 295
fulling mill 50
furze 25, 32, 127, 132
Furze Cottage 262
G
games 155, 199-200
Garrod, Rosalind (née Adams) 40, 178, 180, 227, 278, 285
Gas 158, 198, 223, 245
Gas Masks 213, 214, 223-224
gas works 198
George IV 55

INDEX

German 10, 216, 254, 259, 273, 285
giant 13, 253-254
Gibbs, Alan 246
Gibbs, Eva (née Parker) 246
Gibbs, Charles 242
Gibbs, Elizabeth 230
Gibbs, Richard 116
Gilbert, Virginia 278-279, 289, 291-292, 295
Giles, Bill 99, 114
Giles Square 296
Glove Industry 76, 219, 229-231, 232, 233, 234, 238
Glovers Close 157, 232
Glovers' Close 44
Glyme Farm 65, 196, 225
Goodey, Fred 269
Goodheart, Mr 174
Goodman, Harry 157-158
Great Rollright 16-18, 24, 28, 31, 36, 57, 115, 168, 222, 231, 262, 267, 278
Green, Peter 266
Gregory, Nancibel 263
Gulliver family 178-179

H
ha-ha 31
Hall family 258
Hall, Herbert 263
Hall, Richard 244
Hall, Tom 36-37, 252-253, 262
Halt Farm 16, 266, 269
Hancock, Mr 259
Harris, George 14, 23, 98, 166, 232, 244, 274, 290
Harris, Henry 238
Harris, May Ruby 14, 274
Harris, Rev. Francis 101
Harrison, Wilf 59, 205-206
Hartwells 198, 250, 259
Haslum, Philip 268
Haven Cottage 99
Hayes, Mr W.C. 27, 254
Hearth Tax 7, 55, 60-63
Hedges, Mr G. 42
Heythrop 15-16, 23-24, 33, 48, 52, 59, 101, 123, 134-135, 149, 152, 154, 156, 199, 202, 252, 262-265, 274
Heythrop Hunt 55, 152
Heythrop Mansion 135
Hickey, William 53-54
Higgs, Harry 157
Highwaymen 22
Hill Side Farm 25
Hill View Farm 36, 38, 244, 277
Hippolyte 13, 253-254
Hit or Miss 16-17, 31, 53, 227, 253, 270
Hobbs, Anthony 132, 147
Holy Trinity Church 156
Holyhead 18
Home Farm 8, 35, 44, 114, 116, 123, 135, 202, 214, 216, 244, 258-259, 261-264, 273-274
Home Guard 9, 213, 216-217
Horse & Groom 278
Howse, John 274-276, 278
Howse, Margaret 274-276, 282, 291-293, 295

Hub Ironworks 174
Huckvale family 48, 55-57, 60, 65-71, 77, 80, 97, 110, 130, 149-150, 265, 271, 287, 296
Huckvale, Cuthbert 60, 65-71
Huckvale, Johnathan 65-71, 271,
Huckvale, Samuel 48, 55-57, 60, 65-71, 97, 130, 149-150, 287
Huckvale, William 55-57, 60, 65-71, 80, 110, 149-150
Hudson, Dennis 291
Hughes, Bernard 282
Hughes, Gary 285
Hull Farm 9, 16, 28, 125, 127, 142, 149, 229, 237-238, 240, 267-269, 288
Hyatt, Emily 179
Hyatt, Richard 57

I
Illingworth, Joan 290
Inclosures and Allotments Act 4, 17

J
Jackson, Mr 281
Jackson's Oxford Journal (J.O.J.) 21-22, 53, 55, 84-85, 109, 116, 127, 133, 146, 182, 255, 267
Jacobite 81-84
Jennings, Caroline 292, 295
Jennings, Simon 122
Joines, E.J. 119, 122, 214
Joines, Grace 40-41
Joines, Jack 34, 276
Joines, Josiah 41
Joines, Mrs 34, 175, 178, 218-219, 222, 226, 243, 285, 291
Jupiter 45

K
Kerby, Thomas 53, 56, 237
Kettlewell family 271
Kettlewell, Michael 263, 271
Kettlewell, Nicholas 81, 271
Kettlewell, Peter 81
Kettlewell, R.W. 27, 271, 290
Kiddington 65, 160, 173, 225
Kierkegaard 285
King, Dr. 161
King, William 56
Kingham 14, 22, 24, 84, 158, 257
Kings House 223, 277, 280
Kiteney Copse 16
Knight, Miss Doris 152, 162, 169, 243, 246, 258, 280, 283

L
L.D.V. 9, 213, 216, 223, 298
labourers' revolt 134
Lamb, George Richard 119, 243, 246
Lamb, John 264
Lambert, Fred 128
Land Army 220, 249, 259
Lane, John 179,185, 194
Langlois, Dora (Née Knight) 253-256
laundry 156, 163, 165
Laws of Settlement 8, 106
Lewis, Alan 285
Lewis, Dennis 37, 59, 99, 233

INDEX

Lewis, Fred 279
Lewry, Margaret 279
Liadell, Mr H. 199
lime kiln 31, 267
Little Meadows 260
Little Rollright 17, 129, 167, 266
Littledale, Revd. Godfrey A. 182, 184, 196, 198, 266
Long Compton 18, 48, 54, 100, 167
Lord of the Manor 47, 97, 152, 167
Lower Endolls 47
Lutener, Mr J.B. 37

M

Magic lantern 169
Main Street 17, 44, 125, 127, 165, 232, 264, 276, 285, 288
Major, Murray 203, 278
Major, Noel 203
Mann, Revd. Ralph 65-66, 68, 72
Mann, John 96
Manning, Winifred 279
Manor Farm 142, 149
Mansell, Stanley 279
Marriott, Mrs (née Illingworth) 268
Martin family 178-179
Martin, Thomas 61
May Day 159-160, 188, 192, 289
McCrae, Gordon 284
McCrae, Mrs 122
McDonald, Irene and Gladys 279
McKnight, Dr. 163
men's club 277
Meredith, Mrs 197
Merryweather Farm 269
Messenger, Alf 158, 161
Messengers 23, 277
Middle Farm 125-126
Miles, Florence 179
Miles, John 74, 80
Miles, Sylvia 160
milestone 18
Military Drill 188-189
Millard, Alma (née Joines) 41, 206-207
Millard, Keith 260
mills, water 46-47, 51, 147, 235
Mission Room 37, 119, 156, 160, 174, 202, 243
motor bike scrambles 277-278
Moulder family 13, 27, 31, 37, 41-43, 80, 98-99, 138, 157-158, 162, 164-166, 187, 192, 201, 211, 243, 248, 253, 270, 274, 296
Moulder, Samuel 31, 98-99, 157-158, 164-166, 274
Moulder, William 13, 27, 41-43, 138,
murrel stones 164

N

Napoleonic prisoners 36
Nash, Mrs K.F. 269
New Farm 124-125, 127, 149, 267
New Year's Eve 1999 285
Niven, David 170
Nolan, Nancy (née Shepard) 152, 165, 168, 170, 235
Notgrove station 154
nylons 171

O

Oakley, Mr 154
Occupations 229-239
old coaching road 47
Old School House 163-164, 179-180, 243, 278
Old Shed 38
Osborn, Mr 225
Osborn, Wendy & David 58
Over Norton Allotment Charity 117-119
Over Norton Estate Sale 1918 58
Over Norton History Group 5, 33, 52, 167, 284
Over Norton House 7, 15, 28, 30-32, 39, 41-42, 72, 81, 84, 87, 93-95, 98, 152, 156-157, 162, 165, 178-179, 223, 243, 256, 287, 296
Over Norton lakes 38
Over Norton Parish Council (O.N.P.C.) 14, 26-29, 35, 38, 41-43, 95, 106, 114, 117, 118-119, 138-139, 213-214, 228, 240, 246, 263, 268, 276, 280, 283-284, 298
Over Norton Park 15, 17, 19, 30, 36-37, 45, 81, 84, 86, 88, 99-102, 122-123, 131, 154-155, 157, 165, 191, 214, 224, 228, 242-243, 253, 270, 271, 281-282, 289-292
Over Norton Park Estate 271
Over Norton Women's Institute (O.N.W.I.) 215, 218, 221, 225, 227-228, 293-295
Oxfordshire Yeomanry 7, 81, 100
Oxhill 13

P

Padbury, Freda 197-198
Padbury, Mrs Minnie May (née Burtonshaw) 166, 175, 197-199, 201, 258
Parish Council (H Rider Haggard) 117
Parker family 246-248
Pashley, Doris (née Harrison) 28, 138, 152, 164, 170-172, 180, 205-206, 219-220, 226, 282, 294
Pashley, Glen 138, 282, 284
Pashley, Pam 282
Pashley, Ray 251, 270, 281-282
Pashley, Vince 282
Paws With Inn 16, 58
Paynes Square 277
Paynes Yard 23, 220
Pearce's chemist shop 170
Pearman family 32, 38, 59, 122, 214-215, 222, 253, 260-261, 263-264, 280, 282-283, 288-289, 294-295
Pearman, David 122, 260-261,
Pearman, Ian 32, 38, 282-283
Pearman, Rebecca 59, 260-261, 282-283, 295
Pearman, Phyllis (née Pinfold) 288-289, 294-295
Peckham Town Hall 59
Penfield 28, 285
Penn, The 28, 285
Pennant, Edward 82
Pennant family 87-88
Penrhyn Castle 81-82, 86-88
Pillars, The 30
Pitts, Mr 52, 257
Pool Meadow 16
population 13, 46, 136, 147
Post Office 14, 161, 212, 232, 244, 274-275, 288, 290
Pound, The 28

INDEX

Power, Joseph 162
Pratt, Dave 284
Pratt, Miss 202
Primsdown 157, 264
Prince of Wales 55, 87, 169
Priory Farm 15-16, 28, 33, 48, 52, 72, 132, 149, 229, 257, 269
Priory Mead 50
Priory Mill 16, 28, 34, 50-51, 150, 229, 240, 262-263, 267-269
Protestation Returns 79
Prowse, Pat 280
public baths 170
public house 6, 158, 233, 262, 277-278
Public Rights of Way 4, 7, 25, 27-28
Putmans 159, 168

Q
Quarhill Close 36, 283

R
Radcliffe Infirmary 205
railway tunnel 24
Railways 22
Randall, Pat (née Cambray) 213, 218, 221, 223, 259
Rationing 9, 213, 217-218
Reed, Mr 266
Reg's Cafe 170
ridge and furrow 30, 47
Rollright 50, 59, 222
Rollright Brook 167, 265
Rollright Halt 23-24, 266
Rollright Heath Farm 262
Rollright Stones 17, 38, 162, 166-168, 203, 262, 283
Roper family 52, 253, 257-258
Rose, Mr 259, 261
Rose Cottage 23, 157, 163, 165, 243, 275, 277
Roughton, Peggy 277, 290
Roughton, Joe 122, 138, 273, 277
round barrow 32
Rowell & Sons 42-43, 123, 219, 263, 265
Rudge, Dorothy, Tom & family 35, 43-44, 47, 175, 202-203, 213, 216-218, 221-223, 228, 244, 248-252, 259, 261, 264, 266, 277-278, 282
Runacres, Eric 295
Runacres, Jane 220, 288, 291-293, 295

S
Sale, Marjorie (née Roper) and Reg 257-258
Salford 15-17, 24-25, 29, 33, 36, 87, 96-97, 106-107, 132, 138, 141, 154, 159, 241, 260, 264-266, 283
Sandels, Henry 27, 276
Sanders, Mr 35, 43
Sandfields Farm 27-28, 260-261, 289
Saunders, Albert 34-35, 119, 211-212, 244, 274, 276
Saunders, George Henry 101-103
Saunders, John 249
Saunders, Lizzie (née Webb) 14, 98, 211-212, 290
Scholfield, Frederick 139
School Certificate Examination 207
Schools:
    Banbury County School 175, 204
    Banbury Grammar 204
    Board School 4, 8, 175, 181-182, 184-186, 189
    Boarding School 57, 208
    British School 172, 187, 201, 204, 213
    Chipping Norton Boys' National School 196-197, 240
    Chipping Norton County School 171-175, 203-206, 246
    Chipping Norton National Girls' School 196
    Church Enstone School 199
    Church of England Infants' School 196
    Dame School 8, 175-178, 293
    Green School 172
    Heythrop School 199
    Holy Trinity Roman Catholic Primary School 208
    National School 4, 8, 23, 175, 178, 181, 187-188, 195-197, 201, 240, 242
    Over Norton Council School 166, 190, 194, 197
    Over Norton Sunday School 166, 280
    Public Elementary School 175, 180, 246
    St Cecilia's School 202-203
    Technical School 198
Scots pine 17, 83
Secondary Modern School 203
Servants Taxes 237
Shakespeare Inn 53
sheep farming 64, 148
Sheffield family 152, 155-156, 173-174, 201, 214, 243, 275
Shennan, Claire 155
Shepard family 165-166, 214
Shepherd's Dene Farm 269-270
Shrewsbury 17-18
Shrimpton, Miss 202
Silver Jubilee 10, 273, 281, 294
Slad Cottage 160, 281
Slad, The 17, 281
Slad Lodge 26, 29, 31
Small Holdings Act 240
Smith, Shelley 290, 295
Sole, Fred 152, 156-158, 285
spinning top 160, 168
Springfield House 252
St James' Chapel Group 10, 273, 279
St Mary's Church 114, 122
St. Mary's Primary School 172, 203
Stallard, Miss 155
Stanbra, Thomas 253, 258
Stanley, Adeline 277
Stanley, Chrissie (née Parker) 246
Steane, John 257
Steeple Aston cope 49, 52
Steward, Mr 203
Stickley, Emily 181
Stobart, Edwyn 264, 270, 283
Stonemason 40
Sunday School 166, 175-176, 273, 280
Sunnyside 10, 26, 273, 275
Surveyor of Highways 18
Swimming Pool 170
Symonds, Walter 173

T
Tanner, Frank 157-158

taxes 55, 56, 57, 60, 61, 62, 237, 286-287
Taylor (Long Compton) 100
Taylor, Mr & Mrs 202
Taylor, Thomas 62, 80, 115-116, 229-230
The Folly 25, 72, 244
The Green 17, 23, 25-26, 34, 233, 273-275, 285
The Orchard 285
The Oxford House 278
The Steps 32
The Three Tuns 278
Thompson, Robin 281
Thompson, Sophie 282
Thomson, Joyce (née Shepard) 152, 165-166, 168-171, 275
Thornet family 166
Thornly, Louisa 179
Three Chimneys 44, 159, 178-179, 243, 263, 293
Toll house 166, 235
tolls 20, 105
Top Endolls 47
Torrington Diaries 54
Tourist Information Office 14
Townsend, Lord 'Turnip' 128
Tull, Jethro 128
Turnpike Trusts 18
tweed mill 162, 165, 170, 234
U
Union Row 26, 296
Upper Norton House 7, 81, 84
V
V.E. Day 225
V.J. Day 225
Village Green 13, 17, 13, 25-26, 29, 31, 36, 99, 256, 289
Village hall (opened 1980) 36, 38, 280-282, 284, 294
Village Hall, wooden (opened December 1934) 40, 174, 222, 277, 282, 292
W
W.A.A.F. 170
Walford, A.P. 264
Walford, Wilmot Poole 34, 43, 118-119, 173, 238, 243, 256, 273-274
Walk Farm 15, 262-263, 267, 269
Wall Hanging 288-295
Walter, Mr 279
War 5, 9, 60, 88, 90, 96, 98-99, 133, 164-165, 207, 209-225, 240-241, 244, 251, 254, 255, 259, 270, 273, 276, 282-283, 289, 295
War Memorial 44, 108, 212, 273
War Memorial Hospital 273
Ward, Connie 126
Ward, William 63
warehouse 26, 233
Warne, William 43, 255
Warner, John 149
Warner, Robert 95
Warwickshire 13
water 32, 41-43, 44, 85, 99-100, 126, 147, 157, 160, 163-164, 166, 202, 215, 224, 235, 245, 250, 262-263, 285
Weale, Ambrose 256-257

Weale, William John 35, 98, 253, 256-257
Webb, Thomas 23
Webb, Walty 27, 34-35, 38
Webb's shop 202
Well House 203
wells 43-44
Wells, Mr (a draper) 251
Wells, George 236
West, John 34-35, 277, 283
West, John (Heythrop) 131
West Farm 124-126, 142, 149
Weston, Mr 159
wheelwright 13, 35, 256
whips and tops 168
White Hart Hotel, Chipping Norton 21, 60
White Hart Hotel, Fairford 264
Whitsun 160
Wiggins, Jim 6, 33, 52, 257
Willis, Mrs 31
Wilmot, Mr 157-158
Wilson Mrs J. (née Cambray) 259
Window Tax 5, 7, 45, 55-56, 91
Witts, Francis 152
Witts, Frederick & Margaret 152
Witts, John 53
Witts Farm 28, 36-37, 43, 47, 114, 125-126, 163, 203, 216, 221-222, 228, 232, 242-244, 246, 248-249, 251-253, 261, 266, 277
Witts House 157, 232, 252, 264
Wolcot House 281
Wood Alfred 243
Wood, Micky 170
Wood, Robert 86
Wool Way 16,
Woolliams, Audrey 203, 264
Woolliams, Mr 214, 216, 228, 259, 262, 263, 264
Woolliams, Richard 35, 116, 135, 202-203, 225, 261-264
Woolworths 168, 256
Workhouse 4, 8, 13, 20, 26, 32, 106-112, 202, 285
Workhouse Row 26, 108, 285
Worvill, Jack 157
Worvill, Jean 219-220
Worvill, Frank 157
Worvill, Roy 98, 175, 204-206
Wright, Mary 114-119
Wright, WIlliam 48, 56, 106, 114-119
Wynmere Farm 269
Y
Young, Arthur 22, 123, 128, 130-133
Youth Club 10, 273, 282